D12864417

MARK GERTLER

SELECTED LETTERS

MARK GERTLER
SELECTED LETTERS

EDITED BY

Noel Carrington

WITH AN INTRODUCTION
ON HIS WORK AS AN ARTIST BY

Quentin Bell

RUPERT HART-DAVIS
SOHO SQUARE LONDON
1965

Rupert Hart-Davis Ltd
36 Soho Square London W1
First published 1965

Printed in Great Britain
by Ebenezer Baylis and Son, Ltd
The Trinity Press, Worcester, and London

Contents

Illustrations

PLATES

IN THE TEXT

Introduction

"What a brood I have raised." Such, we are told, was the verdict of Henry Tonks, the formidable autocrat of the Slade, on the students whom he had educated. It is the common fate of teachers to be horrified by the performance of their best pupils, and Tonks, with the Nash brothers and Stanley Spencer, Harold Gilman, Matthew Smith, Spencer Gore and Wyndham Lewis to his credit, may be excused for supposing that he had reared a generation of vipers. None, I think, bit him harder than Mark Gertler. Gertler was a prize pupil, and the outright rejection of all that he had been taught must have been all the more painful from one who had so perfectly learnt that which the Slade hoped to teach.

What the Slade *could* teach, and what Gertler could so triumphantly learn may be seen in the early self-portrait (Plate 1) which he made after a year's tuition. Here was a young man who could do anything. He had taken something from the Pre-Raphaelites—to be more exact from Rossetti (he never quite forgot Rossetti)—and at the same time he had acquired a bold, sharp decisive use of line (observe the treatment of the nose) which comes from France, via the New English Art Club. It is precise and yet free, intelligent but nevertheless a little sentimental; in short it is all that a Slade drawing was supposed to be.

How far the young Gertler was ready to adventure upon this particular path and with what intelligence, with what speed and assurance he was able to travel, may be gauged by anyone who looks at the celebrated portrait of the artist's mother in the Tate (Plate 2). The self-portrait is, in a sense, a preparation for this canvas; Gertler has chosen the same viewpoint, and much the same pictorial problem; but with what assurance he now conveys a sense of mass, how much more subtle and penetrating he now is in his rendering of psychological truth. Look at the hands, remembering that they were painted by a boy of twenty, and consider their solidity and the character that is implicit in their quiet tension.

This portrait of Mrs Gertler is, in effect, the kind of thing that her son's teachers were trying to paint; but rarely with such a fine mixture of brilliance and sincerity. How adroitly he could have played their game had he chosen to stay with it. How well he could have used those low pitched, discreetly sensuous harmonies, so perfectly adapted to the painting of duchesses and generals. In his portrait of his sister (Plate 3) the tact and refinement of the professsional portrait painter is already evident; it is still a little jejeune, a little too sincere, but these are faults of which a young painter is soon cured. In 1911 Gertler had everything that an artist needs to gain him a baronetcy and a dignified mansion in the Home Counties.

And yet, even in the portrait of his mother, he strikes a faint but unmistakably alien note, enough to show us that he was living in a country that was being invaded and overrun by the Post-Impressionists, enough to give pause to anyone who may have supposed that one day Sir Mark Gertler R.A. would take his place amongst the immortals of the Establishment; there is a little sharpness about the planes of the face, a hint of Cézanne about the eyes, the mouth, the monumentality of the pose, enough in fact to make it seem possible that the young man would kick aside the brilliant, glittering, worldly future that lay at his feet, throw away the gifts of fortune and turn to ——

Here the enthusiastic critic halts in some perplexity. To what did this rebellious young man turn, for what did he sacrifice his material prospects? It is not easy to formulate a coherent answer; for although Gertler was certainly one of that company of brave young painters who, when Post-Impressionism was under fire, marched to the sound of the guns, the odd thing is that he appears to have advanced upon two divergent paths.

Look at the illustrations 5 and 6; they are of the same year, the year 1914. They both show a radical departure from the "Portrait of the Artist's Mother", but they might almost be by different artists. The Gertler who painted "Rabbi and Rabbitzin" is a tough, uncompromising fellow, who has looked, not only at Cézanne, but at the Vorticists and, probably, at William Roberts. There is a hint here of what the century was to experience in the way of ruthless, metallic form and fierce sculptural statement, the sentiment—and there is to be sure an abundance of sentiment in those melancholy Jewish faces that look out at us with such intensity—is strictly confined by the austerely calculated design.

How different from this the work of that Gertler who painted "The Black and White Cottage". This Gertler is quiet, romantic, melancholy, full of the shyness and oddity of his adopted country, full of precise angular Pre-Raphaelite detail. Here the chiaroscuro is used, not to impose an aggressive solidity, but rather to induce that sense of familiar things made strange which we find in the best drawings of the young Millais and in all Stanley Spencer's work. The subject has been treated with marked deference, the design is not formal, it is sentimental, it is the work of an infinitely poetical artist.

These two personæ flit in and out of Gertler's paintings. They account in part for its odd charm, and they account also for its disconcerting inequalities; what he needed, I think, was to arrive at a synthesis, but he did not find it until the very end.

During the war years it was the harsh, bold Post-Impressionist of "Rabbi and Rabbitzin" who prevailed; not always, for in "The Dutch Doll" (Plate 9) there is much of his gentler persona; but in general he was at this time trying to curb his talents as a charmer and a romantic. "The Merry-Go-Round" (Plate 10) was his most determined effort in this direction. It was perhaps his masterpiece; the colour is almost unbearably harsh and strident. Gertler seems to have been determined to show how much he could unleash and, looking back at the Tate portrait, one may feel a pang of regret; but how much he has gained in the process. The holiday-makers are deliberately reduced to the same wooden state of rigidity as their steeds, the clouds above are as aggressively Cézanne as they. Everything is held, as though within some whirling, metallic labyrinth, by a system of ellipses and verticals. This compels the artist to insist upon a series of redundant visual rhymes which, with relentless iteration, render the strange, mazed, tipsy reel of the fairground. It is a picture which certainly deserves to be respected; but which is more easily admired than loved.

Possibly Gertler himself felt that he was stacking the odds too heavily against beauty and that he could, more efficiently and agreeably, arrive at his ends by turning from painting to sculpture. At all events, whatever his motives, in the following year he produced "The Acrobats" (Plate 12), a superb piece of sculpture, not far in the manner from Gaudier Brezka, but nearer to Negro sculpture. Here, so it seems to me, he shows all the strength and lively invention of "The Merry-Go-Round" but with a greater subtlety of rhythm and with a sensuous feeling which that painting lacks; of the two works it is the less ambitious but the more perfect and it is, I think, altogether regrettable that Gertler did not pursue an art for which he had, manifestly, such astonishing gifts.

That he did not is due I think to the reappearance soon after of that other Gertler, the gentle romantic, painting pictures such as "Garsington Manor" (Plate 16) and "Trees at Sanatorium, Scotland" (Plate 15). Here he is doing something which could hardly be attained by sculpture. He conveys the softness of atmosphere, the fusion of indefinable shapes, forms that melt into each other, the tender, mysterious ambiguities of landscape in the open air. His mood is soft, delicate and sad; in paintings such as "Girlhood" (Plate 18), or "The Servant Girl" (Plate 17), in which he is looking rather at Renoir than at Cézanne, the painter's sweetness verges on sentimentality. Moreover, at this point, another influence becomes apparent. Like so many other English painters of the 1920's, Gertler was strongly attracted by Duncan Grant. "The Queen of Sheba" (Plate 16) is very close to Grant (the still life in the foreground is almost pastiche) and although this is a very lively and charming essay in that manner the influence was not a happy one, for, as is almost always the case in a relationship such as this, it is the decorative side of the master's work, the manner and the mannerisms of the master which are transmitted, while his underlying vision and strength remain inimitable.

The epoch of Duncan Grant's ascendancy in British painting is one which is not easy for us to admire. It stands at just the wrong distance of time for us to be able to see its virtues so that, today, Grant himself is underestimated. How much more so those painters who felt his influence without sharing his genius. Therefore one must be cautious in estimating

Gertler's productions of the 1920's. Nevertheless, I think that it is a disappointing period. He is still looking for a synthesis which escapes him; his tight, precise forms convey an idea of volume, of solidity, which accords ill with the romantic melancholy that he seeks to express; the effect is one of heavy romanticism, and surely romanticism should always weigh as little as possible.

In effect at this point in his career Gertler is getting the worst of both his worlds; his sentiment robs him of strength, his search for plasticity deprives him of poetical freedom and yet, when one looks not at the reproductions but at the originals of this period, one immediately becomes aware of a very pure, a very honest sentiment. If there was failure, it was a failure of execution not of intention.

Thus there was always a possibility of recovery and in his last years Gertler does recover. "The Mandolinist" of 1934 (Plate 23) is at once massive and psychologically right. The design is as impressive as anything in his work and yet easy, flowing and unforced. He was beginning to do in paint that which he had so magnificently done in sculpture. Gertler's death at this moment, just when he had at last resolved three decades of conflict and perplexity, just when he was becoming mature and might have had another twenty years of superb achievement before him, is one of the great tragedies of British Art.

QUENTIN BELL
1965

Editor's Foreword

Some years ago I was handed a large collection of letters written by Mark Gertler, the Jewish artist who made a name for himself between the wars and who died in 1939. They seemed to me to reveal the story of a strange and unhappy genius, and moreover to throw a valuable sidelight on a then influential intellectual circle. Gertler was a prolific letter writer, spontaneous rather than literary. As with most letters not written with an eye to publication, only a portion is worth reprinting. Omissions are chiefly of repetitions or of day-to-day engagements no longer of interest. Only in a few instances have I deleted passages which refer to living persons or which might give offence to the families of those mentioned.

Gertler's spelling was often unorthodox, especially in his early years, and there seemed no point in adhering to his text in that respect. His punctuation—frequently a series of dashes, as if to indicate that he was drawing a fresh breath—was also unconventional. I have taken the liberty of repunctuating as near the sense as possible.

The bulk of the early letters were written to my sister "Carrington" and came to me on the death of her husband Ralph Partridge, and some thirty years after her own death. Many of these letters were undated. With the aid of Carrington's own letters to Gertler which had also been preserved, approximate dates have not been difficult to fix. Gertler's widow, Mrs Marjorie Gertler, has given me invaluable help throughout, and I have also had the co-operation of his son, Mr Luke Gertler, and of his niece, Mrs Renée Diamond. Amongst Gertler's old friends I am particularly indebted to Mr Tom Balston, not only for the loan of letters but for putting at my disposal his great knowledge of Gertler's paintings. Other principal sources of letters have been the Koteliansky MSS in the British Museum, and here I acknowledge the ready help of the officials in the Department of Manuscripts. For other letters I am indebted to the following: The Trustees of Sir Edward Marsh's estate, and the New York Public Library (Berg Collection); Mr James Strachey, as literary executor of Lytton Strachey; Sir John Rothenstein and Mr Michael Rothenstein, literary executors of Sir William Rothenstein, and to the library of Harvard University; William Heinemann Ltd and Mr Laurance Pollinger, as literary executor of Mrs Frieda Lawrence; Mr Richard Carline; Mrs Valentine

Dobrée; The Hon. Dorothy Brett, and the University of Texas Library; Mrs Kathleen Nevinson; and Mrs Julian Vinogradoff for the letters of Lady Ottoline Morrell; Mrs D. Mewton-Wood for letters to W. J. Turner. Permission to reprint Sylvia Lynd's appreciation of Gertler was kindly given me by Mrs M. Gaster.

I have also received useful information from many of Gertler's friends, notably Mrs Mary Hutchinson, Mrs Barbara Bagenal, Gwendoline Lady Melchett, The Hon. Dorothy Brett, Mr Richard Carline, Mrs Vinagradoff, Mr Maurice Farquharson, and Mr Oliver Brown of the Leicester Galleries. I am indebted to Mrs Frances Partridge, not only for compiling the index, but for most valuable advice and encouragement throughout; also to Mrs Judy Carrington for deciphering manuscripts and typing for the printer. Lastly I must acknowledge the help and consideration I have received at every stage from my publishers, in particular Mr John Knowler and Mr Richard Garnett.

Unfortunately I have not been able to trace letters from several sources which would almost certainly have added value to the book, in particular letters which Gertler must have written to D. H. Lawrence, Gilbert Cannan, Montague Shearman, C. R. W. Nevinson and Lady Ottoline Morrell, as well as some of his own writing that he mentions. Cannan's novel *Mendel*, based on Gertler's early life and the subject of some scandal at the time of its publication in 1916, is discussed in an Appendix.

PART ONE

Childhood

Mark Gertler was born at Spitalfields, London, on 9 December 1891, the youngest by seven years of a family of five—he had two brothers and two sisters. His father, Louis Gertler, was a furrier who seems to have had as little success in that trade as in others that he also took up. The mother, Golda, was the central figure of Gertler's boyhood. She was devoted to him, as were all his family. The parents came originally from Przemysl, then part of Austrian Poland, and were thus able to claim Polish descent during the war.

After Mark's birth the family returned to Austria, where the father kept an inn, chiefly frequented by soldiers, which clearly provided neither a reasonable living nor a desirable home for his family. The father then sought his fortune in America, leaving his family behind in Austria. Eventually he summoned them to join him again in London. Gertler's own recollection of these days has been preserved and is here printed.

FIRST MEMORIES[1]

by

Mark Gertler

18 October 1934

I don't know exactly how old I was, and unfortunately I cannot ask my family to help me because the first incident I remember with clarity contains a certain amount of deception, even slyness on my part, that is if one can call it sly to pretend not to hear what one is not intended to hear and is not in the position to avoid hearing. I say I cannot appeal to my family, because it was them I deceived, and have never since mentioned the incident in their presence. But I could not have been more than four. We were in Austria—that is all of us except my father, who was somewhere in America—and I was supposed to be asleep when I heard the following: Mother to my eldest brother Harry, "Harrish, it is cold and Maxalla will

[1] This manuscript was found in the studio at 5 Grove Terrace, NW5, on the night of Monday, 26 June 1939, and was handed to John Mavrogordato, of Exeter College, Oxford, on the following morning for safekeeping by Gertler's niece, Renée (Mrs Leslie Diamond).

suffer. Could you not bring home with you from the factory a warm little coat?" Harry, "All right, all right, I'll try, perhaps." Mother, "If you succeed we'll say father sent you a present, Maxalla, from America." The next evening at the same time, when I am supposed to be asleep again, my brother arrives. I am terribly impatient—this time it is hard for me to keep up the pretence of sleep. I keep cocking one eye open every second and, sure enough, my brother extricates from inside his trousers a coat!—a coat I was to wear a long time and get to love very much though I knew it was not my father who sent it.

It is curious that I cannot remember anything else at all clearly during the four or five years we spent in Austria. But I should like, before leaving that period, to tell what I subsequently learnt about it and about my birth from my people. Although all my family was born in Austria, I myself was born in Spitalfields, London. My father and mother a few years previous to this decided to leave Austria and "try their luck" in London. They arrived almost penniless with four children and settled in a street called Gun Street, Spitalfields. When I was a year old they decided that there was no luck forthcoming and with the help of the Jewish Board of Guardians returned to their native country with only me, as it were, to show for it. They were not received exactly with enthusiasm by their relations, who realised that something would have to be done and who had by this time decided that my father was a good-for-nothing, especially those on my mother's side, who had often warned her—as she used to relate so frequently—not to marry him, "For if you do, Golda, take warning you will never have enough to eat." However, they clubbed together and between them managed to collect enough money to buy them a small inn on the outskirts of the Town.

According to the stories my family have told me of this inn—and there are many and rich in material—it was doomed from the start, for it was most unfortunately situated. It existed between two other more important drink houses, and the only customers we got always arrived already drunk, with all their money spent, from one of the other pubs and refused to pay for what they drank at our place, which resulted nearly every night in murderous fights between my father and his customers, who were mainly soldiers. Later I shall have more to say about my father's fighting capacity and his build and character, for he was in his way an extraordinary man. But there are one or two things in relation to our short stay in this unhappy inn I should like to tell about.

The first concerns myself. It seems that as a small child I was extremely popular and particularly with these same drunken and dissipated soldiers. Often my mother told me these very rough young men would agree to pay for their drinks only on condition that I was produced, when they would proceed to play and joke with me. As this meant dragging me out of my cradle my mother often cursed them in her heart, but produced me all the same, for sometimes, she said, she would hardly dare to think of what ructions they'd kick up if she had failed to do so. Finally they somehow arranged to have a complete officer's uniform made for me and the correct number of stars fixed to the collar, and amused themselves by very seriously saluting me and awaiting my return salute. This apparently was a great game.

The other story I want to relate is to show the sort of thing that used to happen on really *bad* nights. Once, my brother tells me, we were warned that a whole troop of drunken soldiers were marching towards us in a very menacing mood. My father ordered the doors to be locked and barred and as many heavy objects as could be found to be shoved up against them. Sure enough a few minutes later there were noises, bangings and shoutings, and even swords thrust in between the crevices of the doors. This went on for so long, and my mother and sisters became so terrified that my father decided on a plan to scramble out unseen from a back window and get help from some neighbouring people and officers, who between them managed somehow to restore order and disperse the soldiers.

How the inn came to an end and what happened later my mother used to tell in a derisive manner, in order to show up what a simpleton my father was, for she always used to blame him for our failure and tell us how much better things would have turned out had he waited and taken *her* advice. I will tell the story in the way my mother would tell it me so often when we were alone together. My mother spoke mostly in Yiddish. Even after forty years in England she could speak very little English. But her Yiddish was extremely expressive and in translating it I shall try and keep to her kind of expressions and phrasing—"Oh was an inn that was—what a hell—and how does your tuttalla (derisive way of referring to my father) wind up with this inn? Perhaps sell it? No fear! Not he! One day in he comes with that smile of his—of course I know already what that smile means—and says to me, Golda don't worry any more—no more inn, we've got something better than that inn now. Oh woe me, I says, what have we got better—tell me—be quick—and what do you think he tells to my unhappy self? BOOTS! Oh! God help me, I says, Boots? What do you mean, boots? BOOTS, he says. Well I go and look and what do I see. Oh woe for my troubles. Not even a single pair of BOOTS!!! All odd, all odd, as I live today, God help me. All odd! Why did you not wait for my advice I says—but not he—he even gets angry, if you please, and runs out. A few days later, as sure as I live, he returns with the same smile and says, Golda you didn't like the boots eh? No I did *not* like the boots, I says. All right, he says, come and look here—and what does he show me this time—perhaps something valuable you may think? No, even worse, BUTTONS! A sack full of buttons—and *such* buttons—where could he have got such buttons from—that's all. I have never seen such buttons, not even on Christians' garments, let alone Jewish ones. Well what more can I tell you? You know your tuttalla. Soon there was nothing in the house to eat. He asks me for a clean shirt, and off he is to America—leaving me to starve with five children. Oh woe me, woe me! What a life I've had, only troubles, only troubles, and all thanks to your father."

Her story is hardly an exaggeration of what actually happened. As for the buttons—the story my brothers tell of that used to fill me with pity for my father. Apparently he actually went out into the market place with both my brothers—he a very very proud man—and in this market place where he was so well known managed to articulate in a sort of shy undertone—"Buttons, buttons". My brothers tell me that, during the many hours they stood there, only one customer approached and even that one was unable to find the kind of buttons she wanted.

When his troubles came to a head my father had a way of "Running to America" as my mother used to say. "Let me have a clean shirt, Golda, for this evening I go to America." Well, after the button failure he could stand it no longer and "ran to America", and my mother, as she said, was left with no means and five children. By this time, however, my eldest brother was just old enough to start work and I suppose contributed a little to the upkeep of the household. My mother did what she could to support us. She had many tales of hardship to tell of this period. At one time she slaved away in a Jewish restaurant, her only wages being some food left over from the day which she carried home to us tired and worn out after her long day's work.

At times we were reduced to extremes. One day, for instance, when my eldest brother was seen to be approaching the house, the few crusts that we had were quickly hidden away in case he took more than his share. This story my mother used to tell with tears in her eyes.

The experience I relate at the beginning was the most vivid to me, but there are others which I remember more hazily but which are worth mentioning as sometimes quite small matters in the early life of a child may be of great effect in the making of his character in later life. In this connection there are two things I should like to mention.

The first shows a fear of noise, especially sudden noise. My brothers and sisters used often to take me to listen to military bands. Now although —as I say—the greater of these very early experiences came to me as if in a dream, there are always one or two points that project themselves clearly in my memory—rather as sensations—and which have become part of me. The thing I remember so clearly in relation to these bands is the terrible and overwhelming fear that used to spread and pervade my whole body as soon as the bandmaster raised his arms to arrange and commence the first crash of sound. Somehow it seems to me now that all the music I heard there began with a terrific clash. Just at that awful moment when the conductor's arms would be raised at their highest and suspended there before finally bringing down upon us that fearful bang, I suffered agonies of fright and could hardly even control myself enough to prevent a terrifying yell, which frightened the people around almost as much as the music did me and annoyed my people so much that they used to threaten to leave me at home next time, which added considerably to my depression as after the first crash I enjoyed the music very much indeed.

The other experience is a sort of phantom figure or bogey invented by my brother and sisters with which to frighten me into obedience and keep me in order. When, for instance, I would be naughty or they wished in some way to control my behaviour they would say, "Mickey-Coo will be angry with you. He won't give you any more toys," or, if they were pleased with me, "Now Mickey-Coo will be pleased and soon he will provide you with another toy." This "Mickey-Coo" became a figure of great reality and importance to me and played an enormous part in my life. When, for instance, they would produce some useless bit of tin and say this comes from Mickey-Coo as a reward for your good behaviour, that bit of tin would have for me the greatest significance and would become for me an emblem of such mystery and a source for so much imagination and invention that I very much doubt if the most intricate and expensive toy could have at that time meant half as much to me.

It was in Austria, also, when I was apparently three years old, that I did my first drawing. It appears that my mother who was finishing a letter to my father playfully suggested to me that I too should include a few words to my father. Of course I was unable to write, as she knew, but to her astonishment I seized the pen, drew a watch and chain on the paper and said, "I want Father to send me this!"

We return to England after about five years of struggle and hardship in Przemysl. My mother at last received a letter from my father which raised her hopes and cheered her heart. "I have prospects," it said. "Come, we shall meet in England. I know what to do there and if what I do there is not good we shall go on to America where I know still better what to do." Although my mother usually distrusted my father's optimistic moods and felt that nothing good would come of it, she was at this time ready for any change, as she felt that our conditions could hardly be changed for the worse. Anyway we would all be together again and it is good to be with your man. Actually if she could have gazed into the future she would have seen there many causes for fresh suffering, but certainly, from a material point of view, things were to improve, perhaps not rapidly but surely enough gradually to place her in a position which, for a woman of my mother's experience, could be reckoned as comparatively comfortable, although the business of paying rent or settling the butcher's bills, the grocer's, clothes for the children and many other necessaries continued for many years to remain an insoluble problem. Yet food to eat there was somehow, clothes for our bodies, and a house to live in.

THE JOURNEY

It is curious that most of the journey remains an absolute blank in my memory. I say curious because I can remember things with so much more clarity previous to it and because a great deal happened that ought to have impressed itself upon my memory. I showed, for instance, such a strong aptitude for dancing, and charmed the crew and the passengers so much that my mother used to say if it were not for me she could hardly have got through the journey. Dressed in my Hungarian coat of deep orange-coloured leather, decorated with gold and scarlet braid, vermilion tam-o-shanter and top boots up to the knee, I would suddenly start to any sound of music or song a sort of dance that would so enchant the people that they would get for us any tit-bits that were going in the way of food, or other comforts and even money.

These little extras were very necessary indeed, because the journey, from what I used to hear of it from my brother and sisters, was for the most part like a nightmare. We travelled in some sort of cattle-boat herded very close together, the journey lasting for weeks and most of the time in rough seas, and all of us were sick and in a dreadful plight. This fact seems difficult to imagine where I could have found sufficient place to dance, or an audience well enough to watch me. My mother apparently was terrified nearly all the way of actual shipwreck and was only comforted by a fellow passenger, a Jew, who used to comfort her by pointing to the lamp and saying, "How can you be frightened, Mrs Gertler, when the lamp hangs so straight." Now it is quite at the end of the journey, our landing in fact, where my own memory comes to life and it is from this moment only that I am in the position to relate my experiences—just as they impressed themselves upon my feelings and sensations—without having to depend upon the stories told me by my mother or other members of my family. From now on there are no gaps. All is continuous and clear, and if a good deal of my surroundings and a great number of details are still vague, the sequence of each event remains vivid and the essentials connected and alive.

THE ARRIVAL

I am standing on a wooden floor. There is land—England—England is moving towards me, not I to it. It is sort of gyrating towards me. I am standing surrounded by my family all ready with heavy packages straining from their necks—pressing their backs—all available hands are grasping rebellious packages. My mother strains her eyes and says, "Oh woe is me but I cannot see your father! He is not there, he is not there, what shall I do?" Everybody is pushing and shoving. It doesn't feel friendly—all is chaos, selfish and straining—I am being pushed and hustled, some women are screaming and men shouting roughly. Then a voice emerges: "Golda! Golda! Here I am, Louis Weinig, don't you know me? Leib will be late—at Liverpool Street Station—later—come where are you all? Sacha—Harrish—Max—come—Golda!"

LONDON!

Then later, outside Liverpool Street Station. We had arrived! London! All of us huddled together, looking rather like gypsies. Some passers-by threw coins. But we were waiting, we were waiting for my father. Some mistake—he was unable to meet us at the ship. But his life-long friend and "kinsman"—Louis Weinig—came and helped us and later housed us. On my eldest brother's neck I see a vein sticking out—the enormous bundle hanging from his shoulder is straining it. As long as I live I shall continue to see that swollen vein. The bundle contains most of our bedding—feather beds. My father arrives at last. There is a sort of wave of emotion which entangles us, but I am not very moved by this—only the veins on my brother's neck is telling on me. But later I see a bright coloured shop—Gardiners of Whitechapel. "Mother, does the King live here?" "No, my son, in London nearly everybody has such large and brightly lit houses. This is *London*, my son." Yes, this was London! For some people it may be England my England, but for me it is London, my London. Yes, although I was born in it, I saw London—experienced London—for the first time then, and I was six and my only language was Yiddish! And the year was 1898. Yes, there was a moment in my life when I was actually fresh to London—London where I have lived for so long, experienced so much, London that has become part of me to such an extent that I can almost imagine life more easily without the people I have known than its own embodiment and peculiarity. And it is here then, in London, and at the age of six and in 1898, that my true history commences—my own life as I have known it and suffered it.

FIRST FIT OF DEPRESSION

Louis Weinig lived in Shoreditch. My father's life-long friend and pal, he came from Przemysl also and was therefore our "kinsman". Louis Weinig was a wit. He was famous for his comic stories, though these stories generally made him cut a bit of figure as well as being comic. He would somehow emerge triumphant—having had the last word—or won the fight. He was not the sort of man to hide his light behind a bushel. Fair modesty—or any sort of modesty—was not his, nor was it much indulged in by anybody in his world. When he told one of his stories he was quite frankly the hero and mostly a very glowing hero. Nobody was critical, because modesty was not the fashion and most people used conversation chiefly to boost themselves. The difference between him and the others was that he *was* funny. I remember looking forward to his visits and joining very heartily in the general laughter like everyone did when he recounted his adventures, though I soon got to know most of them by heart. But his *style* was the important element, not the matter, so one could hear him often without getting bored. His wife was a very frail woman, always dying of consumption. There were several children and the poverty so great that the poor little woman was compelled to crawl about and do the housework, bring up the children and even help others who were as poor as herself, when she was obviously feverish and hardly able to stand. In our presence she would often be seized with a fit of coughing which generally ended in haemorrhage, yet she was always cheerful and sweet-tempered. His family lived in two rooms in some very drab tenement in Shoreditch and it was in one of these two rooms that the whole of my family, consisting of seven human beings, was housed for the night.

Louis Weinig and *his* family slept in the other. How *exactly* we were accommodated I don't know, but this is how it *appeared* to me as I awoke in the middle of the night. I remember suddenly awakening and sitting up. I was at the end of the room on the floor next my mother, then the others—

all on the floor covered in sacks. The vision of this somehow filled my heart with overwhelming sadness. I cried, but quietly, not to awaken my mother, and that is the first real fit of depression I remember experiencing. It is curious that I should have felt it like that, for it was not as if I were accustomed to more luxurious circumstances. Yet as I sat there in the quiet of the night I was filled with a sort of pathos and feeling of gloom which remains as vivid today as it was then, and I have always remembered it, besides, as being the *first* fit of depression that I consciously suffered.

ZION SQUARE, 1898

We lived some weeks with the Weinigs before my father succeeded in getting a job. It was the smoothing of walking-sticks with sandpaper. For this work he was paid 12*s.* 6*d.* a week, a poor wage, yet we were all very cheerful, as very soon we were to have a home of our own. I can't imagine how it was managed on 12*s.* 6*d.* a week, but sure enough we got our "home". It consisted of a room with some kind of detached corner where my mother cooked, and managed to produce enough food to keep us all alive, and the street in which our "home" existed was called Zion Square. . . .

Our landlord, Mr Levy, and his wife were kind, decent people and their leniency with regard to our rent was of course a great help. For the 12*s.* 6*d.* did not always work out and often the weekly rent had to be delayed. Their youngest son Moisha, who was about my own age, soon became my best pal and I always remember him as my *first* best pal. For I have always had a "best pal" and I could name them all in succession up to this day.

Mr Levy was a boot maker. He had a workshop in the house, a small room, where about four or five "hands" worked. This workshop was where Moisha and I used to spend most of our time playing about in and around the machines, over which the "hands" used to sit bent and huddled, treading, treading away hour after hour—these "hands", mere boys and girls who appeared to me then as very adult people indeed, worked an incredible number of hours at a stretch cooped up in that dirty airless little room. I particularly remember one youth, whom they called Mara, more vividly than the rest, because he worked more persistently than the others, at what was called "overtime". Probably more ambitious than the rest to make a little extra money in order to save up for marriage and a "home". He worked from early morning until late at night—midnight and sometimes past—not even leaving the workshop for meals. Every now and then a chunk of bread and butter overlaid with a thin spread of pinky, watery jam and a cup of tea, was brought up to him, which he would swallow rapidly so that he could go on treading out more and more of that stuff he was paid to produce. He was tall, very thin, and very white and he came to a tragic end. All that toil and labour was utterly wasted, for one day he was discovered pacing the square, when he should have been working at his machine, spinning a few gold sovereigns in the air, and murmuring as each piece clinked to ground "What is money, what is money?" . . .

MAIDA AND SCHOOL

After we had lived in Zion Square about a year and I was seven years old, I was sent to "*Maida*", a Hebrew class. I hadn't far to go, as this institution existed in the same square, only a few yards from our house. The teacher was an old Rabbi of about seventy with long white beard which ended in two points. The class consisted of one room with a long narrow table, at the head of which the old Rabbi sat and we children all around the rest of it. The Rabbi used to read the Old Testament to us in Hebrew, translating each sentence, or sentences, each word into Yiddish, in a rapid hardly intelligible monotone, and we had to drone on after him, repeating the parts we could catch, and filling up the rest with noises that meant nothing whatsoever. Only occasionally, when he felt like it, would he pull us up and, choosing a boy quite indiscriminately, thump him. I must have been one of his favourites, for not only did I hardly ever get thumped, but he would even select me quite frequently from among the class, and let me sit on his lap while the lesson proceeded. This, for me, was a very doubtful pleasure for, as he gabbled out the Hebrew and Yiddish, his beard would travel up and down my cheek tickling intolerably—making me long even more than usual for the end of the lesson and good riddance to the beard.

The experience that stands out most clearly of my *Maida* days is not the Hebrew lessons or any stories of the Old Testament (we hardly understood a word he was reading anyway) but—*fried fish*! There was always a smell of fried fish in *Maida*, and occasionally the Old Testament would be abruptly closed and put aside as the old Rabbitzin would enter from the kitchen with a piece of fried fish and some brown bread (the sort that contains carraway seeds) for the Rabbi to eat. Now I was always a small eater and my mother had great difficulty in making me eat the food she produced for me, but at the sight of fried fish I always and utterly rebelled. Nothing would induce me to touch it. One day at *Maida*, while watching the Rabbi eating his fish, I somehow became interested—fascinated. And how he smacked his lips—how good it all seemed. And the touch of mustard, by jove, I thought, it *must* be good. The first thing I asked my mother for after the class was fried fish. She was astonished, but her surprise was still greater when she saw with what relish I ate it, and I have never ceased to like fried fish—I mean of course fried fish done in the *Jewish* way, an entirely different affair from the fried fish you get ordinarily in restaurants.

It was of course understood that I must be sent to *Maida* and learn how to become a good Jew, but about the ordinary schools, or board schools, as they were then called, my parents lived in blissful ignorance. They had no idea that a child was, or could be, forced by law to attend them. So one day there came a great knocking at the street door, the kind of rat-tat-tat that forebodes trouble, and when my mother arrived breathless and fearful and opened the door she was confronted by a very angry man, who was quite unable to make her understand what he was angry about, for my mother's English, never very good, was at that time very embryonic indeed. After a good deal of shouting on both sides, Mrs Levy was sufficiently aroused from her cooking to come to my mother's aid. It was then discovered that the angry man was an inspector of board schools, and was demanding my presence at the school *immediately*, and he told them I should have been sent to school long ago. My mother explained, with the help of Mrs Levy's English, that she hadn't the least idea that it was necessary to send children to school at a certain age, but that now she *did* know, she would take me to school wherever he suggested. As all this happened towards the end of the week, it was agreed that I should be taken to school the following Monday morning.

On the morning of that important day both my mother and I awoke much too early—nervous and flustered—to prepare for this fearful event. My mother washed my face, neck, and hands, combed my hair through, with the fine comb she used when looking for things, then again with the ordinary comb and brush, and at last, after a period that seemed an age, I was all ready—dressed in my sailor suit—to set out for school.

The school I went to was called Deal Street School—for the simple reason that it was in Deal Street. From Zion Square it was only about ten minutes' walk, and, when we arrived, we were told to join a queue of people who were waiting there for the same purpose as ourselves. It was a hot day and, as soon as we joined the queue, my mother for some reason lifted me into her arms and held me there in a manner she used when I was younger. I felt uncomfortable but did not protest, and soon I began to notice beads of sweat gather like pearls on her forehead and temples, then join and trickle down her cheeks in thin glistening streams. Then I heard a woman saying, "Why do you carry such a big boy in your arms, Mrs, ain't he old enough to stand!" I felt ashamed and tried to wriggle down, but my mother gathered her arms around me tighter and held me there not deigning even to answer the woman.

At last our turn came to approach the desk, at which a man was sitting, very stern and angry—making us feel from the start that we were somehow in the wrong, and that he jolly well meant to "let us have it". "Put that boy down *at once*. He is not a babe!—Name of Gertler I see, what's his *Christian* name?" Of course my mother could make nothing of it at all, until some woman at the back came to the rescue. "Mux," she said. "Mux!" said the man. "Never heard such a name—no such name in *this* country—we'll call him *Mark* Gertler," and nodding to a woman near by and pointing his pen at me he said, "Next!"

The woman separated me from my mother and taking me by the hand, she led me away. I felt desolate. I looked back at my mother and she tried to help me, but her eyes were wet and I felt worse. I was somehow too young to realize that it was only a day school, not so *very* different from *Maida*, and that I should be seeing my mother again that very day. Anyway the whole thing seemed far more severe and orderly than anything I was used to, and by the time I was given a place between two other children, on a hard seat with a little desk in front of me, I felt more heart-broken than anything I had experienced since that sad night when I suddenly awoke and saw the whole of my family lying in a row on the floor of Louis Weinig's room. I glanced at the children nearest me, as if to discover whether I dare give way to the tears that were choking me, but realized instantly that here was a new situation—that here in this atmosphere one must try *not* to cry and I succeeded in controlling my emotions —perhaps for the first time in my short life.

During the first part of my schooling at Deal Street, I was of course placed in the part of the school they call the "Infants", that is, where the children are considered young enough to be *mixed.* I can't remember exactly how long I was kept there, but before I leave this short section of my life, I should like to describe first how we children were brought up and secondly, an incident that happened in the "Infants" and that was the cause of a great deal of misery and which I suppose is merely typical of most schools anywhere.

My mother was as devoted to us all as any woman could possibly be. I should be inclined to think even above the average. There were five of us—three boys and two girls. I was the youngest, younger than Jack, who was the nearest me in age by about seven years. So whereas the other four were fairly close to each other in years, there was between them and myself a considerable gap, and I was always referred to as the "babe" and was perhaps for that reason my mother's darling. She did all she could for us, within her means, and was completely self-sacrificing, but unfortunately, like most of the people in the world she lived in, some of the most important things in connection with the upbringing of a child were quite unknown to her, and I consider the most disastrous of these was the fact that we were allowed to go to bed at any old hour. The result was that we never got enough rest. I was a very nervous, highly strung, and emotional child, somewhat undersized, thin and pale, yet I would hardly ever be put to bed before the rest of the family, which meant midnight, and on week-ends, when there were gatherings, long past that hour. I decided to describe the early part of my upbringing at this point because it was when I first started going to school that I began feeling the strain of it. I shall always remember the awful mixture of exhaustion and despair I felt every morning when I had to make myself get up in time for school, for I was very concientious and terrified of losing a mark, and every morning the strain made me weep and cry as I dressed, "It is late already, I shall be late."

The second "incident" relates to something quite different. Soon after I started my career at the "Infants", my father arranged as a special treat to give me "pocket money". My pocket money consisted of a farthing a day. This—the handling of money—was an entirely new experience, and when at last I was dressed and got through my cup of tea and bread and butter, I began to feel consoled and happy at the prospect of the farthing, which I used to carry clasped tightly in my fist, happily contemplating which of the various sweets I should buy that day at a special little shop I used to pass on my way to school.

Now for a while all went well. I would, after much deliberation, at last decide upon a jar of sweets and pointing at it with one hand and producing the hot farthing from the other, receive in return the little bag of sweets. But one day, as I emerged from the shop with my little bag, a girl, perhaps a little older than myself, but who looked formidably large to me, approached and quietly, but very definitely, robbed me of my sweets. When I recovered from my astonishment and realised that the sweets had gone, gone forever—and that I could do nothing about it, for it never occurred to me to resist—I howled, and cried, and stamped my way to school, no longer even dreaming of controlling my emotions, as I did on my first day at the "Infants". When I reached the classroom, I daresay I expected to be consoled with and sympathetically received as I would have been at home, but this was school, not home—here was a tight-laced teacher, not mother. So, without even being asked the cause of my distress, I was told very sternly to "stop that noise *at* once!" and sit down. Gradually the sobbing subsided, and when I remembered that tomorrow I would have another farthing and be able to get myself some more sweets, I recovered completely, and forgot almost all about it. But alas, my troubles had only begun.

The next morning as I was hopping and skipping along with my farthing, having by that time completely forgotten about the big girl, I was brought up sharp, only a yard or so from the shop, by the sight of my enemy! Yes, there she was—large and formidable—standing there waiting. I stopped. She approached, and without even allowing me to enter the shop she opened my fist, withdrew the farthing and, as if to add "insult to injury", she smacked my face and walked off! This time I was just stunned. I did not even want to cry, but the injury, the pain, was profound. For the first time in my life I realised the existence of *injustice*. The previous day it all somehow seemed simple. True I had lost my bag of sweets, and it was painful, but I was still able to feel that the loss could be replaced—that an isolated though very unpleasant accident had happened—but today much deeper issues were involved. It seemed that I was being hurt, and was apparently going to be so hurt every day—though I had done nothing wrong to deserve it! And there was nothing, nothing, I could do. I walked on to school brooding and suffering—suffering more deeply than ever I had done before. It still did not occur to me to resist, and the situation itself became too important—too painful even—to divulge or complain of. And so the thing grew into a dreadful secret inside me, and daily I suffered the same injury, the same indignity, carrying the whole weight of it alone. This unfortunate episode came to an end somewhat abruptly. Although each day when I reached home I made no complaint, my family must have noticed at last that something was very wrong, and began cross-questioning me. At first I just refused to give up my painful secret. They then tried to guess—is it this? is it that? No, no, I kept shaking my head. At last I broke down under their sympathetic enquiries, and told them the whole story. It was arranged then that my sister Sophia should accompany me to school next morning, catch the girl and give her "what's what", but next morning, as we approached the little shop, my tyrant soon realised the situation, turned tail and fled as hard as she could, and never again waylaid me.

[*Gertler's manuscript ends here.*]

PART TWO

The Young Artist

Gertler made his first drawing, he believed, at the age of three when in Austria, and in London soon showed his talent by drawing on the pavement of the yard.

His family, poor as they were, encouraged him with paints and material. Indeed the pride shown by his brothers and sisters in his talent, and the sacrifices they had made for him, were always fully acknowledged by him all through his life. He attended classes at the Regent Street Polytechnic without very much benefit.

In 1907, when just sixteen, he was apprenticed to Clayton and Bell, glass painters. No doubt his family thought that even at five shillings a week this was a magnificent opening, but Gertler found the work as frustrating as Dickens had found the blacking factory. Letters from the firm show that, though shocked by his determination to break his apprenticeship, they put no serious obstacle in his way. Fortunately the Jewish Educational Aid Society heard something of his case and decided to take advice from William Rothenstein. As a result the money was found to send him to the Slade School, and Rothenstein undertook to supervise his progress. It should perhaps be mentioned that one version of Gertler's early years is to be found in Cannan's novel *Mendel*, but the picture is grossly overpainted and distorted.

The Slade was the Slade of Brown and Tonks and certainly the most stimulating art school in the country at that time. Here he won several scholarships and prizes. Not only was his ability recognized but a whole new world was opened up by new friendships. He continued, however, to live with his family in the East End, and nearly all his early drawings and paintings are of his family or other Jewish characters. Of the Slade period proper, 1908–12, the only surviving correspondence which I have been able to discover is that with William Rothenstein, who continued to give him encouragement. Rothenstein in his own memoirs records the help he gave to many young artists, including Epstein, Paul Nash, and Gertler, and his grief that they seldom saw fit to repay the debt with gratitude. Artists are notoriously able to forget their early patrons, and the relationship is seldom an easy one to maintain.

To William Rothenstein

[? *1908*] *14 Spital Square, Bishopsgate, E.*

Dear Sir, I have of course started work in the new school and found everything all right when I went there last Tuesday and spoke to Prof. Brown. It was arranged that I start with drawing from the Antique, but every day from 4 to 5 everybody is allowed to do some sketches from the life (figure), which I think is excellent practice and also much more interesting than the Antique. You will excuse me worrying you but I saw Mr Lesser[1] and we thought that it would be best to ask you when it would be convenient for me to come and see you next, and would you kindly mention whether I am to bring any materials in order to do some work.

Yours faithfully MARK GERTLER

To William Rothenstein

Sunday [? *1909*]

Dear Mr Rothenstein, On behalf of my mother I desire to express to you her most heartfelt thanks for your kind letter,[2] which completed the overwhelming happiness my success brought her. When she reflects on all that you have done for me she does not quite know how to express her gratitude. Her entire happiness is bound up in my progress. She feels how true is what you write and for your words of sympathy she cannot adequately express the gratitude she really feels. My people, too, beg me to add their thanks to that of my mother. As for myself, I cannot sufficiently express my own gratitude for the kindness you have shown me. Yours sincerely

MARK GERTLER

P.S. Hoping it is convenient for you, I shall come and see you on *Wednesday* afternoon.

[1] Secretary of the Education Aid Society.

[2] The letter referred to here was probably the following:

22 May 1909 *11 Oak Hill Park, Frognal*

Dear Mrs Gertler, How proud and happy you will be feeling at your son's success. You may be quite sure he has deserved it, and that his beginning is an indication of the path which he is to follow. Everyone who meets him feels that he is one day going to express the beauty he feels so deeply, and I am sure he owes a great deal to you all for your devotion to him and to your wise encouragement of his bent. I hope and believe that he is to give you many more pleasures with his success; and as life is not only made up of them, I feel he will have in you a wise comforter and a patient sympathiser. He has already made for himself many friends, and the honourable place he has now won in the Slade School will be an immense stimulus to him in his work. Please see that he gets out as much as possible; we shall always be glad to see him here. With many congratulations to you all.

Believe me to be most sincerely yours W. ROTHENSTEIN

Many thanks to your son for so kindly writing me announcing the good news.

To William Rothenstein[1]

Sunday [*May 1909*] 14 *Spital Square, E.*

Dear Mr Rothenstein, I have a question to ask you which has been worrying me the last few weeks. Fothergill[2]—I will say it right away—wants me to send my "Onions" to the New English[3] and on that account made the frame for it. The idea has always seemed so absurd to me that I was ashamed to ask you when I saw you, but what will he say if I don't send it? What shall I do? For the scholarship, Brown says I have no need to send things he has already seen, amongst which are the "Onions", so I am free to send it to the N.E.A.C. if I like.

I may mention that I have been passed as eligible for competing for the scholarship. Yours sincerely MARK GERTLER

To William Rothenstein

Wednesday [? *1909*]

Dear Mr Rothenstein, I must indeed thank you for your most kind and encouraging letter. It made me feel much happier and braced me up like the sea an invalid. Reading it, I felt encouragement dancing in the very atmosphere about me and the earnest interest you take for my benefit are there convincingly displayed. My World is a World of Beauty and Joy, marred only by one thing, "Progress", and if at any time I am encouraged on that point, my world becomes perfect: all is bliss and I am in ecstasies of joy. So I must thank you once more and only hope that *you* may always have cause for happiness as I have today. Lastly I must thank "Providence" for one hundred times for being able to put my heart and soul to such an *Art*. Yours sincerely MARK GERTLER

Best wishes from all.
Regards to Mrs Rothenstein.

[1] This letter received the following reply:

[*12 May 1909*] *11 Oak Hill Park, Frognal*

My dear Gertler, I am delighted to hear that the school question is not going to prove a difficulty in the way of the Slade scholarship. I feel sure you have a good chance of getting it and you are doing quite rightly in submitting your still-life to the jury of the N.E.A.C. You must not worry too much about your progress, about which I have no kind of doubt; the great thing is to *care* very much for beautiful things, and to carry a pencil and sketch book about with you always and to live as much with nature as possible. Painting is done in the studio, but inspiration comes from outside, and you must get away into the fields whenever you get a chance spend as much of your time as you can in the open air. Come up to Hampstead some day soon. We will go for another walk on the Heath. Please remember me kindly to your people. Yours always sincerely W.R.

[2] John Fothergill, who later kept the Spread Eagle, Thame.

[3] The New English Art Club, at that time the goal for Slade students. Generally referred to in these letters as the N.E.A.C.

To William Rothenstein

[*Wednesday ? 1910*] *14 Spital Square, E.*

Dear Mr Rothenstein, I was indeed very pleased to hear from you, and shall be really happy to see you again. As for myself I am in "Paradise". Everything is going excellently and could not be better. Tonks has been encouraging me greatly. Besides praising some paintings I have done in holidays, he told me that I had made good progress in school and that I can tell my people so. Imagine my joy. I shall come and see you next Tuesday and bring some drawings *only*, although I should like you to see paintings too; but for them I am going to be impertinent enough to ask you down to *my* place for tea, where we will make you taste some Passover food, which I am sure you will like. Will you come?

With best wishes from us *all* to yourself and family. Sincerely yours
MARK GERTLER

To William Rothenstein

[*? 1909*] *Post Office, Andover, Hants*

Dear Mr Rothenstein, I suppose you have received my first postcard although I now write again to let you know a little more about myself. The country here is very beautiful indeed and I am enjoying it immensely. Lately I am enjoying it still more because at first Mr Goyson kept me at painting little bits around a farm, but now he lets me paint in the meadows near little streams which are beautiful beyond words. I can actually see the fishes swimming in the water. To sum it up in a few words, everything is very beautiful and ideal-like.

The following is how I spend each day.

Paint from 10 a.m. to 1 p.m.
Draw from 2 p.m. to 4 p.m.
Paint from 5 p.m. to 8.30 p.m.
Work altogether from 10 a.m. until 8.30 p.m.

If it rains I paint stables and other interiors.

Now I should very much like to hear how you are spending your holiday.

Best regards to Mrs R. and children. Yours sincerely MARK GERTLER

Mr Lesser has bought my "Onion" still-life for £1.

To William Rothenstein

[*? 1909*] *Post Office, Andover, Hants.*

Dear Mr Rothenstein, I was indeed glad to hear from you and to hear that you are all so happy. I was getting quite anxious about you all—I did not know what to think. Thinking that you were somewhere in Dorset I was greatly surprised to learn that you are in France instead. I was very glad also to know that the children are enjoying themselves. I can almost see Rachel's eyes beaming with pleasure as she settles down—only for a short time—to play one game. John I suppose will be rather reluctant to go back to school after mountain climbing and imagining himself all sorts of brave personages. Mrs R. and Albert[1], are they very happy too? I have had an excellent time here and what is more important I have gained a great deal of experience in landscape which will be of use to me in my other works. I have also done a great deal of useful drawing. The number of canvases I shall have to bring home will be quite large.

My people are all quite well, thank you, but longing for me to come home and I shall not be sorry to see all their dear faces again.

I am going to London on next Tuesday. I have heard from Fothergill—he is quite well. Shall be glad to see your work. My best wishes to you all.

MARK

To William Rothenstein

[? *1910*] *14 Spital Square, E.*

Dear Mr Rothenstein, I should like to come and see you on Thursday afternoon and we could arrange about getting a "Jew". I went to see Mr Samuels but he didn't offer to buy anything although he promised to let me paint his wife after he returns from his holiday, that is in about four months' time. I didn't like the man very much—a sort of "touch me not" person. He has a nice big house, but he does not deserve it. I was never more socialistically inclined than when I came home with my two loads of pictures, which weren't by any means light. He let me go home without buying one! Those are the *nice* people!!

If this appointment does not suit, could you let me know which day would? I want to come and see you. Yours sincerely MARK GERTLER

To William Rothenstein[2]

[*10 May 1910*] *14 Spital Square, E.*

Dear Mr Rothenstein, Although my praise, I know, has not much worth, I feel that as a "brother brush" (if you will give me leave to call myself

[1] Albert Rothenstein (afterwards Rutherston) brother of William.

[2] Rothenstein's reply to this letter was as follows:

21 May 1910 *11 Oak Hill Park, Frognal*

My dear Gertler, Many thanks for your letter. Believe me nothing touches me more than to get the acknowledgement of younger men that one's work has not been all in vain. I hope you and yours are all well. Please give your good people my kindest regards. I shall be freer these next days and will come down to see you at Spital Square soon. I think I sent you tickets for my show; yours always

W.R.

Self-Portrait
Pencil drawing (10 × 8 in.) 1909
Reproduced by permission of Mr Kerrison Preston

The Artist's Mother

Oil painting (26 × 22 in.) 1911

Reproduced by permission of the Tate Gallery

that) I must congratulate you for the two very fine pictures you have at the Whitechapel Art Gallery. It is really impudent of me to write you this, but believe me it is from the bottom of my heart that I do so, for of all the fine things of that *very* fine show I like your pictures *best*. Of the two I like the "Jew" picture best—I spent all my time, nearly, looking at it. It is one of the finest things I know of *all* pictures and very proud am I to be able to say that the man who did it is my *kindest* friend.

Believe me to be yours very sincerely MARK GERTLER

To William Rothenstein

[*Probably 1910*] *14 Spital Square, E.*

Dear Mr Rothenstein, I think that I have not yet written to tell you that I am now the proud possessor of a beautiful studio. It is situated in Commercial Street round the corner of where I live. Although it is on the top floor of a house, in the middle of a noisy market place, it is very comfortable. I am very happy and proud of it indeed. I am so independent! I sit at one end of the room and look across to the other and say, Look! this is all my own. I can do what I please. Sing, run, place my feet on the table, anything, and there is no one to stop me. I of course don't do these things, but sit and gloat over the quiet solitude of it. It is exactly what I used to look forward to, for what more does one want but a room, materials, and the National Gallery?

On the whole I am awfully pleased with my existence. I live almost spiritually, looking down with a cynical smile at all the petty little worries of mankind, for I feel that I gracefully float above all these, touching only what is beautiful and worthy. When I look at other men and see what are their worries, their ambitions, their outlooks, I feel that they have in life got hold of the "wrong end of the stick" and that I am really in a way a superman, for in order to be happy they seek unworthy and impossible things whilst I can go out and thrill with happiness over a tree, a blade of grass, a cloud, a child, an onion, any part of nature's innocent work. Have I not the advantage?

Just one other thing that makes me so happy, that is my nice friends amongst the upper class. They are so much nicer than the rough "East Ends" I am used to. My chief friend and pal is young Nevinson,[1] a very very nice chap. I am awfully fond of him. I am so happy when I am out with him. He invites me down to dinner and then we go on the Heath talking of the future, oh! so enthusiastically! Then Sassoon,[2] who has done me many little kindnesses. He is a chap that does you a kindness *without fuss* from his heart. Yours very sincerely, a happy friend MARK GERTLER

[1] C. R. W. Nevinson, son of H. W. Nevinson, the journalist.
[2] Probably Siegfried Sassoon.

PART THREE

Friends and Patrons

The earliest letters of Mark Gertler to Carrington which have been preserved date from the spring of 1912, when he was twenty and when he had just finished his time at the Slade and was still living with his family in the East End, which at that time was in outlook and customs almost a world apart. During his first year or so at the school he seems to have been extremely lonely, no doubt through pride and shyness. I do not think there was any snobbery at the Slade. His exceptional ability was, however, soon recognised. His first intimate friend was C. R. W. Nevinson, who introduced him to the brilliant group of young artists, Paul and John Nash, William Roberts, Stanley Spencer and John Currie. Nevinson himself was something of a lone wolf, introspective and often despondent about his work. His friendship with Gertler had meant a great deal to him and the break over Carrington, whom Nevinson had been the first to know and to love, was a loss to both artists.

The artists used to meet in Soho or at the Café Royal, and it was there Gertler came to meet Edward Marsh and his first patrons. In a letter to Rupert Brooke (July 1913) Marsh describes Gertler, whom he has just met, as "a beautiful little Jew, like a Lippo Lippi cherub", and in another letter: "He is rather beautiful and has a funny little shiny black fringe, his mind is deep and simple, and I think he's got the *feu sacré*." In his biography of Marsh, Christopher Hassall credits Currie and Gertler with the conversion of Marsh from old master drawings to an interest in contemporary art. During 1914 Marsh was active in trying to match his Georgian poets with a volume of Georgian drawings, which was to include Gertler along with Stanley Spencer, Paul and John Nash, Nevinson, Gaudier-Brzeska, Roberts and about twenty then unknown artists. Unfortunately, perhaps because of the war, it came to nothing.

Gertler's meeting with Carrington (as she was known at the Slade and for the rest of her life) was fateful for him, whether for good or ill the reader can decide. Their friendship covers nearly ten years of his life, when he was developing as an artist and a person. It may help to understand the rather complicated nature of their relationship if I give something of her own background. She was some two years younger than Gertler and came from a very different *milieu*. Her parents were middle class and Victorian. By the time this correspondence opens her father, of whom she was really fond, was over eighty and crippled. Dora Carrington was one of a family of five, all educated at Bedford, a town favoured by ex-colonials for its cheap education, a town which also retained some of the puritanism of Bunyan. Carrington's talent for drawing won her a scholarship at the Slade, an event her mother never ceased to regret, at least in private (even if at tea parties it scored a point in prestige). From the moment Carrington left home there was a constant struggle to avoid returning for holidays and to evade by some ruse maternal discipline and inquisition. It was this, perhaps, which developed her aptitude for broken engagements and minor deceptions, habits for which Gertler (and not only Gertler) so often reproached her. It also schooled her not to sacrifice her independence, but to pursue her career as an artist and to choose her own friends. This was to prove the everlasting stumbling block in the prolonged love affair between her and Gertler. Gilbert Cannan, who knew both, was not far out when he wrote a final assessment of the affair in his novel *Mendel*:[1] "Of the two, she had the better brain, and indeed the stronger character. She had been toughened in the struggle to break out of the web of hypocrisy and meaningless tradition of gentility in which her family was enmeshed, and the freedom she had won was very precious to her."

Her own letters to Gertler have also survived and some of them have been chosen to give a fairer picture of their relationship.

To Carrington

6 May 1912 — *32 Elder Street, E.*

Dear Carrington, Please come on Friday at 5 o'clock with Barlow and Ruth.[2] I hope you will find my picture worth seeing. I have worked very earnestly at it, and put in a lot of love and care, but it still falls far short of the beautiful things I want to do.

I have just come home from Cambridge and I have never before enjoyed a train ride so much. I enjoyed mostly when we passed the "slums" of Hackney and Bethnal Green. It reminded me so much of my early life and all its simplicity. The poverty, although striking, had a beautiful simplicity which was to be envied.

In one back-yard there was a little girl minding a child. In another there was nothing but a dear little bird, who, with much curiosity, was inspecting a chimney-pot. It must have taken it for some huge and ruined tower. One yard interested me very much. There was a Jewish boy taking his Hebrew lesson from an aged Rabbi. As usual, the Rabbi was doing both the teaching and the learning, whilst the boy was vacantly thinking of his "pals" outside.

[1] For a further account of this novel, see the Appendix on page 253.

[2] Two Slade students. Ruth Humphries was daughter of a Bradford printer.

How like my youth! Only instead of "pals" I thought of *art*.

Oh! Carrington! How curious life is! Well, until Friday, I am

MARK GERTLER

I may see you Friday morning as I am coming to the Slade with Nevinson to see Tonks. Bring Ruth on Friday.

To Carrington

19 June 1912 — *32 Elder Street, E.*

Dear Carrington, I have thought of ourselves, and I've come to the conclusion that I love you far too much for us to be merely friends. Therefore, unless you would agree to marry me, or in some other way be more than friends, I am afraid we must part for always.

Of course I need hardly tell what misery that would cause me, but it can't be helped. When I look at you, you look so beautiful that I feel that I must kiss you. You have taught me to expect this by having favoured another man that way—a thing I shall never get over.

Before I finish this letter let me place before you the advantages you would have by marrying me.

1. I am a very promising artist—one who is likely to make a lot of money.
2. I am an intelligent companion.
3. You would not have to *rely* upon your people.
4. I could help you in your *art* career.
5. You would have absolute freedom and a nice studio of your *own*.

I know of course you would not agree to this.

I shall see you twice more, when you come to tea and when we go to the Opera with Brett.[1] Try and keep Thursday evening free, so that we could have a *last* talk. I shall of course send you those two reproductions I have ordered for you and will always be glad to help you. MARK GERTLER

To Carrington

[? *June 1912*] — *32 Elder Street, E.*

Dear Carrington, I am writing to ask you if you will be my friend again.

I will tell you why I want you. I find it almost impossible to paint without having some person at the back of my mind. I mean that ever since I got to know you I thought of you in every stroke I did. Now I find that I want you badly to see all that I paint and I keep wondering what you will think of my work. I can't bear the idea of developing without you and

[1] The Hon. Dorothy Brett, daughter of Lord Esher, and also a Slade student.

I am developing so quickly. You can't think how difficult it is to have no one to work for, no one to share one's real successes with.

Now, I only ask you to come if you want to yourself. By now, you must think me a very tiresome, weak and inconsistent person, and you are perhaps tired of me. In that case you *must* tell me and then we could part for ever. In which case I should struggle through this lonely and friendless period of my life and wait until someone else comes to take your place. I could do this, so if you don't want me tell me. Whatever you do, *don't* come back out of kindness to me.

I have nothing more to write in this letter. What I've written is badly expressed, because I am desperately unhappy. This afternoon my work has gone particularly well, but, I thought, who is there to care about it, who can I share it with! And you, I suppose, have forgotten me by now or are tired of me.

MARK GERTLER

To Carrington

2 July 1912 *32 Elder Street, E.*

Dear Carrington, If you can see me on Wednesday I would be glad.

Because I want to say good-bye to you. It may be good-bye for a long time—longer than three months, I am afraid.

I don't think that often these last few times I love you quite as much as I used to. I have suddenly begun to think that you simply use me as a help to your work and for myself you don't care a scrap. Your affections are given completely to Nevinson. I must have been a fool to stand it as long as I have, without seeing through you. I have written to Nevinson telling him that we, he and I, are no longer friends.

I have just had a letter from a Jewish girl I once knew. A girl that is simple and beautiful, who is, thank God, not "*arty*" and of my own class. She will not torment my life.

I want to see you on Wednesday because I want to say good-bye. If you can't see me in the evening, I shall be in my studio all day. Let me know. If I am to come to you I will come 6.30. Yes, after Wednesday I shall leave you in peace with Nevinson. You can do what you like then.

Well, in case you cannot see me on Wednesday, let me here say good-bye and I wish you every success. When you come back, go often to the National Gallery and look at the pictures we both used to look at together.

MARK GERTLER

To Carrington

2 July 1912 *32 Elder Street, E.*

Dear Carrington, I wouldn't have written my last letter, without I knew that I could be *just* friends.

All the adversity I have had against my love, for you, has so pitilessly crushed it, that I now can easily fall in and say "*Let us be just friends*" and certainly I *do* want you as a friend. You must never say, though, that I ceased loving you because I tired of you. No! it was merely crushed by the cold treatment it received. *Love is very sensitive!* Even a lover possesses dignity: I was no exception. When, time after time, you would write "We are *merely* friends" or actually come down to my studio and say "We must part"—why? *Because you love me!* What treatment! What a reason!—My dignity was so outraged, my love so hideously rebuffed, that my love took wings and, terribly insulted, flew for ever away, leaving me rather limp and astonished. I cannot help thinking that it was a pity to so have crushed it, because it had beautiful points. It was then that I knew I could be friends and so I wrote. So now we are friends! Ordinary friends! As cold as you like! Yes! I will treat you *exactly* as I would a man. I hope you will like it.

Please don't think I am blaming *you, not in the least.*

Well, from now we will *for ever* drop the subject. We better start being friends at once. I shall never mention to you again that I ever loved you. So that you won't be bored by me, as you of late must have been by my confessions of love.

As regards Nevinson, I am afraid I cannot go back to be his friend—it is not jealousy at all. You see I have lost interest in him—for no definite reason—so why should I be with a person for whose company I do not care? You see I have a way of changing my friends. He was once my friend, but now my *greatest* friend is Currie[1] and Currie would consider it rather funny if I said tomorrow night I shall go out with Nevinson! It wouldn't be fair to Currie.

Besides Nevinson will soon forget me. I shall soon pass out of his life, as he has passed out of mine. When you come back he will be able to have you as a friend all right and I don't see why I should deputise until then.

I have now completely finished my long picture and the "Musical Girl". New ideas are now being born in my head which will not be ready for some days. I will write you more about my work in the next letter.

Let me know how your work is getting on—send me a small one if possible. Write often and I will do the same. Let me know your "Ruth" address, and also remember me to Ruth. Yours sincerely MARK GERTLER

To C. R. W. Nevinson

[*July 1912*] *32 Elder Street, E.*

Dear Nevinson, I am writing here to tell you that our friendship must end from now, my sole reason being that I am in love with Carrington and I have reason to believe that you are so too. Therefore, much as I have tried

[1] John Currie, a close friend of Gertler, highly thought of by Marsh. Gilbert Cannan depicts him as "Logan" in his novel *Mendel.*

to overlook it, I have come to the conclusion that rivals, and rivals in love, cannot be friends.

You must know that ever since you brought Carrington to my studio my love for her has been steadily increasing. You might also remember that many times, when you asked me down to dinner, I refused to come. *Jealousy* was the cause of it.

Whenever you told me that you had been kissing her, you could have knocked me down with a feather, so faint was I. Whenever you saw me depressed of late, when we were all out together, it wasn't boredom as I pretended but *love.*

Yes! I have become the most sentimental hero in the most sentimental drama on the "Halls". I who was so cynical and caricatured those heroes. A music-hall sketch makes me—now—weep, I weep over its truth and realism. I devour little love scenes in penny novelettes.

I have, in some of my passionate letters to Carrington, told her how easily I could worship her. Yes, I argued, the Gods and the Christs one reads of, one cannot see or understand, but you, my beautiful girl, you I can see and feel and therefore you are my God!

To touch her hand is bliss! to kiss it Heaven itself! I have stroked her hair and I nearly fainted with joy.

That, my dear Nevinson, is my unfortunate condition! From this, you must see that I cannot bear *any man* who has anything to do with her. Rivals we are destined to be and rivals we must remain. We must be rivals openly, really rivals dramatically and theatrically and not friends. I am sorry but that is how it must be.

You are now evidently saying how silly Gertler has become! I know it and I cannot help it. If we meet in company we need make no fuss and just pretend that we are the same.[1] MARK GERTLER

[1] Nevinson described his break with Gertler in the following letter to Carrington:

Thursday *4 Downside Crescent, Hampstead*

My dear Carrington, I am distinctly amused at you two. I congratulate Gertler on his delightful ease and facility he is able to change from the role of a passionate and over-jealous lover to that of a philanthropic platonic friend. However only leopards can't change their spots and I believe snakes when affected by heat and other adverse circumstances are proverbially gifted with casting their skins, so why should not poor human men masquerade in different emotions if it amuses them. Of course you will not take my advice: that is why it is so freely, invariably, and safely given by all our friends and enemies. But one thing I do earnestly beg you; may I in future be kept absolutely outside all your future lapses and quarrels and depressions? Your acquaintance with Gertler I don't think can affect my old friendship with him as I feel there is not much hope of it being regained. I have managed to exist this week without it so I presume next month it will still be possible. All this worry has again succeeded in enlarging my liver, as unfortunately I have felt this loss of Gertler more intensely than I thought possible. I suppose I am cursed with an abnormally affectionate temperament, which naturally after my first and only experiment of letting it loose on a girl five years ago, I have naturally ever since realised the hopeless misunderstanding and eventual quarrel that is bound to happen with a girl immensely liked. That my nature slowly and silently and almost unknown to myself has been letting itself loose on Gertler is my folly, never dreaming that

To Carrington

[*July 1912*] *32 Elder Street, E.*

Carrington Dear, Listen to what I have to say! Ever since I wrote you that last letter, I have been doing nothing but repent for what I wrote. Here then will I state my real feelings and emotions. Emotions that come from my innermost heart.

1. I love you *more* than ever.
2. I never ceased to love you for one second ever since I met you.
3. I only said I did at moments when I was in a rage.
4. You are the best, the most good and the most beautiful woman I *ever* knew.
5. My only desire is that you should forgive me for my last letter. I shall die of misery if you don't.

I shall do *my best* to remain friends with you, but whether we do or not, I shall always think of you as a person I loved.

You can't imagine how difficult I find it to remain friends. Believe me I do my best, because I know you would prefer it so. However, I shall *really* try and am quite willing to sacrifice, in so doing, all my own feelings to yours.

---

sex would as usual come and ruin all, as it is bound to between man and women. Does not Oscar Wilde say something about "All men kill the thing they love, a brave man with a sword, the coward with a kiss", though I suppose you are still too innocent to realise the whole power and truth of this, as I do not suppose you understand what the words "kill" and "kiss" symbolise. As I dare say you can gather from the tone of my letter I still have not altered my mind one atom of what I originally thought, but of course you will do what you want, so I will not waste any time saying anything except please remember "to men women have always proved that triumph of matter over mind", and if Gertler does admire your looks, and there is fortunately no accounting for taste, he will always prefer your looks and all that concerns your looks over *everything* else. Now I suppose this letter has thoroughly annoyed you, as I have spoken too many unsugared truths and there is nothing that irritates all of us more, but I merely wanted to state my point of view, so I have done. I will try and be nice on the next page. On Monday we start for Havre, if I am well enough. I have been working like Satan drawing my own and my mother's head and one model whose repulsive turn-up nose and over-heated and badly-kept body made me rid of her before I had completed. I am really improving in my drawing. If only I could feel some hope that I might some day do a fairly good drawing I think my life would be more tolerable. Even if I lost everything and gained some hope, which I feel dimly stirring within me. My dear honey, I know I am about to say a maiden and auntly phrase, but do always keep a belief in yourself besides your critical faculty. I can warn you it is quite the lowest ebb of misery to become always a passive onlooker of your own incompetence or to be fatuous, hopeless. Write to me again before Monday if it does not bore you. I always wait for your letters but you can rely on me always nipping my affection in the bud and make it run nicely and pleasantly in a small and babbling brook; a Japanese tree form of affection, stunted but beautiful and nice to have about the house and no danger of ever growing. I am your affectionate friend C. R. W. NEVINSON

Nevinson also wrote me, in return to my letter to him, how miserable my letter has made him. His letter has made me wretchedly miserable. I shall have to do my best to be friends with him too.

Give me, please, the whole evening tomorrow, as it may, after all, have to be a long good-bye. MARK GERTLER

To Carrington

13 July 1912 *32 Elder Street, E.*

Dear Carrington, I have had one or two more successes, which I feel I must write you of, as I feel you are now my most intimate friend.

1. I have sold one of my early pictures for £35.
2. I've been approached by the Society of Portrait Painters asking me to put my name down for election.
3. The last and *most important* is a congratulatory letter from *Brown*[1] about my pictures, and asking me if I would care to put *my name* down for *election to New English*!!!

I am so happy! It is such things that make me think for a *moment* that my ambition to become a true artist may yet be realized.

I shall see you on Friday at 7 o'clock when we shall have a good dinner on the strength of it. I am MARK GERTLER

To Carrington

19 July 1912 *32 Elder Street, E.*

My dearest Carrington, Thank you for your flowers.

Now tell me, Carrington, why should we so foolishly part?

You see, from what you have told me I now see that I cannot expect anything from you but friendship: *Great* Friendship. Having realised that I now will expect *no more.* But to part altogether really strikes me, Carrington, as being theatrical and absurd. Don't you see! your friendship alone gives me so much pleasure. Why should I lose that? How nice it will be to write to you all my little troubles and pleasures?!

Do you know that every time I paint a picture I say, Oh! Won't Carrington like this, or I hope Carrington will like this. You see *that* is so necessary to me. Every man ought to have a woman confidant and friend. I must have you.

Really, Carrington, I will not bother you any more with my love for you. Then will you please let me continue? I should be much happier really. Do let us continue and not be foolish. After all, those nights we had

[1] Professor Brown of the Slade.

together were very beautiful weren't they? I don't ask for more. I don't want to marry; that would be rather stupid.

Well, dear, let me know soon what you think. MARK GERTLER

Thank you *so much* for *Les Misérables*. The thing I ought to have mentioned firstly is that your friendship *inspires my work*, *Not*, as you say, spoils my life and work. You are *wrong*, *wrong*.

To Carrington

[? *July 1912*] *32 Elder Street, E.*

Dear Carrington, Don't be unhappy, as life is very inspiring and beautiful. That it is hard, is true. But isn't there something grand about it being hard? Isn't there something grand to try and bear up and give to the world all we can? Think of the good company we are in. Think of Christ, Michael Angelo.

Angelo's life was very sad. How grand it is to think that a man that gave such marvellous things to the world got nothing in return but sadness and ill treatment from it! When a great friend of Michael Angelo's died, Michael said, "Now that he is gone and left me alone in this *deceitful* world I shall end my last few years in abject misery."

Think of that! When he said that he had already given us that marvellous creation the "Entombment" in the National Gallery! So you see we have to try and see something beautiful in this hardness of life. In writing this I am *sure* that we will be much happier in sticking together. Friends like ourselves cannot afford to part.

I am trying to get you a photograph of Epstein's statue.

I am happier already. MARK GERTLER

To Carrington

[*July 1912*] *Hôtel-Restaurant Taverne Charles, 36 Rue du Quai, Ostende*

My dearest Carrington, I thank you very much for your letter. It was to me *extremely* interesting. It in fact excited me to such a pitch that I feel I must come over to Bradford for a day to see the Exhibition and other works. Would you please ask Ruth if she could see me if I came across on Tuesday next?

Also would you ask her to let me know particulars about fares and from where I start, etc. I should be extremely pleased if she would help me, and could arrange to see me and show me round that day. If necessary I should stay in Bradford the night, as I should like to see Charles Rothenstein's[1] collections. Ruth could give me an introduction. Also tell me if you will be there that day. Let me know soon.

[1] Brother of William Rothenstein, later known as Charles Rutherston.

I am enjoying my stay here extremely. Our plan is to have a complete rest from work. This place is like one huge Soho! *Beautiful* children. It is very healthy. We bathe each morning in the sea. I have bought myself a very beautiful shirt. If I come to Bradford I shall wear it.

I, of course, find it extremely difficult to go without work. Some moments hang heavily and wearily upon me. And my hand itches for the brush. I have just come from a French café, where the music played so beautifully that I should have given much to have you, my dearest Carrington, with me. Do you still, Carrington, like me a little? I like you, so much, oh! very much.

Carrington, before I came here Epstein took me to the British Museum and there revealed to me such wonders in works of art that my inspiration knew no bounds and I came to the conclusion that Egyptian art is *by far, by far, by far* the greatest of *all* art. Oh! Carrington it is, it is. We moderns are but ants in comparison. But ants!

As I think of this great art my ambition doubles and redoubles! Oh! Carrington, if I am given many years in this world, I think! I think! I shall do great things! Things so great that they will surprise all men! But Carrington! I shall have to have your companionship! You must, you must like me a little. I do not ask for more from you, Carrington, because as soon as I do not hear from you the sun has no rays for me, the flowers no scent, all beauty flies from me and all is blackness! Black as Hell. Remember I do not ask much from you, for as I have already told you I now know that I cannot expect your love. It was a terrible realisation! But what could I do?! I know now that nature has chosen to illtreat me from that point of view.

But I shall make up for it by producing great art! You see! The photo of yourself sitting on the beach is beautiful. You are certainly a beautiful little person. I don't know anybody to equal you.

I have succeeded in getting the Boxer of the "Dieppe" to sit for me! I shall do a good thing of him. When you come back, we can draw him together. . . .

Remember me to Ruth and tell her that I am awfully sorry but I still don't know Wadsworth's[1] address.

Well I may see you on Tuesday.

I enclose photos of Henry[2] and myself. MARK GERTLER

To Carrington

[? *August 1912*] *32 Elder Street, E.*

Dear Carrington, I had a very exciting time this morning. Went to see

[1] Edward Wadsworth, the painter.

[2] Dolly Henry, Currie's mistress. Currie and she had gone to Ostend with Gertler.

"Cupid";[1] "Cupid" took me to have a drink and behold! *John*[2] was there.

John immediately came up to me and we talked and talked. I never knew what a beautifully simple man he was. He took me to see his work—asked me what I thought. But I was so excited and nervous that I didn't know what to say.

Then we had lunch together and got so confidential that we told each other all about our lives. I even told him that I loved a beautiful little girl and that she had left me for three months. He was very sympathetic. I told him that my little girl's face was always like a beautiful flower encased in a form of gold. He told me that he loved his wife and, with *tears* actually in his eyes, he told me how he had just lost a charming little boy of his.

He then proceeded to give me some very useful "tips" on tempera, of which I will, when you return, tell you. We parted great friends and he told me he likes me very much. Isn't it splendid!

My mother is home and I am pleased. Tomorrow I go to the country until Wednesday. My address will be until then c/o Waley Cohen, Courtlands, East Grinstead, Sussex. Yours ever MARK GERTLER

To Carrington

2 September 1912, midnight *32 Elder Street, E.*

My dear Carrington, I have not long come from a Wagner concert. What a wonderful man is Wagner!! What a wonderful art is music!!—Oh! it was beautiful and inspiring! Love, sorrow, despair, hope, joy, all were expressed—oh! too wonderfully for me to tell you how much it means to me—look at it yourself. Excuse, please, my own *foolish* attempts that I send you. My only excuse is that I am but twenty.

I have lately discovered much about tempera. So much that within a fortnight I hope *actually* to be painting in *tempera*. It has cost me so much time and trouble to find out that I have done but little work. In the meantime whilst my grounds, etc., are getting ready, I shall be employed on a big picture I am very keen on—"The Coster Family"—this in oil. I have done two little paintings which are not altogether bad for a beginner like myself. Though, to speak the truth, everything I have done so far is *nothing—nothing*. Unless I do something far, far greater soon I shall be very miserable and unhappy. The more I go on, the more difficult does my art become to me. I have had such miserable nights lately. You don't know—some nights I couldn't sleep at all, so hopeless did my work and the future seem. Yet some youths would be happy in my position—everybody seems to praise my work and yet, and yet—!

Tonight I am happy, though. I must now finish. The light of my candle is beginning to throb, like an excited heart. How like a dying man—it

[1] I cannot trace to whom this refers.

[2] Augustus John.

seems to make great efforts. Up and down it goes! Poor, poor candle, how like us you are.

Well it is much past midnight and one restless and sleepless cock that an old woman keeps next door in a yard has already crowed. So good-bye

MARK GERTLER

To Carrington

12 September 1912 *32 Elder Street, E.*

Dear Carrington, Thank you so much for your letter. You mistake to think that anything you tell me about yourself bores me. Few things interest me more. I was a little sorry to hear that you do not intend coming out much next term. Although I wouldn't dream of asking you out more than you would like. As I don't want—*in any way*—to be a worry to you. In fact, I shall do my best to be a help, and so show my thanks for your friendship —for I love you above all my friends—*I mean even as a friend.*

Next term, I should like you to come and study with me in the galleries etc. That, I am sure, would give us both pleasure, besides being *time gained and not lost*. Also if it is too much trouble I should like you to write as often as you can to me—it only takes a few minutes. Surely you spare that time for *me*?

It would be difficult to give you my state of mind just now about my art. All I can say is that each day I am struck with the enormity, the difficulty, and the greatness of *our art*. My own incapacity appals me. Yet each day I learn so much that I wonder at the little I knew yesterday. I have on my desk as I write some reproductions of Fra Angelico!—that beautiful monk knew how to paint!

Dear, dear man! How I love you and your work. The dear man gave up his whole life to *religion and art* and did pictures on the walls of each fellow monk's cell.

I abandon most of my ideas now. So critical am I just now. I am painting in tempera. Oh! the difficulty! The little picture I am painting now I call "Hagar". The ones I am about to do are (1) Coster Mother and Child, (2) An Adam and Eve, (3) A portrait of my mother in which I shall try and get all that I feel about my mother. They will all be in tempera except my mother. Of course my output will be very small now—very small. You see I do a complete picture in oil first then copy it in tempera. So little can you alter in tempera. In fact you can't alter it *at all.*

I am so interested in my work that I see *nobody*—not even Currie. I live in a sort of beautiful, half melancholy loneliness.

Keats is interesting me enormously just now. Have you his poems? If so read his poem to *Fanny*, the woman he loved. He and his love are as unfortunate as myself. Here are small quotations from this:

> I know it—and to know it is despair
> To one who loves you as I love, sweet Fanny!

Whose heart goes fluttering for you every where,
Nor, when away you roam,
Dare keep its wretched home,
Love, love alone, his pains severe and many.
Then, loveliest! Keep me free,
From torturing jealousy.

This is only a bit from a beautiful poem. He is wonderful!

Please do not think I insert this as an appeal. You and I are *but friends* and I love you for being my friend—enough!

I think I can get you a little model—a child.

When are you coming to town? Will you, I wonder, be good enough to come and see me soon?

Well I must do some more tempera—so good-bye.

Please, dear Carrington, write *soon*. Your great friend MARK GERTLER

To Carrington

24 September 1912 *32 Elder Street, E.*

Dear Carrington, Thank you for your letter. It gave me great pleasure, because you don't know how conflicting and worrying are the emotions that pass through my mind—I mean concerning my art! Carrington! as I write this my eyes are aching with trouble. I could weep about it all.

You see, I am so dissatisfied about my work.

So troubled am I lately and so useless do I feel as an artist that, although —it may seem funny—I seriously thought of taking up some simple trade, and so justify my existence and be useful. What's the good of living if you are no use!? And mediocre art is not only useless, but *criminal*. For we are merely imposing! I thought of being a *baker*; three days a week bread is a *necessity*. No, I am at present more useless than the simplest baker! Oh! great is my trouble! Please God! Give me some more talents so that I may be of some use.

Please, Carrington, excuse this doleful letter, but as I once told you, I want you to be a friend in my troublesome moments as well as the happy. But, God knows, I can't help writing this—so deeply do I feel it. But I suppose I am young and there is yet time.

Fancy, in the midst of all these thoughts, a poor woman and her son, a boy of fourteen, came to ask my advice. She thinks the boy has talents— ought he to be an artist?

Oh! Carrington, what could I say? The mother looked at me and envied me! They both thought what a happy man this must be. They were both nervous and "Sir'd" me. Did they know that, though for so many years I had been studying, studying, working, working, pouring my very brains out into my art, yet there I stood feeling more ignorant than when

I first started as a boy of fourteen like the little fellow that was asking my advice at that moment.

"It's a hard life, it's a hard life," was all I managed to mutter to the anxious mother. They went away more bewildered than they came. I dropped exhausted into an armchair, thinking, thinking of all my past life! How strange it all seemed! I remembered my childhood in Austria. The great *poverty*. No bread and my poor striving mother—my father was in America at the time. Then I remembered my school days in London with my little urchin friends. They now sell newspapers at the Mansion House. Then came my Polytechnic days. Then I worked in a designing firm for *a year*! which nearly broke my heart. Then the Slade and that awful ghost Tonks, and here I am now an artist—supposed to be—yes, I thought to myself, "Be a tailor, anything, my dear boy," but not an artist. By this time the room was in gloom and my pictures all looked like mocking spectres that were there to laugh at me. I could stand it no longer. So I went out and saw more unfortunate artists. I looked at them talking art, Ancient art, Modern art, Impressionism, Post-Impressionism, Neo-Impressionism, Cubists, Spottists, Futurists, Cave-dwelling, Wyndham Lewis, Duncan Grant, Etchells,[1] Roger Fry! I looked on and laughed to myself saying, "Give me the *Baker*, the *Baker*," and I walked home disgusted with them *all*, was glad to find my dear simple mother waiting for me with a nice roll, that she knows I like, and a cup of hot coffee. Dear mother, the same mother of all my life, *twenty years*. You, dear mother, I thought, are the only *modern artist*.

When you come back I will tell you a lot about my mother.

MARK GERTLER

Excuse this terrible long letter. How I must *bore* you with all this egoism!

To Carrington

[? *December 1912*] *32 Elder Street, E.*

Dear Carrington, I hope your leg is better—you probably cut it whilst dancing with Pincher. The joy of dancing with him was so great that you jumped for joy! thus cutting yourself. I am nothing! I can be kept waiting a whole hour in a *lonely* studio. The excuse being that Wadsworth's work was *so* interesting, that, that, honestly, Mark Gertler was completely forgotten! Also, the last night, you go to a *rotten* dance in preference to seeing me. That is how you treat me. You take every opportunity to annoy and hurt me. Yet you are the *Lady* and I am the East End boy.

In the future you are not going to any dance without *my* permission.

I am sending you 10*s*. for your fares to London on Thursday or any other day. If it isn't sufficient, let me know. Come if possible because it would be so nice to arrange about P[aris]![2]

[1] Frederick Etchells, post-impressionist painter, architect and translator of Corbusier.

[2] Gertler planned a visit there with Carrington but it came to nothing.

I have suddenly taken up again my big picture, with extraordinary fresh vigour. It is now practically finished. I think it is the best thing I've done. Therefore I haven't had time to do much else, but there are many new things brewing in my mind. I have done a little sketch painting of a child, which I think is rather amusing.

Oh! Carrington, how I should love to be able to express myself simply and beautifully in paint. I have no ambitions in life but that. I once told you how simple my desires are. I shall keep doing little pictures for a long time—simple things—so that I can put my whole soul into trying to express my own feelings as forcibly and beautifully as I can. But oh! it makes me so sad and unhappy—I mean my incapacity. Today after work I took a walk and went down to Tower Bridge to look at the water and ships. I enjoyed it very much—it was so quiet. There was a beautiful half moon out. I was rather surprised to hear a tiny little child, sitting on a bench next to me, shouting to its mother "Oh! Muvver, ain't that nice?" and it was pointing to the moon!

Last night I finished *The Widow in the Bye Street*.[1] I liked it enormously. It only added to my idea that you women are the curse of our lives. I hated you all last night.

Well, although I have lots to write I shall stop now, for fear of boring you. Were it a dance that I was writing about I should write more fully, for *then* you could *not* be bored.

Please write at once about coming to London and remember I *want* you to come.

MARK GERTLER

To Carrington

Thursday midnight [? *December 1912*] *32 Elder Street, E.*

Dear Carrington, Monday will do very well. Come if it rains or not. I thought we were to start the 2nd for Paris. Why are you making it so late?

Never mind the affection of your people. Be more independent!

I have four things on hand now. One—the family group—is quite large.

Since the trouble I had with my last big picture, I have not been quite well. Today I got up with a very bad headache, which prevented me from working. In the afternoon I got a lot better, and as I sat by my fire, thinking, I happened to notice how beautiful the little patch I got from my back window was. From where I sat there were just a few chimneys coming most serenely against the sky, which was that indescribable luminous grey with little rose flecks peacefully travelling across it.

I got up, walked to the window, opened it wide and sat on the sill dangling my legs outside. How can I describe to you the beauty of it all?! There were lots of chimneys of all shapes and sizes. Here and there one would send out little puffs of smoke: purple smoke, blue smoke, creamy smoke, all done quietly, quietly, as if in a whisper. In the yards below a

[1] By John Masefield.

The Artist's Sister

Oil painting (40 × 30 in.) 1911

Reproduced by permission of Mr Thomas Balston

Jewish Family

Oil painting (20 × 20 in.) 1913

Reproduced by permission of the Arts Council of Great Britain

Presented by the Contemporary Art Society to the Tate Gallery

woman would be hanging washing of beautifully faded colours—pink drawers, blue shirts, bright green skirts. Later, the sky turned into beautiful rose, and lights appeared at the windows which made little oblong shapes of the palest lemon. Oh! I sat there and thought and thought. I just enjoyed it and cared for no person or anything. It was one of those moments when one even enjoys that horrible loneliness and isolation of life, the thought of which in the ordinary way gives one great pain.

Yes, my isolation is extraordinary. I am alone, alone, in the whole of this world! Yes, if only, like my brothers, I was an ordinary workman, as I should have been. But no! I must desire, desire. How I pay for those desires! Oh! God! Do I deserve to be so tormented? By my ambitions I am cut off from my own family and class and by them I have been raised to be equal to a class I hate! They do not understand me nor I them. So I am an outcast. As I look at my desk I laugh, for there are dozens of notices of me in the daily papers, a lot of them praising my talents. Oh! yes I am quite well known, and yet *alone.*

But do not think I decry my fate. No! For in life, I have only one ambition, to justify my existence by paintings of great Beauty. BY MY DEAR, DEAR ART. You see if I don't do it before I am done. I am only a boy of twenty-one. I am sorry I said dear, dear art—it is not dear, because it gives me so much pain, but then all things we love give us pain.

I have been seeing a great deal of Currie. He is a great joy to me and really my truest friend.

Write me a letter before Monday. Well, shall see you at my studio on Monday? I have *no* sympathy with your leg. MARK GERTLER

To Carrington

December 1912 *32 Elder Street, E.*

Thank you, my dearest Carrington, for the little book you gave me on Millet. It is interesting me enormously. It is so like my own life, where he says: "I do not know joy: I have never seen it"—"The most cheerful things I know are calm and silence." How true that is!

The more I go on the more I seem to realise that outside my *art* there is nothing to hope for—nothing! What sometimes fills me with dread is that more and more do I seem to get severed from my fellow creatures; sometimes it seems that I have nothing in common with *anybody* on earth. My real friends seem to be, rather, the sun, the moon, the trees, the sky and other things of natural beauty.

I send you a sketch of a picture I have nearly completed of my mother. This is really the very best thing I have done. Although I am sure everybody will disagree with me. They will say: "It is not as *carefully* finished as usual." I do not care what anybody says. It was done in fever heat. Never was I so inspired as when I painted this. It is quite different in technique to anything I have done. You see I sacrificed *everything* to the spirit. I know that, had I gone on and finished it, it would have died a horrible death. So I was content to get a little of something into it, rather than finish and please the foolish buyers. But that little that I have got is surely there.

I find that there is a train that runs from Victoria at 11 o'clock. But I will let you know definitely in my next letter.

I do not mean to hurt you, my dear girl, when I find fault with you. You must overlook my critical faculty, as you must surely know that I love you dearly. It is a great regret to me that God made you unable to love me, as I love you. Had you loved me, you would have been a blessing and a happy addition to my life. However, as it is, we can be friends, perhaps for quite a *long* time, but one never knows.

Write and tell me how you are. I hope your leg is better. You were looking a little pale on Monday.

Keep well dear. Yours always MARK GERTLER

My drawings at "Chenil"[1] are selling like hot buns. I have sold seven drawings. *Gill*[2] bought one.

To Carrington

March 1913 *32 Elder Street, E.*

Dear Carrington, Thanks very much for your very interesting letter. It was very good of you to think of me and to write so soon.

The little statue of yours must indeed be wonderful. Thanks for the drawing you did of it for me. I shall look forward to seeing it. I am so glad that it is making you happy.

Thursday night I went to the Indian Museum by myself. How I enjoyed it! I have discovered a lot of new little things there which are simply magical!—I wanted you so much to be with me. Tears came into my eyes as I looked at them, all alone, in that deserted gallery. Oh! how genuine is the art of these ancients! You must come with me when you come back.

MacNamara,[3] who suddenly came to see me, asked me to come and sail with him on the river at Hammersmith. I went and we had a most adventurous time—it hailed and rained and I got drenched! Once we got blown on to a little island and were both nearly drowned! But when we got to Kew we had *such* a good lunch, lamb and boiled potatoes, mint sauce and all sorts of nice things, also a lot of whisky, after which we got so lively that we sat under a macintosh, regardless of the rain, and told each other stories.

Saturday night Currie, Henry and myself went up to Schiff's[4] for dinner.

[1] The Chenil Gallery, Chelsea.

[2] Eric Gill, the sculptor and engraver.

[3] Brother-in-law of Augustus John.

[4] Sydney Schiff, rich connoisseur and patron of artists, also wrote under the name of "Stephen Hudson" and translated the last volume of Proust, whose friend he had become. His wife, Violet, was a singer.

There were a lot of people there, also a very graceful girl, who made me dance a ballet with her. I took the part of Nijinsky. I had on a jersey and a belt. We did it so well that everybody applauded very much. They told me I looked *very nice*! Then we did a music-hall sketch, and they roared with laughter, including the girl with whom I was acting. They thought I was very clever.

Currie could not go to Ireland as he is not quite well, so I am not so lonely. Odle[1] asked me up to his people for Easter, but I could not tear myself away from my work, so I wired at the last moment to say no.

I have turned my "Jew" picture into a different thing altogether. It suddenly occurred to me how wonderful it would be to have my little girl's head near to his. So now the scheme is just two heads together: his very old, pale and wrinkled head near that healthy, fresh, young face of my little girl. The old man will be with one hand most delicately touching the girl's face, the other will be round her shoulder. I am terribly inspired with the idea and feel sure it will be one of the best things I've done. The big picture is still in the making.

My people wish to be remembered to you and my mother is waiting for her letter.

Well, good-bye and *write soon please* MARK GERTLER

To Carrington

2 April 1913 *32 Elder Street, E.*

Dear Carrington, Thanks for your letter. I am sorry that you cannot come to London. I enjoyed my few days at Brighton very much. I met there a very beautiful and charming young girl. She made it even more pleasant for me. I saw many very beautiful girls there. Beautiful girls always make me happy. They seem to be more plentiful in the spring—they come out like flowers.

I know nothing more beautiful than a beautiful girl—a beautiful face and round soft yellow neck, and fine arms, are to me the most ravishing of sights. In Brighton I felt one continual desire to kiss these beautiful creatures. However, this one that I found I did kiss. Next to being a great artist I should like to be a beautiful girl. What wonderful creatures you people are, when you are beautiful. To my mind, those that justify their existence most are the beautiful girls and the great artists. A man should be a great artist, and a woman beautiful, I see nothing in between. They are really both the same. The artist creates beauty and the beautiful girl is beauty. Beauty, therefore, is the king of life. My God is beauty, I worship him. A philosopher would immediately stop me here and ask me, "What do you mean by beauty, what is beauty!?"

I would answer, Go to the Devil!!! Beauty is what looks beautiful to *me* and what looks beautiful to *you*. Enough! don't pester me with your

[1] Alan Odle, an illustrator.

horrible and logical and tiresome philosophy. Yes, beauty rules my whole life. I paint because I want to create beauty, I love you because you are beautiful and so on.

There are many depressing sights in Brighton. I mean chiefly those horrible old emaciated women who sit upright in chariots, drawn by degraded and shabby men. These women, I believe, are called invalids. Tell me, is there a more depressing sight than this? I feel that I want to kick the man's bottom and chuck the old lady, chariot included, into the sea.

My mother thanks you for your letter. She is writing a Yiddish letter to you, which I will translate.

Write *as soon as possible*. Your letters make me happy. M. GERTLER

To Carrington

9 April 1913 *32 Elder Street, E.*

Dear Carrington, I am still working on my little picture, I have now added another head—a girl—so there is the Jew and two girls. I am working very hard indeed on it and there is still a great deal to do in it. I have not started anything else yet, as I find that I cannot concentrate on two things at once.

Currie is still ill with rheumatism, so most of my evenings are spent with him in his rooms. Henry makes supper. I enjoy these quiet and peaceful evenings very much.

I could not buy a Voltaire's *Candide*, so I stole one for you from the dentist's waiting-room library. He won't know. I will let you have it when you come back. MARK GERTLER

To Carrington

[*9 April 1913*] *32 Elder Street, E.*

This is a literal translation of my mother's letter.

Dear Miss Carrington, I thank you very much for the trouble you took to write me a letter. I am pleased to hear that you enjoy yourself and that you have nice weather there. This is nice for you to smell the good scents of the nice flowers that in your garden grow. You ask me if I like Mark's picture, then I write you that I like it very much, and I hope that everybody will like it. I wish you well and hope soon to see you.

To Carrington

[? *June 1913*] *32 Elder Street, E.*

Dearest Carrington, Thanks for your letter. I only wish I was in the mood to write you a nice one, but today I have had a hard day. My work went very badly and I was disgusted with my horrible incompetence. Sometimes it is really difficult to go on living!

Today has been bad: I've felt wretched: I am practically repainting the whole of my picture and it won't be done for the N.E.A.C. God knows when I shall do something that will please me! There are times when everything I do seems loathsome to me. However, I felt happy, through all, to know that I had your friendship and I believe that you would like me even if my work sometimes did go wrong. That is a great comfort!

I am still young and full of energy, and I know that tomorrow morning I shall get up with renewed vigour and go for it like a warrior! How wonderful that renewal of vigour is!! Just when one thinks that all is over and that there is nothing but death, suddenly, suddenly, it comes, it comes, like dawn it breaks! The heavy cloak of depression that so weighed and oppressed one's limbs drops, and eagerly with raised arm we embrace the New Hope!—that renewal of energy! How wonderful that it should happen so often! Ah! That's the beauty of youth!

But *you* make me more happy than *anything*! You helped me through my today's trouble—more than you ever can guess!!!

Well, dear, on Saturday at 7 o'clock MARK GERTLER

To Ruth Humphries

[1913] *32 Elder Street, E.*

Dear Ruth, Carrington wrote and told me about your wonderful success. I can't tell you how glad I am. Your picture had extremely promising points, and as long as you don't do anything silly—such as getting married or something ghastly like that—you ought to do good pictures. Remember, though, that good painting is so rare and beautiful an art, that it needs *tremendous* work and self-sacrifice, Ruth, to paint well—remember this!

Yours sincerely MARK GERTLER

To the Hon. Dorothy Brett

June 1913 *32 Elder Street, E.*

Dear Brett, Thanks for your letter. I find that you have bought two of my drawings—thanks very much. I have sold two others, so I have a few pounds still. It is very uncomfortable to have to worry, though, to have to worry over every penny one spends. I am working very, very hard, and yet—would you believe it—if you were to come back this moment I would have *nothing* to show you! No sooner do I finish a picture than I paint it out. As I go on, I get more and more critical about my own work—nothing satisfies me. My people look upon me as a complete lunatic!!

I have made a very interesting friend lately—a Mr Marsh (Winston Churchill's secretary). He is a very nice man, but I am afraid he likes *me* more than my work—I do not share his taste in art. He buys everybody's work except my own. He knows your father.

Last Monday to hear the first Wagner Promenade Concert, Queen's Hall. *Simply wonderful.* Oh! so inspiring! Some moments I wanted to weep with emotion! You must go as soon as you come back—mind you do! I wish I too could express myself so tragically and yet so beautifully! . . .

One of the things I have at present on hand is a picture which I call "Christ and the Elders"! Don't be surprised! It's merely a study of a lot of old Jews' heads round a young one—my brothers. It's really a technical study of heads and hands, although I am interested in the subject more than you would think. I have hopes for this picture. . . .

Mr Marsh took me to a first night of a play. Evening dress!! I felt so awkward! Everybody in the theatre looked at me. I felt ashamed. I feel so uncomfortable in evening dress, especially as my friend wore a monocle!! My face looks so dirty in comparison with those well-washed gentry. I must use that hard sponge again that I bought. . . .

With best wishes

MARK GERTLER

To the Hon. Dorothy Brett

July 1913 — *32 Elder Street, E.*

Dear Brett, Thanks very much for your most encouraging letter. I certainly did not like the Albert Hall show. Those cousins of yours who do not like the type John paints are idiots! You must try and avoid the society of such people. They lead such soft and uselessly happy lives that they know nothing about life. Their life is too easy. They have had no hardships. God! They don't know what some experience here on Earth—the same Earth. "One touch of Nature makes the whole world kin," but some touches put miles of space between us.

But Brett! *The worst kind of person is the rich English Jew*!!! Ugh! those patronizing horrors! Let me tell you what one lady of that class wrote me a few days ago. She said she had been and seen my "New English" picture and that she thinks my eyes *must be wrong* to paint like that, and that I would do her a great favour if I would—at her expense—see an oculist! Oh, Brett! What do you think of that? That has settled my dealings with the upper-class Jew.

I am getting very poor now. I cannot even afford models or outings in the evenings, and there is no hope of selling anything more, as my work is getting more and more personal, and therefore less and less understood. You see the curse is that even the most cultured buyer almost unconsciously looks for a little prettiness. Oh, he must have a little bit of it, else how can he hang it on his dainty wall! How could his white and scented wife look at it! How could one possibly go on eating asparagus in the same room! My types, they say, are *ugly*. But withal I am not a bit unhappy. I am working desperately hard and learning, learning daily.

The thing I hate looking forward to is *living on my people*. They are so poor! If only I had a little income!

I am painting a portrait of my mother.[1] She sits bent on a chair, deep in thought. Her large hands are lying heavily and wearily on her lap. The whole suggests suffering and a life that has known hardship. It is barbaric and symbolic. . . .

With best wishes MARK GERTLER

To the Hon. Dorothy Brett

September 1913 *32 Elder Street, E.*

Dear Brett, . . . I don't think skill, that is superficial skill, has much to do with the greatness of a picture. It has, in fact, been the cause of so many centuries of bad art. Thank God we "moderns" are finding out and soon, I think, we shall have art as great as it has ever been before, and *in our own way*. We have much to thank Cézanne for. He was a great, great man.

I am quite willing to be friendly with Carrington, if *she* is. But I think she considers me nothing more than a dissipator and drunkard, and not a fit companion for her. Perhaps she is right.

As regards the conduct of artists, I am sure that every *real* artist knows what is best for himself. A real artist is "beyond good and evil". Heavens! do you think that a real artist could become *merely* a dissipator and a drunkard?!! It would bore him stiff!!! Show me the drink that is more intoxicating than his *work*. Where is the dissipation that is half as ravishing? No! I am afraid that you girls only too often entertain groundless fears for us men.

Currie and Henry sometimes amuse me terribly. Sometimes I feel I want to break that tie between us. Friendships are terribly difficult to manage and I don't think they are worth the trouble. Henry is not intelligent at all, that's the trouble. Frankly I prefer to stand alone. I need no great friend at all. Ties are a terrible nuisance and hindrance to an artist . . . .

MARK GERTLER

To Edward Marsh

[*September 1913*] *32 Elder Street, E.*

Dear Marsh, Thanks very much for your interesting cards you sent me. I am glad you enjoyed your holidays, and from your cards I should say you enjoyed it very much.

[1] Gertler painted several fine portraits of his mother besides that illustrated (Plate 2, facing page 33).

Since you have been away, I have done extremely little work. The chief things I have done are two "still-lifes" and drawings. At the same time I feel that I have been working so hard that I intend now to rest for some time.

Knewstub[1] came down the other day and bought quite a lot of my things, so I am rich again! He was very disappointed to have to go without that picture that you bought, but as he sells everything to America I am glad that you had it first.

Do come down and see me whenever you can, just drop me a card to say when. I am so glad to have got some money again. I think poverty is a terrible tragedy! How unfortunate I was to be born from the lower class—that is to say without an income! A modern artist must have an income.

MARK GERTLER

To Edward Marsh

[*1913*] *32 Elder Street, E.*

Dear Eddie, "Cookham"[2] has written to me. Monday, apparently, was all right, but in his letter to me he was so insultingly critical about my own work that I've done with him and could not think of going down to see him. You can go on Monday by yourself if you like. His address is: Fernlea, Cookham-on-Thames.

MARK GERTLER

To Edward Marsh

October 1913 *32 Elder Street, E.*

Dear Edward, About the "Cookham" affair I have finally decided that I cannot forgive the insults he sent me in that letter. His second letter says that it was not meant insultingly. That makes it *worse*. For then what he wrote were not insults, but *truths*. In that case I do not want to know a man who has such ideas about me as he has. I have more respect for myself than that; no, his personality interests me no longer. He seems to have already adopted the "Great Man" attitude, which I loathe like poison—I hate it!!! He has had much praise lately and he is spoilt. I will have nothing more to do with him. His personality will prejudice me against his work also. I intend dropping the subject now, as I must get on with my work. I have no time for petty quarrels.

What about Friday?

MARK GERTLER

[1] John Knewstub, brother-in-law of William Rothenstein and owner of the Chenil Gallery.

[2] Stanley Spencer.

To Edward Marsh

[*1913*] *32 Elder Street, E.*

Dear Edward, Would you mind coming rather one morning next week than this? My picture is in a very incomplete state and a week will make much difference. Also I want to be alone this week to think. I'm in a peculiar state of mind just now and suffering much mental strain. At such times I only worry people and I am best alone. I enjoyed this week-end very much and I am thankful to Barnes.[1] But it's always the same. Always here exists that bridge between people and myself. I can't analyse the reason for this.

They seem to be clever—very clever. They talk well, argue masterly, and yet and yet there is something—something—that makes me dislike them. Some moments I hate them! I stand alone! But if God will help me to put into my work that passion, that inspiration, that profundity of soul that *I know* I possess, I will triumph over those learned Cambridge youths. One of them argued *down* at me about painting!

Let me know which morning of next week you will come. Perhaps you can come one tea-time? Let me know. Write soon. I value your friendship. Don't be offended with me—never be offended with me—for with my friends I must be frank. Frankness walks arm-in-arm with rudeness, and if ever I am rudely frank, don't think that I am insincere. Insincerity makes me so miserable that it pays to be sincere. Those are my feelings. Now we are friends, aren't we? MARK GERTLER

To Carrington

October 1913 *32 Elder Street, E.*

Dear Friend, I am writing to thank you for your kindness in consenting to come with me on Thursday. It made me so happy that I "skipped" home the whole way, like Nevinson's Girl. I only hope that I am not a worry and nuisance to you. I will do my best *never* to worry you, if only you will agree to let me see and talk to you *sometimes*.

You cannot imagine how important you are to my work. You say you like my work, then will you be surprised if I tell you that I think of you in *every* stroke I do?! That you have been a tremendous source of inspiration to me—you are the only personality I've ever met that I've liked *whole-heartedly*.

Having told you this, you will not be surprised at my persistence in knowing you, in spite of your indifference and coldness towards me. There is only one thing—I feel that I am not worthy of your company. I feel that I am *far* too vulgar and rough for you. But I am hoping through my work to reach to your level.

[1] James Strachey Barnes, brother of Mary Hutchinson, and a cousin of the Stracheys.

The point is this—if you will *occasionally only* let me see and talk to you, you will be doing something that, apart from making myself happy, you will *never* regret. I mean the work you will make me produce.

I will tell you more when we meet on Thursday.

There is one thing more. If ever you have an appointment with me and something more interesting turns up, you can *always* put me off. Although I shall be unhappy, I shall understand. Yours ever MARK GERTLER

To Carrington

Christmas 1913 *32 Elder Street, E.*

My dear Carrington, I cannot tell you how happy I was to get your present. Thank you very much indeed. They are beautiful coloured ties, especially the one with the spots.

But I was very distressed to read in your letter than you are unhappy with your people. I cannot bear to think that you, my Carrington, are unhappy. It is of course not at all surprising that you should find it difficult to get on with them. You are so different from them. However, try and bear up and remember that it is merely your *superiority* which causes the difficulty and unhappiness.

You know that I have the same trouble with my people. I think it is hopeless to expect any spiritual understanding between our parents and ourselves. Although in your case I should have thought that they would appreciate you more and would feel happy to have you with them. I am sure that you must make their home less dull and prosaic by your presence.

It is extraordinary that you should have had the same feelings about Sunday evening as myself. To me, too, it was the Finest Evening, and I also felt that our friendship was more than ever confirmed and that it would now take more than a little to disturb it. Yes. How splendid it is!

Between us there is the finest link possible between one human being and another. Friendship!—*The Spiritual Linking Together of Two Souls!*

How long it has taken us to reach that exquisite state!

Oh! but if only you knew how thankful I am to you!

If only you knew how useful you have been to me!

If only you knew how awful and black life would be without your friendship and how much courage you give me to go on with this hard life and what noble ideas and thoughts the sight of you inspires me with! Will you please forgive this outburst? I feel so thankful to you and so happy that I should have for my friend *just* the person I love most in the world. When I am with you I seem to feel that I am in the country and that I hear the birds loudly singing!

Ruth and Brett have been also very kind to me. I like them enormously. Ruth gave me a beautiful plant with a great big red flower on top besides that book. Brett gave me a beautiful jersey-vest, which I always wanted.

It is nice and warm. I have not seen Brett yet, but I am asking her to tea next Monday to see my little picture.

Monday and Tuesday were wretched days. Horribly dark and foggy. Too dark to work and too wretched to go out. So I sat for hours on end in my mother's kitchen moping by the fire. This made me rather unhappy because I couldn't work and I wanted so much to finish my picture. However yesterday and today were finer days and I worked so hard that I have now practically finished it. I have improved very much the dress by putting more precision of drawing to it, which has made it more alive.

I have scarcely yet started anything else. I am just playing on a composition. In the evenings I have not gone out. This evening I have been reading that dear little Millet book that you were so beautifully kind to give me.

Today my father gave me a big row and almost wanted to hit me, because, whilst painting my mother, I forgot the dinner hour and went on painting till 2.30! Oh! he was wild—he was so hungry. He dines at 1 o'clock! The meat and potatoes got burned! Everybody was annoyed with me. They said I love my art more than them!

Dear Carrington, write to me *at once* please. Your letters make me happy, write me about *your work*. Send your Gauguin next time.

MARK GERTLER

To Carrington

Sunday [*December 1913*] *32 Elder Street, E.*

My dear Carrington, How thankful I was to get your letter last night! I had just had a depressing night with Marsh at the theatre. To begin with I was in evening dress and the play, *Doctor's Dilemma*,[1] disgusted me. I cannot tell you how I hated Shaw last night for writing that play and for allowing such an insipid youth as Dennis Neilson-Terry and such a terrible woman as Lillah McCarthy to act in it! It was the artist part of the play that horrified me—the doctors were very good. I couldn't stand that terrible middle-class audience laughing in an enlightened way, when that insipid young artist was standing with painted lips and "charming"—justifying his artistic immorality in Shawese witticisms! How terrible! I wanted to scream, but I only got a terrible headache instead. How I should have loved to throw a rotten tomato at that weak and painted face of Terry! All this time Lillah McCarthy was standing on another part of the stage, wriggling into so-called beautiful and classic attitudes. It is said of B. Shaw that he has broken down the conventions of the upper middle classes, but I say that he has taken them out of the frying pan only to drop them into the fire!!! I could write you volumes on this subject, but I won't, chiefly because it makes me ill to think of it all. Last night I couldn't sleep and I wanted to *weep* so it upset me!

[1] Revived at the St James's Theatre, 9 December 1913.

I feel that I should like to excite all the working classes to, one night, break into these theatres and *destroy* all those rich *pleasure seekers*!

It was a relief to come home into my mother's kitchen. I looked at my father's thin bony suffering face and his working hands, all rough and hard, and I loved him. I thanked God that this *man* was my father. My father has never heard that name Bernard Shaw!—lucky man!

Thank you very much for troubling to do a sketch for me of your next picture. It looks a splendid idea—you must certainly work hard at it.

My picture is now finished. I finished it yesterday. I worked very hard at it indeed and I think that I've succeeded to get something good into it. Anyway I've got the character of the woman and that's a great deal. I know it is not new, and our revolutionists would say of it that was academic. I don't care. Newness doesn't concern me. I just want to express *myself* and be personal. When a bird is inspired it sings, it sings: it does *not* wonder if its manner of singing is different to a bird that sang a thousand years ago—it just sings. As for realism—my work is real and I wanted to be real. The more I see of life, the more I get to think that realism is necessary. There was not much reality going on in that theatre!

I don't want to be abstract and cater for a few hyper-intellectual maniacs. An over-intellectual man is as dangerous as an over-sexed man. The artists of today have thought so much about newness and revolution that they have forgotten art.

Besides I was born from a working man. I haven't had a grand education and I don't understand all this abstract intellectual nonsense! I am rather in search of reality, even at the cost of "*pretty decorativeness*". I love natural objects and I love painting them as they are—I use them to help me to express an idea. . . .

The very same night that you went for a walk with your brother—Friday—I walked for hours on the Heath and stood on Parliament Hill enjoying that strong wind! I have not yet been to the S[outh] K[ensington] Museum, but I am longing to go and see our wonderful tapestry.

I should think you ought soon to earn some money by your work. Work hard and steadily and you will do it. Keep an eye on Nature the whole time.

Brett has not been to see me yet. I've asked her for tomorrow Monday tea. Marsh tells me that he met Brett. Albert brought her to his flat! . . .

Ever yours, my dearest Carrington MARK GERTLER

To Carrington

1 January 1914 *32 Elder Street, E.*

Dear Friend, I am very happy that you should like the Gauguin so much. It was no sacrifice at all for me to give it you—only a happiness for me to be able to do so.

I liked the Doctor's part of the Shaw play also. I hope you did not find my last letter tedious, but the play as a whole upset me so much that I felt I had to tell someone about it.

You must not bother yourself about belonging to the upper middle class; you ought only to congratulate yourself on being such a wonderful exception—it must be very trying for you to be up there with your people. I wish I could help you.

You must not talk of becoming a teacher with spectacles or of going back to your people. You are quite capable enough a person to become independent. Have you thought of going in for the B.I.[1] scholarship? Brett agrees with me that you ought to. Do you realise that that would mean a £1 a week for two years?! You could easily make the rest, but some families down here live on much less than £1 a week.

Don't think of the Prix de Rome; that is *useless* to you and would spoil you for life. That would mean three years in that decadent city Rome! A city that exists merely on its *past* glories. All the time you would have terrible academicians like Sir William Richmond, R.A., etc. looking after you—far worse than your own people! What an imprisonment it would be—three whole years!!! No! one must always live in cities that have a future, not merely a past—one mustn't be out of things.

The B.I. allows you to do what you like and you can stay with *your friends* and work however you like!!!

Brett came last Tuesday at 3 o'clock and had tea with me—she liked my picture very much. We had dinner afterwards at Tilney Street.[2] I left about 10.30, having spent a wonderfully interesting afternoon and evening —we had so much to say. Tonight we are meeting at the S.K. Museum to see the tapestries.

Ruth sent me a long letter and very interesting.

Apart from Brett I see nobody. I hardly go out at all.

Gilbert Cannan sent me a nice letter asking me to come down. I hope to be able to go in about a fortnight for a few days.

I have suddenly got so fascinated by a funny doll belonging to my little niece that I have put everything aside in order to paint it, with some other objects. The whole makes a most interesting still life.[3] I am working hard at it and am *furiously interested* in it, but I don't know whether you will like it.

Best wishes for New Year — MARK GERTLER

To Carrington

January 1914 — *32 Elder Street, E.*

My dear Carrington, I am very glad that the tapestry reproduction made you so happy. I knew it would, so I sent it at once. It is indeed a wonderful

[1] British Institute. A scholarship Gertler had won a few years before.

[2] The London home of Lord Esher, Brett's father.

[3] A later version (Plate 9, facing page 128) is now in the Brighton Art Gallery.

Caricature of Carrington by Albert Rutherston, 1914

picture. The last time I saw it with Brett it was even more wonderful than ever.

I do not know yet about Gilbert Cannan. I have written to him, suggesting my coming down Wednesday a week for a few days, but he has not yet replied. On the whole I am not keen to go there. I would really rather go by myself to Brighton for a few days. The seaside air is more refreshing and healthy and then I wouldn't have to be engaged in intellectual conversation, which I hate so. However it is extremely good of him to ask me.

I envy you having a friend with you. It must be wonderful to have a friend to live with. You are so fortunate that way. In London for instance you have your great friend Ruth with you. I am always alone. This makes me feel sometimes that I should like to find a great friend with whom I could live. It would be so nice after being all day alone in the Studio to have somebody always to interchange an idea with. The loneliness of man is appalling!

I am working hard on my still-life. There is of course a lot to do to it yet. These days are so short and dark that one can only do very little each day.

I don't know what Brett wrote you about me, but if she gave you wonderful descriptions of me or my work, you are right not to believe her. As for being conceited: I must tell you that if you knew how much I suffer from feelings very much the reverse of conceit, you would not even suggest such a thing in jest.

I cannot say that I like you teasing me. Sometimes you tease me about things I am very sensitive about. In your letter for instance you "tease" me about the letters I've been writing you these holidays. Well, those letters were written in moments of loneliness when I was full of feelings and no one but you to tell them. One must tell those sort of feelings to somebody. I really did not like you jesting about them. Sometimes I feel that you are spiteful—forgive me for saying so. Yours always

MARK GERTLER

To the Hon. Dorothy Brett

January 1914 *The Mill House, Cholesbury, Herts.*

My dear Brett, I am sitting by a huge fire in this very nice country house of Gilbert Cannan's. Gilbert Cannan is an extremely nice man and ought to do good things. I have got on with him very well—we talked and talked last night. I told them all about myself. They were so interested in my life, I told them all about where I came from and all about my people. Cannan thought I was extremely fortunate to live in the East End amongst *real* people. He loves the Jewish theatre and agrees with me that it is far and away more vital than the English, in fact that there is no comparison. We discussed also the milk and water outlook of Roger Fry and his followers and most of the so-called "advanced" people. I am enjoying my stay here very much, but I always long to get back to you people—my dearest friends. Carrington had tea with me last Saturday—she made me so happy. I am coming to tea with you in your studio, Sunday 4.30. Make Carrington come. Tell her she *must* be kind to me or else I shall be unhappy. MARK GERTLER

Remember me lovingly to C. and R.

To Carrington

1 April 1914 *32 Elder Street, E.*

Dear Carrington, The evening with "Cookham" was most successful and inspiring. We got on very well together and had a long talk on art. He talks remarkably well about it. Paul Nash was there too.

Tonks has written me some very nice letters—most encouraging. Yesterday I had to go and interview the Art Master and Headmaster of the school—Boys Foundation School—about a job. It was all very frightening and very official and rather depressing. They said they will let me know. The salary is very small, about 28*s*. a week for three days, but I can't afford to grumble. Every day my people have to scrape together a few shillings for my models. They are very poor themselves just now. The position is very trying. Sometimes it all becomes very, very difficult, but I am trying hard to bear up and am working very hard. Today I spent the whole day painting the man's back. But of the two the model triumphed most, because he went away with my people's hard-earned 7*s*.

I am working really hard and my picture is, I believe, coming along, but very slowly. The more I do, the more there seems to do. What frightens me about it is when I think of the *money* it's going to cost!

I have now *definitely* decided to move to Hampstead as soon as I can afford it. If only I could get a little money and settle myself at Hampstead I should be happy.

I am so glad you enjoyed being with me on the Heath last Sunday. I enjoyed it very much too. MARK GERTLER

To Carrington

April, Monday, 1914 *32 Elder Street, E.*

Dear Carrington, It was a great pleasure to hear from you again, but how slow you were in answering it. I was getting unhappy.

There isn't much more to tell about the meeting between "Cookham" and myself, except that it was very successful. He was very glad to make it up again with me. He wrote and told Marsh so.

Black and White Cottage

Oil painting ($19\frac{1}{2} \times 13\frac{1}{2}$ *in.*) *1914*

Reproduced by permission of Mrs F. C. O. Speyer

(*For a description of the painting of this subject, see page 73*)

Rabbi and Rabbitzin

Oil painting (19 × 15 in.) 1914

Reproduced by permission of Jeremy Hutchinson, Q.C.

Photograph by courtesy of the Phaidon Press

I do not know the "Resurrection" by Bobby.[1] I have not seen it. I do not dislike Paul Nash now—I quite like him. He has invited me tomorrow to come and see him in the country.

Carrington, you must not blame yourself for my poverty! If you mention that again you will hurt me beyond words.

Unfortunately I failed to get that job I wrote you about, but it doesn't matter—I shall struggle through somehow. Most of us have to suffer in this world and we ought to try and bear it without grumbling. I cannot work every day on my picture as my people can't afford the money for the models. I take care of every penny now, so that I should not have to lean too heavily on my people. One of my brothers took out £3 from the bank—all that he had there and which took him a long time to save—to help me. My picture, I think, is making progress. I have worked mostly on the man's back.

Yes we must go on the Heath together a great deal. It is wonderful there. How wonderful the spring is! Everything so full of fresh life and vitality, every blade of grass so fresh and green, what a green! I cannot pass by any patch of green without stopping to look and admire. I think that God reveals himself more in the spring than any other time of year. I am very happy.

How much more I would enjoy all these things if you were near me, Carrington! What a pity that we must be parted the best times of the year. Don't you feel that? I cannot tell you how much I love the spring. I am so glad you are drawing the rocks carefully. Stick to nature and don't listen to art theories. How I should love to bring into the backgrounds of my picture some buds of the springtime, little twigs, leaves and flowers! I would paint them very carefully and accurately.

I go to Gilbert Cannan next Sunday. I am looking forward to it immensely. Brett's portrait is coming along very slowly, she is very difficult to do.

I have seen the Edna Clarke Hall[2] show, it is rather good. Knewstub has sent my old kitchen picture to Leeds to a show there. Everybody likes that picture now. It is getting quite famous. Brett's brother[3] and Zena thought it wonderful.

I have not been to S.K. lately.

Last Thursday afternoon I painted Brett. Albert came in to tea. We had a very nice tea. I like Albert very much. After tea Brett and I had a walk in the park which was very enjoyable.

Friday before sunset I went on to the Heath. It was fine! But I longed and longed for you. Are you looking nice now? How lovely your hands must be now they are brown. Saturday afternoon Brett and I went to Shapiro's concert. It was rather dull and we both felt ill. After the concert we went to Albert's to tea. Many people were there. After that I had to meet Marsh.

[1] William Roberts.

[2] A Slade artist.

[3] The Hon. Maurice Brett, married to Zena Dare, the actress.

That evening was the opening night of the Crab Tree Club,[1] so we went. I think that club will fail. It seems just an inferior cabaret. John came in with his followers, he unusually drunk—very drunk. He came up to me and was very friendly, but he behaved disgustingly and cheaply. I stayed until 4 o'clock and then went home to sleep at Mrs Hebbon's,[2] with Bomberg[3] on one side of me and Flanagan[4] on the other. The next morning I was very annoyed with myself.

Sunday I had tea with Brett's sister[5] at Wimbledon. Captain Brett and Zena were there. I enjoyed it very much—they were so kind and nice to me. In the evening I dined with Marsh, Cathleen Nesbitt[6] and Jeanette Ross Johnson; then we went on to a play by Frank Harris.[7] The play was very bad. After the theatre Albert joined us and we had an excellent supper at the Waldorf. I had my black suit on and your other white shirt. I must have looked nice because Albert asked me to sit for him. I enjoyed that evening enormously.

Everybody is being very nice to me just now. This makes me very happy. I have a lot of friends now. Mrs Shufrer, the woman who has that nice little boy, also wrote me a very long letter and asked me to come and see her. Well, this is all I have to tell you. . . .

When you get this letter just sit down and answer it, there's a good girl.

MARK GERTLER

To Carrington

9 April 1914, Thursday, Midnight — *32 Elder Street, E.*

Yes, you are indeed a good girl to write so soon, Carrington. But if you knew how much I appreciate you for doing so, you would feel amply repaid. Thanks very much.

I enjoyed my visit to the Nashes very much indeed. What a splendid way to live. What beautiful surroundings.[8] How beautiful the country is. It will be my ultimate aim to live in the country. We went for a walk and got caught in the rain, but it was very splendid all the same. He took me to see the lake. Before I went Jack gave me some flowers to take away and said perhaps my mother would like them.

After tea the sister played the piano and then a wonderful rainbow appeared in the sky. It started with a blaze of different colours from one field, made a complete and most accurate semi-circle and finished up with another blaze in another. The sky in the meantime was black-blue.

[1] A night club started at Augustus John's instigation in Greek Street.

[2] Mrs Patrick Hepburn, "Anna Wickham" the poetess.

[3] David Bomberg was at the Slade with Gertler.

[4] John Flanagan, Slade student.

[5] Brett's sister was the Ranee Brooke of Sarawak.

[6] The actress, friend of Rupert Brooke.

[7] *The Bucket Shop* by Frank Harris was given one evening performance by the Stage Society at the Aldwych Theatre on 5 April.

[8] Paul and John Nash then lived at Iver with their parents.

In the garden there was a little tree full of brilliant white blossoms which stood out strong and light against the sky. The whole effect was divine! They have also in their garden a certain yellow flower with a little brown check pattern on it. The wood, before coming to the lake, was also very beautiful. Some of the trunks of the trees were bright green, whilst others were purple. The ground was orange-brown, with the fallen and faded leaves. Some of the trees had very unusual trunks. One trunk looked like a bundle of many-coloured snakes. On others, where the rain had fallen, the colour was beautifully spotted, with green, purple and orange. Between the trees and branches the sky could be seen through in brilliant white-light spots and shapes.

This evening I was out with Brett and her sister. We dined at the Savoy! The richness of the place embarrassed me very much, and I did not feel at all at ease. There was a lot of footmen in grey plush coats and stockings. They all looked at me suspiciously. The dinner was excellent and with that at least I felt at home. I had pea soup, oysters, lamb and potatoes and then a baba with rum and coffee. When I came to my cigarette I had completely forgotten all my worldly troubles. I don't suppose that the waiter there had any idea that I hadn't a penny in the world! After dinner we went to see a play which was very good indeed. . . . Yours very sincerely

MARK GERTLER

To Carrington

Sunday night, April 1914 *The Mill House, Cholesbury*

Dear Carrington, Thank you very much indeed for writing to me about that job. I wrote at once, but I am afraid that nothing will come of it. You see it is practically clerk's work that they require and I really don't think I could do much as a clerk. Although I wouldn't mind trying it, if they took me on, but as it was too late even to get recommendations I stand no chance.

Well, I am now here and writing in a very pleasant little bedroom. Today was a beautiful day. Coming down here in the train was wonderful. The sunshine, the fields and trees of the country fill me always with vague longings. It makes me long, long, for something I don't quite know what. It made me feel that to live in town was decadent. I love all the beautiful things that grow and the sunshine most passionately! I want so much to introduce all these things into the backgrounds of my pictures.

This afternoon we all went out in the little car for a drive. We got on to some high hills, from which vast stretches of landscape can be seen. It was fine, although I must say I am not interested in panorama in landscape. I preferred much more a big shiny blue-black and fat pig waddling on some bright green grass that I noticed as we were coming along. Aren't pigs fine?!

This is a gorgeous night—there is a big moon hanging in the sky. It is quite light. There are innumerable stars out too. The sky in places is so light that the trees can be seen in strong silhouette against it. We must certainly go a great deal on to Hampstead Heath. One can so much more fully enjoy much beautiful things in the company of an intimate friend. Do you know, whenever I go to the country, I always feel how very paintable Hampstead is! This country, although beautiful, isn't anywhere near as paintable as the Heath! . . .

Yours sincerely MARK GERTLER

To Carrington

Wednesday, April 1914 *The Mill House, Cholesbury*

Dear Carrington, The recommendation arrived far too late and when it did I am here in the country and cannot use it! However I really don't believe that the job would do at all for me. My position as regards money seems rather hopeless at present, but something may turn up soon—I hope so. The worst of it is that the worry of having no money gets into one's head, and one cannot work so freely as when one could feel a little more settled in that way. I have reached a queer stage of my life now, I don't know how it will turn out. Some people say it is good for a young artist to be poor! I entirely disagree! Poverty makes one's mind sordid. However, I thank God for at least having endowed me with the true spirit of an artist. By means of this true spirit I am raised for the most part of time, far, far, above all these sordid and material cares and worries into a wonderful and higher world. A world of imagination and infinite beauty! It is in that world that I really live! It is only that part of my existence that makes life worth living for me. However, against my will though it be, I have to descend from my higher world into this—the material and the sordid—and it is here that I suffer. Yet in spite of much discouragement my life's plan is very simple. I just want to devote my whole life in working at what I feel and experience during my momentary stays in that higher world by means of art. I have not expressed myself as clearly here as I should have liked to, but it is enough to give you a glimmering of the feelings and emotions I experience.

But why should I worry you with all this, for as you said in your letter you are far more interested at present in the landscape and the wood-cutting.

I am enjoying my stay here in a peaceful kind of way. But what I enjoy most here is the company of Gilbert Cannan and the talks with him. He is a *true man*. There are not many like him. I like him truly. In the evenings we sit in the dimly lit mill, where he plays Beethoven to me and then we talk and talk. Last night he read some of his poems to me. They sounded to me very good. I feel about him as if he was my greatest friend. He tells me I can use his cottage as if it were my own! I am doing no work here at all. . . . MARK GERTLER

To Edward Marsh

May 1914 *32 Elder Street, E.*

My dear Eddie, Lady Ottoline[1] wrote me today and asked Carrington and myself to come with her to the *Magic Flute* on Monday, 25th. Unfortunately I think that falls on the same day as our opera. It's terrible but I feel I can't refuse Lady Ottoline the very first appointment. Could you possibly excuse me?

I am coming to breakfast to ask your leave. I shall be with you 9.30. I hardly need tell you how sorry I am. How much I wanted to see the opera! But I feel it is so difficult to refuse Lady Ottoline—then there is Carrington too.

Well, I'll come and talk about it to you. MARK GERTLER

To Edward Marsh

June 1914 *32 Elder Street, E.*

Dear Eddie, Again I must put you off, about seeing my picture next Sunday. I am very sorry, but I really cannot get myself to show my work to anybody.

I showed it to Lady Ottoline simply because I hoped she would buy it. As for Gilbert Cannan he came to see me and it would have been silly to hide away my picture from him, but in each case I hated showing it. I am very sensitive about my work and, even if I would have money, I wouldn't exhibit. Besides, at present my work is very "studentish" and, really, I hardly think it would interest you. Next Monday is sending-in day of the N.E.A.C. and if they accept it, you will see it there. You must forgive these curious ways of mine—I can't help it. I like to be friends with people, apart from my work. I am your friend and yet I do not want to come down to the Admiralty to see what you are doing!

Please excuse this long and serious letter. I know you prefer funny ones.

Yours sincerely MARK GERTLER

P.S. Please may I have eggs and bacon for my breakfast on Wednesday?!

To Carrington

Sunday, June 1914 *Yorkshire*

Dear Carrington, I am sitting now writing this to you on a lonely moor. Enormous white and black clouds are rolling through the blue sky and disappearing into black grey on the other side.

[1] Lady Ottoline Morrell, married to Philip Morrell, Liberal M.P.

Yesterday we walked about twenty miles. In the morning of yesterday I had to walk ten miles to get shaved! The barber was a big fat yokel but very nice. As he shaved me his enormous belly pressed against me and I wanted to laugh. With one large hand he grasped my head, with the other he scraped me as if I were a lump of wood. In the shop there was a farmer who, after complimenting me on my hair, offered to walk part of the way back with me. I enjoyed his company *extremely*. He was so frank and open. When I told him that I was an artist he said, "Artistry is not in my line, I was brought up on a farm."

Some moments I get terribly depressed here—the landscape is vast, so endless, so melancholy. It makes me feel so small, so utterly alone! My only comfort now and here is that I know you. I can't tell you how much I miss you, dear Carrington. I wonder if you are thinking of me. You were so harsh with me the other night, when I tried to help you to find your latch key. You brushed me aside! It made me very unhappy!—because I want to be allowed to help you in many ways.

As I am getting cold I shall walk on and continue this letter later on. The post is not until tomorrow.

11 o'clock Sunday night

I continue this letter in my bedroom—it is a wonderful night! From my window I can see the beautiful round moon in the most lovely blue sky—clear and light. The moors stand out forebodingly and black. They look endless and mysterious—they frighten me. I have taken down the little curtain so I shall be able to see the moon from my bed. I have to sleep with most of my clothes on to keep warm.

Well, good night MARK GERTLER

To Carrington

July 1914 *c/o Mrs C. Cooke, Old Coast Guard Cottage, Pett Level, Near Hastings*[1]

Dear Carrington, I have not written to you because I have been very occupied in my mind thinking things out. I have not written to anybody except my mother.

I like this place enormously. The air is splendid and I am feeling much better. My face is very burnt and painful as the skin is peeling. I have bathed a great deal. What I enjoy most about bathing is drying in the sun. That is a wonderful feeling.

I am not a bit lonely here, as I love the inhabitants. They are wonderful people. The people I am staying with are extraordinarily lovable. There is the old mother, monumental and big. She rules the house like some queen. Her dignity is splendid. When she walks, she seems to sail along like a big ship. Then there are two rather beautiful daughters, healthy, big and

[1] The Knewstubs had a house at Hastings and no doubt had arranged this holiday.

brown, with simple unaffected minds. Then father and son. The father is very like [Augustus] John, but genuine. He drinks pints of beer. The son is a splendidly made young man, very, very strong. Amongst these people I am more at home and more happy than I've felt for a long time. They remind me so much of my own people, and, by the way, through them I love my own people more. Through them I see beauties in my own people which I never saw before.

My place is by these sort of people. I belong to this class. I shall always be unhappy if I try to get away from this class to which I belong. There is a little inn a little way along in which the fishermen and sailors come to drink beer. They are wonderfully beautiful. It is a pleasure to look at them. Yes, it is a long time since I've so truly loved men and women as I do here. Well, from them I've learnt my place. It is a great thing to know which is our real place. I've also learnt that I must go on in the *East End*. There lies my work, sordid as it is. When I get back, I'm going to spend some days in the country—quite near London—because I want to find a little place where I can hire a room, to which I can run some days in the week for peace and landscape work, for I am getting to love trees and fields and cows more and more. So I want to find a second home in some little country village. In that way I shall be able to combine the beauties of the East End and country. The thought of this plan is making me very happy. I think I shall be able to manage this as Knewstub has sold my early Kitchen picture and is going to give me some money.

Epstein is the one fault in my holiday here. Somehow he puts me off working. So far I have done nothing, but I've learnt a *great deal* all the same. Epstein has a filthy mind and he always has some girl living with him, *including* his wife. Now he has a horrible black girl. She tells me she's sat at the Slade. She's like a Gauguin. I hate her more and more every day!

For painting, this country does not suit me, as it is a little scenic, but it's splendid to be in.

In the evenings I go for a walk with one of the daughters. She is a fine girl. She is very kind to me and does all sorts of things for me. They are all kind to me here.

I hope your work is going well. I *loved* that nude painting of yours. What a good painter you are! Carrington, you must not expect much to happen between us. I am afraid that our roads lie in different directions to a great extent. The difference of class will always be against our being real friends. You don't know, Carrington, what a difference there is between us.

If you will be writing to me again, please let me know Ruth's address, as I have lost John's[1] last letter and therefore his address.

Yours sincerely MARK GERTLER

P.S. I hope your father is better. I am very sorry that he is ill.

[1] John Selby-Bigge, later second baronet, engaged to Ruth Humphries.

To Carrington

Sunday, July 1914 *Pett Level, Near Hastings*

Dear Carrington, Your design, as far as I can judge it from your sketch, is quite good enough to build up a picture on. I would not say so unless I thought so.

I have two landscapes going. I shall not go back until I finish them. This may mean staying here a week or so longer. One of my landscapes I have nearly finished and one is only begun.

If it wasn't for Epstein I would settle here for some time, but I really can't as long as he is here. The black girl, thank God, is gone.

This place makes me hate London. I think London is a horrible place to live in and it is with horror that I look forward to going back. However, it is as well to realise as soon as possible that we can't have everything as we should like it. I have a passionate desire now to live in the country, but I can't manage it for many reasons. So I *must* go back to my East End, where only God knows how many discomforts I suffer. However, if my plan works, about getting a place in the country, it would improve matters for me considerably.

I have written to Gilbert Cannan asking him if he could help me to get something near him. That would be splendid. If there was a country place that I could get to know, I am sure I would do very fine landscape. But you must get to know the country first. I was just beginning to see things in Gilbert Cannan's country, so it would be fine if I could get something there. What do you think? Do you know any better place near London? Let me know if you do.

I shall try and be your friend if you want me to, but you see the last few years of my life have been so wretched that sometimes I feel like cutting away from everything and everybody I have been associated with, in order to try and make my life more tolerable. You can't imagine how much I've suffered. Anyway it is always a pleasure for me to hear from you and I like very much writing to you about myself.

Well I hope your picture will go well. With best wishes MARK GERTLER

To Carrington

Sunday, July 1914 *Pett Level, Near Hastings*

Dear Carrington, Thank you very much for your letter. I am working hard here. I am only doing landscape as yet, I find that sufficiently absorbing. The first landscape which is nearly finished is of a black and white cottage against a dull sky—silver and lead. The foreground consists of a golden elder seen through another plant, called pampas grass. The picture finishes up at the bottom with a dark green gate and fence.[1]

[1] This painting (Plate 5, facing page 64) was given by Lady Hamilton to Violet Asquith on her wedding. See page 107.

The scene, as it is in nature, is most beautiful. The pampas grass is a strikingly beautiful plant. It is made up of long, elastic and needle-like leaves which are most graceful. It looks most beautiful when it flirts with the wind—then it looks like a ruffled head of hair! I am trying my best to get the exquisite grace of this plant. No matter how the wind blows it about, it always retains the beautiful and graceful curves of its leaves! It is indeed wonderful. I have worked for many days on this plant alone, but it is as difficult as it is beautiful. I feel very tired after I have worked at it for a day, with mahl stick and sables. It needs a very steady hand.

The other landscape is only just started. It is a group of white cottages and red roofs against a revolving wall of trees—high and upright. There is no sky in this picture.

Mrs Epstein tells me of a beautiful little village near Rickmansworth in Hertfordshire. I shall, then, make a point of exploring there and in Gilbert Cannan's part. I don't suppose that in the future I shall live more than a few months at a time in London. London will be very useful in the winter. If ever I get enough money, I shall get a pianola for my country home! How I look forward to all this!! The thought of it gives me great pleasure.

I do not agree with you about "Cookham" being the *only* individual artist. That is rather unfair on some of us other artists who work. But of course it is a matter of opinion.

You say I am now going to do so much better work. You are mistaken, for although I admit that there is much room for improvement in my work, I still do not think that one can improve by leaps and bounds. One can only improve little by little in true art.

Also do not expect too much from me, as you are likely to be disappointed. I would rather you expected little and, perhaps, be pleasantly surprised than expect much and be disappointed. After all, I do not paint to keep up to people's expectations but because I *must* paint: because it is as natural for me to paint as it is for a bird to fly, but that does not necessarily mean I *must* paint great works. For although it is natural for all birds to fly, some fly higher than others.

Thanks very much for the Flaubert extract on Originality. It is in some parts very good and true, but I doubt very much whether "originality" can be acquired. Also I think it is very dangerous to strive too much after originality for its own sake. This mad striving after originality at all costs has been, I am sure, the cause of a great deal of what is bad in so called "advanced" art.

Epstein does not worry me now. I do not know when I return to London. Not before next Wednesday a week in any case. Next Wednesday I have to move to another cottage as these people have visitors. Then, as I do not know my new address, will you please address your next letter as above.

Please do *not* send me any photos of yourself, as they might disturb the peace of mind I enjoy here. Do not be annoyed at this, as I would very much like to have them, but they might awaken emotions in me that, for the sake of my work, I would rather keep under.

I have had a little trouble with the daughter here, as she is a flirt and she tries to encourage me to flirt with her, when we are out walking at night, but this does not appeal to me, so I now avoid her, although otherwise she is very good to me and does a lot for me. It is my intention to have nothing to do with women physically until I am married, if ever I do marry, and I must say I am very anxious to. It would be so useful to have a wife and so companionable, especially for my country plan. I must really try and find a girl in the East End when I return. . . .

Yours sincerely MARK GERTLER

To Carrington

August 1914 *Pett Level, Near Hastings*

Dear Carrington, It is very kind of you to write me so often. Thanks very much. I appreciate it immensely.

I am afraid I gave you too glowing a description of my landscape in my last letter—now you are sure to be disappointed. To begin with, let me tell you it is only 20 by 14 inches—quite tiny and colourless. Remember also I have never done landscapes seriously before.

I loved painting landscape although I've done so little. It was fine painting things I've so long pined to paint. I should imagine the pleasure akin to that of a lover embracing, for the first time, the girl he for so long loved and longed to embrace. Just as he would passionately and lovingly linger over parts until then forbidden, so I lovingly lingered over those beautiful greens, greys and whites I knew so well but never before had the opportunity to paint.

I go back to my little den in the East End on Wednesday: so will you address your next there. . . .

Yours sincerely MARK GERTLER

To Carrington

August 1914 *32 Elder Street, E.*

Dear Carrington, I arrived in London last Wednesday. My heart sank as soon as I arrived. My first desire was to immediately return to the country, where I was so happy.

The war is indeed terrible, but how ludicrous! If it continues much longer, the working classes will starve. My own father's little workshop is closed! Isn't it strange that such a thing as war should still exist?

But I am happy. Today I heard from Gilbert Cannan. He wants me to come to him and he has a cottage for 4*s*. 6*d*. a week for me on the common. I know the cottage, it is Beautiful!!!

I go on Friday. Oh! I am happy for I love the country!

My heart is in the trees!

Do not be unhappy about the war. The best way we can help is to *paint*.

MARK GERTLER

P.S. If you could manage or would care to, you could come and stay in Hertfordshire with either Gilbert Cannan or me.

P.P.S. Don't be unhappy, because you have always me for your friend. *Always open your heart to me.* You are safe doing so. My best wishes to you and your work.

To Edward Marsh

November 1914 *32 Elder Street, E.*

My dear Eddie, I can't tell you how thankful I feel to you.

It isn't the actual money that pleases me, but the generous and friendly feelings that prompted you to help me. I feel that you are a real friend and that makes me very happy. I do hope that some day I shall be able in some way to help you. I hope also to do such good work that you will feel that I was worthy of your help. Yours very sincerely

MARK GERTLER

To Carrington

[*1914*] 32 *Elder Street, E.*

My dear Carrington, I can't help writing to you again. I feel rather happy now. I have just started a picture of a mother feeding her baby. I am full of it. I am going to try and paint *not* the beauty of maternity, but the hardness of existence. I shall try to express all the poverty, strife and horror of life in the mother's face, whilst the child will be brutally and unconsciously sucking the very blood of the mother. Yet there will be a resignation about it all, a resignation that all we poor humans have to adopt, to make life tolerable. I shall not paint hurriedly but meditatively and shall take my time. If I get what I want it will be a fine picture.

Oh! Carrington, how could you say that I only cared for you sexually? It has hurt me very, very, very much. You don't really think so, do you?

How happy I shall be on Saturday, when you will come and talk to me. Yours ever MARK GERTLER

PART FOUR

War and New Friends

The impact of the First World War on Gertler was not very great and on his work it was negligible. He seems to have felt that it simply did not concern him as a painter, though artist friends like Nevinson, Paul Nash, and Stanley Spencer became involved and gained in experience and reputation. Gertler's letters hardly reveal him as an active pacifist, but undoubtedly he was affected by the propaganda of friends, for in his immediate circle were the leading—or, as they were described in the press, most notorious—pacifists of the time, Gilbert Cannan, Lytton Strachey, D. H. Lawrence and Bertrand Russell. No doubt it was through their influence that he was led to make a not very graceful break with Eddie Marsh. Carrington, also, especially after the death of her second brother on the Somme in 1916, was a convinced and vocal pacifist.

During these years Gertler made friends chiefly amongst writers and intellectuals: hardly at all with artists. He became a regular guest at Garsington Manor, near Oxford, the beautiful home of Philip and Ottoline Morrell, probably one of the few homes in England at that time where pacifism was not only respectable but the orthodox religion. If he appeared to make slow progress in reputation as an artist, it should be borne in mind that in the First World War all art and culture was under a cloud. Even music, if German, was taboo.

His letters already seem to stress constant fits of depression and ill-health, but one should also record the impression he made on many of his friends at this time. His gaiety, charm and wit are recalled in several memoirs, notably those of Ottoline Morrell and Lady Glenavy (Beatrice Campbell of these letters), who writes: "Gertler had a great talent in telling stories about himself in which he appeared in a ludicrous light, e.g. stopping in a great house and pretending he had had a bath when he couldn't make the taps work. . . . His laughter was a glorious thing." My own recollection of meeting him some time in 1915 at a studio party of Brett's (vivid perhaps because it was the first such party for me) is of his brilliant impersonations and of his skill as a dancer.

It was of great importance to Gertler's development that he now secured a room of his own, a studio in Hampstead. The atmosphere of his own studio always meant something special to him, and he was seldom entirely happy working away from it. He remained proud of his East End Jewish background, but he did not hide the fact that his life there had become frustrating.

To Lytton Strachey

First day of 1915 *32 Elder Street, E.*

Dear Strachey, Thanks very much for your letter. I am home already! Couldn't stick out the fortnight. It was very, very cold. At night I used to almost freeze with cold. Then Mrs Gomm's rooms[1] looked so hideous this time. Texts and pictures crammed all over the walls—"Simply to Thy Cross I Cling"—"Sweet Seventeen, Sweeter Seventy". Portraits of Queen Victoria in china and so on! Too bad. On all the chairs were pieces of intricate lace. Every time I sat down on my chair, my hair would entangle in the lace and I would look like the portrait of Queen Victoria over the mantelpiece on china. I tried in many different ways to get rid of these pieces of lace, but of no avail. I told her I might dirty them with my paints, but she assured me that they were only cheap. Having started with soft arguments, it was difficult to be outwardly angry. So there they remained. All this prevented me working. The only exciting thing that happened were parties—one given by Lawrence[2] and the other by Cannan.[3] These were really fun. On both occasions we all got drunk! The second party, I got so drunk that I made violent love to Katherine Mansfield! She returned it, also being drunk. I ended the evening by weeping bitterly at having kissed another man's woman and everybody trying to console me. Drink has curious and various effects on me. This party was altogether an extraordinary one. So interesting was it that all the writers of Cholesbury feel inspired to use it in their work.

The parties left me so weak and dissipated that I feel as if I'd been to "Iris's Paradise" for a week on end! So I mean to lie low for a bit in order to recover.

Write and tell me when you will come back. In any case write.

I got on extremely with *Hamlet*. I understood far more than anything of Shakespeare I've ever read. I liked so much the grave-digging part.

I don't think Iris Tree[4] and myself will ever get on. She is so very different from me. I am afraid that we should have come to blows. Besides, do you know, I've had enough of woman and love for a bit. I am going to rest from that.

Well, shall expect to hear from you. MARK GERTLER

[1] At Cholesbury.

[2] D. H. Lawrence.

[3] The Cannans' Christmas is described by J. Middleton Murry. A sucking pig was served and Murry started them acting a play dramatising the actual situation between Katherine Mansfield and himself, and casting Gertler as his successor.

[4] Sir Herbert Beerbohm Tree's daughter, also a Slade student.

To the Hon. Dorothy Brett

[*January 1915*] *32 Elder Street, E.*

Dear Brett, . . . I am sending you these photos Carrington sent me. They are of her studio. She asked me to show them to you. You can keep them. I had since to write and tell her plainly that our friendship was over—she didn't seem to understand why I was silent.

I wonder why life should be so ghastly. I mean why one should have to chuck the one person one really loves!

This morning Eddie introduced me to Winston Churchill. He was coming out of St Paul's as we were going in. How plain he is—a cross between Clive Bell and Knewstub. He was quite nice though. In the church we met Mrs Churchill. . . . MARK GERTLER

To Carrington

January 1915 *32 Elder Street, E.*

Dear Carrington, I am sending you, here, the fourth volume of *John Christopher*,[1] not yet *Jude the Obscure*. I have got it for you, but should like to read it again myself. It is such a beautiful book, so subtle—not so vulgar and ordinary in subject as the usual modern novel.

I am glad that you are so happy in your new home.[2] It sounds ideal. How splendid it must be to feel settled and comfortable! Besides, I think the country suits you better than London. It is therefore so wise of you to settle there. Anyhow it is so healthy, and health is one of the two most important things in life (the other most important thing is money). For myself I've never known what it is to be comfortable—except perhaps for moments in other people's houses—in all my life. It is rather hard on me as no one loves comfort more than I do. It is a pity also from a point of view of work, for I am sure that, were I comfortable, if I had a good home and good food, in some healthy part, I could paint interesting pictures. As it is, I am continually struggling against being overcome by the sordidness of my surroundings and family and by poverty. How I loathe poverty!

However, I shan't grumble, for although there are so many people who have every comfort, there are also thousands of poor devils far more wretched than I.

My holiday in Cholesbury this time was not altogether a success, I think mostly because of Mrs Gomm's wretched and uncomfortable rooms. I took my work with me, but couldn't work, so I came home some days before the fortnight was up.

The most exciting things that happened were the Christmas parties. They were real fun. Katherine Mansfield was so good. Gilbert Cannan's

[1] Romain Rolland's long novel.

[2] Carrington's family had moved to Hurstbourne Tarrant in north Hampshire.

party was most extraordinarily exciting. Katherine and myself—both very drunk—made passionate love to each other in front of everybody! And everybody was drunk too. No one knew whether to take it as a joke or scandal. Fortunately, the next day everybody decided to take it as a joke—the Lawrences were the last to come to this decision, as they were most anxious to weave a real romance out of it. Seeing that Katherine's man and myself were just as friendly afterwards, they *had* to take it as a joke. They were very disappointed to have to take it so. I like Katherine Mansfield.

Since I am back I have spent most of my time searching for a studio, as I want to move. But God! what a depressing occupation that is! Everything is frightfully expensive. There is just one I am thinking of taking opposite the Tube Station, Hampstead, three minutes from the *Heath*!!! A place I have been wanting to live near all my life. This one I may take. I shall decide in a day or two.

Shapiro, whom I have seen much of, wanted me to share a place with him. Although it sounded good at first, I afterwards found that it would be much better for me to live alone. With those people one could have no privacy.

So, in writing to them, please do not mention that I want to move. I have seen Iris Tree and I like her very much. She is coming here to tea today. I'm having a large tea party. Iris wants to see my "Eve".[1]

My two great friends are Eddie Marsh and Brett—they are both godsends. Eddie offers me as much as £10 a month during war-time!!! He is also giving me a bedroom in his flat and a latchkey so I can always sleep there!

My "Eve" is finished; those few people who have seen it have liked it more or less. Am not working at present—too excited and unsettled about studios.

Well, good-bye. Write whenever you care to. Yours sincerely

MARK GERTLER

To Edward Marsh

[*January 1915*] *32 Elder Street, E.*

My dear Eddie, It is very good of you to let me have a bedroom with you if I live in Fitzroy Street, but today I have been more successful. I have found what I think two excellent studios in Park Hill Road, near the Hampstead Heath, one at £45 and the other at £40. Tomorrow I go with Brett to choose. Even then I should want your bedroom pretty often, so may I have a key in any case? Shall let you know result on Thursday at breakfast. MARK GERTLER

[1] Almost certainly "The Creation of Eve" (Plate 7 facing page 80) referred to in later letters, e.g. pages 83, 92 and 106.

To Carrington

20 January 1915 *32 Elder Street, E.*

Dear Carrington, It was no sacrifice at all to send you the *John Christopher*. I have read it so many times that I really almost know it by heart. I here send you *Jude the Obscure*.

We are having very exciting times here in London just now. Last night we danced again at Brett's studio. There was Barbara,[1] her friend, and Brett and myself. Barbara was in fancy dress—trousers—she looked quite well. She is awfully good to dance with. I must confess that I enjoy these hilarious evenings. We are trying to arrange to all suddenly appear tomorrow at Lady Ottoline's with masks and fancy dress. I don't know whether it'll come off. It'll be rather awful if we come upon them when they are rather in a quiet mood!

Well, we searched and searched for studios. Just as I was feeling half dead with it and about to give it up and remain here, we suddenly came across a really good one, which I've almost taken for certain. It is in Hampstead. Practically on the Heath! I am only waiting for a formal acceptance from the landlord.

If, by any chance, something happened to prevent that studio being mine, I shall stay here again. I have no more patience left—for a fortnight I've been searching every day! I am quite ill with it. Really these gay evenings are a great relief and almost necessary.

Poor Brett, she is so good, she came with me every time—her little startled face would go quite white with exhaustion and she never heard a word the agents would say. I don't know what I would have done without her. . . .

Of course if ever you come to London you can come and see my work. If you came in May you could see it in the "New English", where I shall send it. I hope all that part about the Lawrences and the party didn't bore you in my last letter. I shall not write about them again.

I've got to go to Cholesbury on Saturday for the week-end to stay with the Cannans, as the Murrys[2] are giving a party and I'm acting in a certain play we are going to give. . . .

Yours sincerely MARK GERTLER

To Carrington

January 1915 *c/o Edward Marsh, 5 Raymond Buildings, Gray's Inn, W.C.*

Dear Carrington, I have taken the studio and am moving in on Monday. I am extremely pleased with it. It is a fine studio and if everything goes well—if I have no desperate money troubles—I ought to be very happy there. It'll be splendid to have the Heath so near me to walk on. Also I am *immensely* relieved to leave the East End and even my parents, although

[1] Barbara Hiles, later Bagenal, a friend of Carrington, and also at the Slade.

[2] J. Middleton Murry and Katherine Mansfield.

The Creation of Eve

Oil painting (33 × 26 in.) 1914

Reproduced by permission of Lady Ridley

Gilbert Cannan at his Mill, Cholesbury

Oil painting (40 × 28 in.) 1915

Reproduced by permission of Mr Thomas Balston

I like them. There, I shall be free and detached—shall belong to no parents. I shall be neither Jew nor Christian and shall belong to no class. I shall be just myself and be able to work out things according to my own tastes. I was beginning to feel stifled by everything here in the East End, worried by the sordidness of my family, their aimlessness, their poverty and their general wretchedness. I used to get terribly depressed also by my father, in whose face there is always an expression of the sufferings and disappointments he has gone through. I keep wondering why they are alive and why they want to live and why nature treated them so cruelly. All this, you see, was depressing and that is why I am relieved to get away. It'll be good to get all that change and yet be in London. Yes, I'm excited about it. It feels like the beginning of chapter one of the second book of my life. It is quite a change for me.

For the present and until I am settled I am staying with Eddie. I have never been so comfortable before in my life and never before had a bath every morning, for over a week. Every morning at 9 o'clock Eddie comes and says, "Mark! Bath ready!" and helps me into a PURPLE SILK DRESSING-GOWN! OH! How good a thing is comfort!

At Lady Ottoline's things went off rather badly. Fortunately I myself was *not* in fancy dress. Brett ran away abashed at once. But I've never seen Brett look so well as she did that night. . . . However we couldn't altogether have been a failure, because Lady Ottoline invites us, this Thursday, to dine! And the girls are to come in fancy dress as before.

Last week-end I stayed with the Cannans. There was no party. All the same I enjoyed it immensely. They want me to come down some time with Brett.

In London, I'm sure, everybody must be wondering at the large and varying train of my girl friends. Barbara is a great success. At Lady Ottoline's they thought she was my sister. Everybody wanted to know who she was. The other night I went to Café Royal—never again—just as horrible.

I've been trying to sell some drawings for Bomberg, but Eddie won't have them.

The Lawrences have moved to Sussex!

I am so sorry for your father. My father's eyes are much better, but his constitution seems to be breaking up rapidly. My mother is ill in bed.

You certainly ought to learn something about cooking. I should always prefer my girl friends to be better cooks than artists. Don't let this annoy you. Yours sincerely. MARK GERTLER

To Carrington

[*23 January 1915*] *Penn Studio, Rudall Crescent, Hampstead*

Dear Carrington, I thank you for your letter, in spite of your not making it affectionate. Affection does not seem to come easily from you at any time.

I am glad you are enjoying the week-end. I am working hard. Yesterday Mr and Mrs Hutchinson[1] came to tea unexpectedly—they have invited me to dine with them on Wednesday. I've accepted.

I had a long letter from Lawrence. He is not very well again, but he likes Cornwall. He says that he liked you very much the last time he saw you and he sends greetings to you and Brett.

Well then, I shall see you on Tuesday at Brett's. MARK GERTLER

To Lytton Strachey

27 January 1915 c/o Edward Marsh, 5 Raymond Buildings, Gray's Inn, W.C.

Dear Strachey, I am glad you are back. I have found a studio at last in Hampstead and am moving in next Monday. I feel both sad and immensely relieved at having to leave the East End and my parents. But the feeling of relief is greater than the feeling of sadness.

Could I come and see you instead of you me? Because everything in my studio is "topsy turvy".

Please let me know when. Perhaps you will be at Lady Ottoline's Thursday. Write here, as in the meantime, until I'm settled, I am staying with Eddie Marsh.

I could come Friday to tea. MARK GERTLER

To Carrington

February 1915 c/o Edward Marsh, 5 Raymond Buildings, Gray's Inn, W.C.

Dear Carrington, I moved into my new studio last Monday. Already I feel very at home there, although I have not slept there, as the bedroom isn't fixed up yet. I am well pleased with it all. Last Monday the Heath looked superb! What a wonderful place it is. How good to live near it. Later on when it gets warmer I shall get up very early in the mornings and go out to paint on the Heath.

Brett, as usual, was a splendid help to me during moving time. It was so good to have somebody who was as interested in it all as myself. I did not feel so lonely and lost as I would have done without her—she dusted all the books and did many things which I shouldn't have thought of myself. She is altogether a wonderful help. I don't know really how I should get on without her. However unhappy or unnerved I am she always brings peace and happiness to me with her presence—she has simply grown a part of me.

Barbara, who lives near to me, is also a help. She is going to recover my cushions for me. Barbara is a good and affectionate girl.

[1] St John (Jack) Hutchinson, K.C., and Mary Hutchinson.

Today I started painting Brett again in my new studio. It is a very good studio to paint in. The light is excellent.

The other day Lady Ottoline came to see my "Eve" with her husband. She thought it "quite beautiful" but what delighted me was that she liked very much my "Husband and Wife", the one nobody liked. You know, the one in which you didn't like the stomach. She is thinking of buying it!

Last Thursday, at Lady Ottoline's, was the wildest of all nights!! I smashed Dodgen's glasses, kicked Miss Strachey so that her foot bled, and made a Belgian girl's arm black and blue!!! John was there.

Lady Ottoline is stopping her Thursdays. She asked me to send you her love and thank you for the Christmas card you sent her. She misses you and wanted to know your address.

Tonight we danced at Brett's. That little German girl you drew nude, dances *excellently*. She has a lovely little figure to clasp.

Barbara is going to sit nude to Brett and me! That will be useful as I can't afford a model. Dodgen, Chile[1] and young Spencer[2] all thought that my "Apples" was the best thing in the New English.

I let Lady Hamilton have my "Cottage" for £12. It hurts me to part with those things as I think that the "Apples", the drawing of "Old Jew" and "Black and White Cottage" about the best things I've done and I loved them myself very much and should have liked to keep them. Eddie now has the drawing and, the more I look at it, the more I like it, but I should have loved to keep the little landscape. However, I am having it well photographed. It is nice to feel that I shall be able to keep my "Eve" for some time, as that is the best of all.

No, Eddie does not admire my legs. My legs are far too thin and hairy! He is used to the legs of Jim Barnes and Rupert Brooke, whose legs are as pink and plump as yours! I cut a very sorry figure after those people. However Eddie is very kind to me in spite of my figure. . . .

I am in the future going to stay nine months of the year in London, the rest—the summer—in the country. Then one can paint out of doors. I think that is the best plan. And after all it is good to meet people after one's work—it's so stimulating. One mustn't begin being a hermit too soon.

MARK GERTLER

To Carrington

Friday, February 1915 — *Penn Studio, Hampstead*

Dear Carrington, Thank you very much for the flowers and the ties. It was good of you to send them. I am glad you sold your drawing. I am sure it proves that you will very soon be able to earn your living at your work.

I have the last month been suffering from pains in the head very badly. The excitement of moving and then this wretched damp weather we've been having have been too much for me. Today it all broke out in the form of a bad cold, so I locked up my studio, bade farewell to Eddie and came

[1] Alvaro Guevara, the Chilean painter.

[2] Gilbert Spencer.

home to my people, Spital Square, to be nursed until I'm better. I expect in a few days to be better. I need rest badly.

I am fed up with Lady Ottoline and her parties and dancing: I only want to get better and retire into my studio to work.

The "London Group" have at last thought it time to ask me to be a member. I got a formal letter from Wadsworth who, it appears, is secretary, commencing with "Dear Sir". I accepted, but whether I shall exhibit I don't know. Today also I heard from the magazine *Colour* asking permission to reproduce my "Blue Flowers" at the Friday Club.

Barbara has sat; she is quite good to draw.

Make your visit to London whenever you like. MARK GERTLER

To Carrington

Sunday, February 1915 *Penn Studio, Hampstead*

Dear Carrington, You do not write to me for a fortnight, yet you ask me to answer your letter very soon. Long letters about yourself would not be tedious to me at all, as you suppose. However I am good, you see, and am writing to you almost at once. I am much better now and have been living altogether in my studio and very much so. I like my studio immensely, but everything is so much more expensive. I eat out and that's very expensive. I have, however, a marvellous landlady. She does all the cleaning for me, lights my fire and makes my bed, all for two shillings a week! She has taken a fancy to me and mothers me. Today being Sunday, she thought the restaurants would be closed, so she cooked me a splendid dinner and sent it in to me! Perhaps that means that she will be willing to cook always for me! That would be splendid. Then I should be as comfortable as a Duke! I shall ask her tomorrow. It feels wonderful getting these sort of things done for one. I have been very lucky in finding this place. It is awfully good for light too.

I must explain once and for always to you, that I do not write you about my work, simply because I think that painting thoughts, or pictures, cannot be written or talked, but *painted* and that only with *great* difficulty. Of course I don't mind telling you the objects or the subjects of the picture I happen to be painting, but more I cannot—you must see them whenever you come to London. As you know, I've been so busy moving that I haven't had time for painting. Now I am doing a portrait of Brett, a small colour study, perhaps for a large picture, of my "Rabbi and Rabbitzin"[1] and a picture of daffodils. Nothing large as yet.

Last week-end I stayed with Strachey[2] in his country cottage in Wiltshire—I enjoyed that. The country was covered with snow and was very beautiful. Just green, white and black. The white snow made lovely shapes on dark bushes.

[1] Plate 6, facing page 65.

[2] Lytton Strachey had rented a cottage at Lockeridge, near Marlborough and was writing *Eminent Victorians* there.

But the Heath also looks very beautiful. Really it's like the country here. From the top lights of my studio I can see the bare black branches of trees against the sky, and the branches are always full of screaming birds. In my bedroom also there is a top light and from my bed I can see the moon, branches and the sky, also hear the birds. It is pleasant as I lie to look up through the branches and see the bellies and chests of the birds. Later on it'll be still better when the leaves are out.

Whilst with Strachey I read Keats' letters. They impressed me very much, so sad! He suddenly got very ill and knew he was going to die! and he wanted so much time for his poetry. He was so near the end, tormented with love for a girl—Fanny Brawne. He wanted her so much that he couldn't bear to correspond with her! She only just admired him and didn't have the slightest idea how great he was. The letters made me very unhappy—he died when he was only twenty-six.

The other day I met Nevinson in uniform! He had come back from the Front! Told me in five minutes *all* about it, and you can imagine how ghastly it sounded in "Nevinsonian" language.... MARK GERTLER

P.S. The other day I picked up a piece of African sculpture wood, like they have in B.M., for 10*s*.! It gives me great delight and is like my work.

To Edward Marsh

[*March 1915*] *5 Raymond Buildings, Gray's Inn, W.C.*

Dear Eddie, This picture is the work of a young Jewish artist. He is almost penniless and wants to go back into the country to see his people for next week, which is Passover week. Passover is a very important festival with us and most Jewish parents like to have their children with them on this occasion.

He seems to be an artist of promise. His name is Kramer.[1] He is a friend of Mr Sadler.[2] I like this drawing, especially the figure of Christ, which is so well drawn. He wants £5 for it. If you like it at all, and would care to help him, please write to me soon, as Passover is early next week. I feel very sorry for the poor fellow. Forgive me for bothering you so much. But he wrote to me and asked me to show you this. He has heard of you. MARK GERTLER

To Lytton Strachey

2 March 1915 *Penn Studio, Hampstead*

Dear Strachey, As I am here all alone tonight I am taking the opportunity to write to you. Things are improving here. My landlady now cooks for me! That saves me a lot of trouble and money.

[1] Jacob Kramer, a Leeds artist. There is a bust of him by Epstein in the Tate.

[2] Professor Michael Sadler, then Chancellor of Leeds University.

Sunday she gave me an excellent dinner, but today I've been unhappy. After the first course, I waited and waited and nothing else came. Now, I simply must have sweets. After waiting for about fifteen minutes I gave my mouth a final wipe, got up and walked off in despair. What if I never get sweets! I sat and brooded all the afternoon about it and couldn't work.

Tomorrow I shall approach her about it. If only I succeed in getting a second course out of her I shall be very comfortable here. At tea time I livened up a bit. I had a party on. The Ranee and Rajah of Sarawak, Brett, and Gilbert Cannan. Tonight I have so little inclination to do anything that I am going to bed in a minute although it's only 8 o'clock!

The Possessed[1] is getting more and more difficult. I simply can't think why everybody in it is so excited about everybody else in it. You think that they might all murder each other any moment. They are all in absolute terror of one another and for no apparent reason. However, I shall struggle through—perhaps the key is at the end....

No, I shouldn't be a bit surprised if, in the story of Susanna and the Elders, Daniel himself was all the time the young man in the garden—as you say. Anyway I am altogether on the side of poor old "Elders".

MARK GERTLER

To Carrington

4 March 1915 *Penn Studio, Hampstead*

Dear Carrington, ... Well I am still more comfortable here. My landlady now cooks for me and very well too. The other day I proudly asked Brett to lunch! She liked it very much. I get excellent breakfasts. After breakfast I go for a long walk on the Heath. That is fine! How different from the East End! Here I stand a much better chance of keeping healthy, as the air is good and the food regular. The Heath is magnificent really. Such good and varied ground. It is so good by the ponds. Sometimes for days on end I don't go into town at all.

Last night was another exciting Thursday. Brett had John, Iris Tree, Barbara and myself to supper in her studio! John arrived with two large bottles of wine. Of course we got drunk. Iris looked very beautiful in a pale-lemon-coloured evening dress. She is so beautiful. I had a love scene with her, which I am afraid I must confess I enjoyed. I like Iris more than is good for me. I have come to the conclusion that it'll be better for me not to see her much. If she was like other girls it wouldn't matter, but she is so capricious and loves hurting one.

Gilbert Cannan came here to tea the other day. He thought my studio "simply splendid" and he loved the Heath. He wants to buy my charcoal study of "Abraham and the Angels". But I must keep it as yet, as sooner or later I will paint it. I promised to reserve it for him. How he does like my work. He seems to understand me more than anyone.

[1] By Feodor Dostoevsky.

Please, by the way, do not think me awful for getting drunk etc. last night. Do not think that I like that sort of thing. If you knew my nature you would be surprised how difficult it is for me, especially with women. I always suffer agonies the next morning—of remorse. As for Iris I shall not see her hardly at all. *I am by no means trying to excuse myself to you.* You can think of me exactly what you like. Only you are apt to misunderstand that sort of thing. Just because you are young and inexperienced and rather, if I may say so, cold or sexless.

I have become great friends with Lytton Strachey. He spends a large part of his time in his cottage, which is in a place near Marlborough—all alone. We carry on a correspondence. He is a very intellectual man—I mean in the right sense. I should think he ought to do good work. He writes such good poetry. He mentions me in one of his poems! . . .[1]

MARK GERTLER

[1] Lytton Strachey sent the following poem to Gertler, and this may be the one referred to:

Happiness

Sometimes it so befalls that ruthless chance
Relents, and in the swiftly-gliding dance
Of life's strange atoms wields a wand benign
And waves them marvellously to combine.
Most happy, happy fortune! Oftenest known
To those in whom the waiting soul has grown
A little weary, and whose deep desires
(As in black coal sleep unextinguished fires)
All joy's rich possibilities ignore,
And, not despairing, yet expect no more.
Ah then, when haply on the listless ear,
Insidious music murmurs and draws near,
And knocks, and pleads, and will not be denied,
Until the spirit's portals opening wide
Admit voluminous harmonies enwound
With long, triumphant mysteries of sound,
—Or, when, upon a sudden, in a breath,
Like a soul caught from out the lap of Death,
A secret silence, for a second's space,
Lives and reveals a heaven in a face,
—Then, then, like the remote, dissolving snow
In Spring-warmed Alpine vales, begin to flow
The softly-trickling rivulets of delight,
Scarce felt at first, but with a gathering might
Hurrying, and the urgent torrents press and pour
In multitudinous gladness, more and more,
And join, and spread, till lo!—deep, calm, and strong,
Beatitude's full flood is rolled along.
The Time, with withdrawn breath, stands still, and smiles;
And, like a vast soap-bubble that beguiles
With gilded nothingness destruction's power,
Quivering and safe hangs the miraculous hour.
And oh! then gently, with familiar art,
Through the swooned brain and the enchanted heart,
Pale Passion weaves her way, while over all
Tears shed from inaccessible glories fall.

April 1915

To Carrington

Easter Monday, 1915 *Penn Studio, Hampstead*

Dear Carrington, Thank you ever so much for your kind letter. I loved helping you into that train. I was only unhappy that you were going away from me.

The stay at Gilbert's was certainly splendid. You seemed somehow so much more sympathetic than usual. Now I love you more than ever, dear girl. Your friendship is the best thing in my life. But it is terribly difficult to get on without you. You must come up and see me at least once every month. Anyhow come at the end of this month. Come at all costs, if only for my sake. The last time you were away too long, you can't think how I suffered, though I *did* not tell you so.

I will send you Gilbert's *Butler*[1] and some photographs tomorrow. Do send me a photo of your "Still-Life". Perhaps you could send the original?! Why not? I could keep it here for you. I should love that. Your brothers sound splendid, I am sure I should like them. I want to meet them so much. Anyhow I love them already because you do and because they are your brothers. . . .

The other night I dined with Mrs Delliba. They are back from Italy. She showed me dozens of most awful reproductions she'd brought back! Andrea del Sarto etc. She screamed enthusiasms about Italy at me in a way which made me wish never to see that country. The dinner, however, was good and we had jumping games afterwards, which was amusing, although I once nearly broke my neck. The Shapiros seem quite friendly again. They, Mrs Parker and myself dined out last night and then went on to the cinema. The cinema was splendid! There was a war picture, some French victory—actual fighting! It was terrible to see long rows of black spots running along the snow and then some "spots" dropping down dead or wounded. There was also a boxing match—Wells and Moran.

Strachey came to tea twice running. He is splendid to talk to. . . .

Yours ever MARK GERTLER

To S. S. Koteliansky[2]

[? *1915*] *The Mill House, Cholesbury*

Dear Koteliansky, Although I came here very unhappy, I have now recovered and am feeling now comparatively happy. Gilbert is a good

[1] Gilbert Cannan's study of Samuel Butler.

[2] A Russian Jew living in London and earning his living by translation. He translated Russian literature for the Hogarth Press. He was also a friend of Katherine Mansfield and many of her letters were addressed to him. Gertler's portrait of him will be found facing page 144.

companion. He is soothing. I like him immensely. I shan't rest until I also have a good wife and a comfortable house. *Plainly* that is what I want. I don't care what *you* say.

My cottage here is very nice, but sometimes I get a curious desire to chop it up and burn it and watch it burning until there is nothing left but a small heap of ashes!

I have been studying Philosophy lately. Spinoza and Berty Russell. But I still can't understand it. Tell me, did Spinoza ever love a woman? As I sit here I can hear Gilbert playing on the pianola. He is writing a long book and is very busy on it. Some moments I feel like running back to London and dipping into a large canvas. I love London. I think of you all sometimes in the evening, talking "plainly".

Best wishes and remembrance to Katherine and Jack.[1]

MARK GERTLER

Have you Kant to lend me?

To Carrington

April 1915 *Penn Studio, Hampstead*

Dear Carrington, I can't thank you sufficiently for your letters. They made me so happy. Yesterday morning, when I got the first of the two, I was so excited that I couldn't eat my breakfast. My hand shook so with excitement and pleasure that I couldn't hold the spoon to eat with. I was glad when breakfast was over and when I at last got on to the Heath. There I could think it all over in peace. I thought how very fortunate I was to have you for a friend. I think of you all day. All day I am having imaginary talks with you and writing you imaginary letters. I do nothing without consulting your mind.

This morning when I got out of bed I rushed to the door for your second letter and there it was, as you promised. I was excited—I read it shivering with cold, standing on the floor with my bare feet. I love your letters so. But how terrible for you, that wedding![2] But I am glad you told me, because I want you to confide everything to me. You must tell me *always* when you are unhappy. Are you happier now, dear, that the wedding is over? How I wish I had money. I should settle you comfortably somewhere near me in a nice studio and see you *every* evening. . . .

Yes, Strachey talks a great deal to me when we are alone. The other day we went for a walk on the Heath together. But it was a Sunday before Easter Monday and so it was crowded and some people shouted at us—imitating a goat. This was aimed at Strachey's beard!

Last Thursday the Shapiros took me to a home at that Jewish artist's

[1] Katherine Mansfield and J. Middleton Murry.

[2] Her sister's wedding to R. C. Elmslie, the surgeon, which was of a very formal kind.

house where I got terribly bored, but his wife is interesting. She has had about half a dozen children and paints far better than her husband.

Early on Wednesday afternoon, just as I was busy painting, I heard a knock at my door. I went to see who it was and there stood Brett herself!! I must say I was pleased to see her funny face again. We had tea and went for a walk on the Heath. Do you know she has become more sensible now; she actually does not altogether look forward to going to Sarawak!

Our talks about her must have had a hypnotic effect on her. She had not much to say about Paris, except that she came across a good Cézanne book. So I am making her send for it at once. She brought me back a pair of corduroy trousers. They are very nice but very heavy. . . .

I talked to Brett about you having her studio for a bit, when she goes, so that you can paint your "Bull and Bush" picture. She seemed delighted at the idea and said that she would much rather you had it than let it. How splendid if you could come for a month. MARK GERTLER

To Edward Marsh

Saturday [*1915*] *Penn Studio, Hampstead*

Dear Marsh, I shall be very glad to let you have my "Interior" as part payment of what I owe you. But I should be very thankful to you if you would let me keep it one week after it comes back, as I may be able to sell it. This may sound horrid to you, but I know you will understand when I tell you that I am at this moment penniless! The last thing I sold was that still-life of the doll, but that was sold a long time before it was exhibited and of that money I have nothing more now. At the Friday Club I only sold a drawing for £5 that won't go very far when I get it. I am only going into these details because I want you to see the reasons of my not letting you have the picture at once, which is what I very much want to do.

The picture comes back today and if I don't sell it by next Saturday you will have it then.

According to my accounts I owe you £64 and not £70 as you say, but I may be wrong, although I doubt it as I have kept them very carefully.[1]

I hope you are well. Yours very sincerely MARK GERTLER

To Lytton Strachey

10 April 1915 *Penn Studio, Hampstead*

Dear Strachey, I am more or less all right, only I wish painting wasn't such a worry. I can't tell you exactly what worries me when I paint, because my worries are altogether too extraordinary and complicated. The

[1] Marsh paid Gertler a small monthly subsidy and Gertler paid him back in paintings.

strange part is that I seem very often *most* worried when my picture goes most well! The most difficult thing, I find, is to control my excitement. My ideas seem so wonderful and exciting that they make me feel wretched! They are too much to bear.

I looked on to the Heath on Easter Monday. Wonderful ideas for pictures! Girls with brilliant feathers and youths swinging in coloured boats!!! The effect was like a rainbow!!! God! give me patience and enough powers of control.

Goodnight. I am unhappy. Come and see me soon. MARK GERTLER

To Carrington

April 1915 *Penn Studio, Hampstead*

Dear Carrington, Thanks so much for the flowers and photographs. The eggs also were a beautiful colour. I am glad you are happy. Yesterday was a beautiful day. I spent most of it walking on the Heath with Strachey.

Tuesday I saw Koteliansky and last night Koteliansky and myself went down to see the Murrys who now live in London. Katherine, however, was out. I was disappointed. They are coming to have tea with me and Koteliansky next week. I like these people and Strachey—they are real and not dull as so many people are.

I heard from Lady Ottoline again! She has, it appears, still one more Thursday tonight—the little Jap. is dancing. Yesterday I had tea with Ruth. How she loves John! Her relationship with John seems to make all others unreal.

Brett is now not going to Sarawak and even uncertain if she is going to Japan! So no pianola for me or studio for you.

Is it your intention to come up at the end of this month in any case or only if Brett goes?

Yours MARK GERTLER

P.S. On Sunday Eddie and myself are going down to see the Spencers. Stanley has asked us. I shall be interested to see their work. Stanley writes that he has four pictures ready!

To Lytton Strachey

23 May 1915 *Penn Studio, Hampstead*

Dear Strachey, So you've had a cold. I've had a terrible one. Last Wednesday I got up in the morning shivering from head to foot. In the afternoon I had a frightful headache and that night on getting into bed I shivered so with cold, in spite of my Jewish bed, that I literally jumped—I thought I was going to die. I got out with terrible difficulty and put all the clothes I could find on, until I must have looked like a "Teddy Bear".

Then, only, by degrees did I get warm! Since then my temperature has got normal, but I've had bad headaches, and like Charmides, chiefly in the mornings. Also it had left me very weak. The other day for instance, after copulating only *once*, mind you, I was left prostrate on the woman, unable to move! My breath coming and going with such rapidity that I thought I shouldn't survive it. The woman, knowing my usual vigour on such occasions, was more alarmed than me at my condition. All the while I lay there I was cursing my fate for not having been born a Eunuch! Which I know is very different from the Eunuch's desire in *Candide*. Tonight, Sunday, I am really feeling well and I think my cold is quickly going. Eddie, however, was alarmed this morning at my appearance and has written to Winston Churchill's doctor for an appointment for me! So now I'm in for it.

This coalition business in Parliament has caused me great anxiety. Never was I so feverishly interested in a political move, simply because it was the only one that stood any chance of directly affecting me. What affects Churchill, affects Eddie Marsh and what affects Eddie Marsh affects me!

However, although they have both been driven out like Adam and Eve from the Garden of Eden, all is not black yet. Anyhow it is not going to affect me, but poor Eddie is rather unhappy and I am sorry for him as his goodness to me has really made me love him. He hates Lord Fisher now and has burnt his photograph! He seems to think the other post they will get will be so dull; whilst at the Admiralty "he did feel he was doing something for his country but now . . ." Poor dear Eddie!!!

The N.E.A.C. have refused my "Eve"! I was absolutely amazed and very vexed because I had hopes of selling it there, and any extra money would have been very useful just now. They refused it, I hear, because the figure of Eve was considered indecent! Of course I've not done much work on account of my cold but I hope to start tomorrow.

My people have now turned Poles! No more are we alien enemies! There is a Polish Society that can officially turn all people that come from Galicia and that can speak Polish into Poles. So that's all right now.

I am afraid I must agree with you about Gilbert Cannan's book,[1] but that it is so depresses me very much. MARK GERTLER

To Edward Marsh

May 1915 *Penn Studio, Hampstead*

My dear Eddie, I have been to the doctor. He says there's nothing much the matter with me. In fact, he says, I am very strong, but have been drinking too much tea and over-smoking. He has given me a nerve medicine and something for my bowels.

I feel extremely grateful to you for all this. I really cannot express my

[1] Probably *Samuel Butler* referred to on page 88.

thanks to you for your extraordinary goodness. I must tell you that I feel that what you are doing for me is *far* more valuable to me than anybody else has ever done. The only thing is that you shall have to have patience with my work. Although I get such little done, you must always know that I am working *extremely* hard and that I never stop working. It being the only thing I have to care for now.

You see I am terribly sensitive about my work and I cannot leave a picture unless I feel that I have got it as near to my conception as is possible. With your present help I am able to carry this out. Of course you must not expect to like everything I do, I do not that myself, but I hope to always turn out a thing, now and then, that you will like. I have faith in myself and I hope to do really fine things some day, but in painting nothing can be hurried, at any rate I find I can't hurry with any success. And after all, quantity doesn't matter, you have only got to go to the N.E.A.C. to see that there are no lack of pictures!

There is just one thing more I want to say and that is that if you find that you are hard up or that you do not feel inclined to continue your help during the war you must *immediately* tell me. I mean, supposing my work disappoints you or you get hard up or supposing the war lasts too long! Anyway you must not let me be a weight on you.

As it stands, however, I must thank you again and I hope I may some day be able to do something for you.

Excuse this long and badly expressed letter but I've long wanted to write it, firstly to tell you how grateful I am, secondly to tell you that if you feel you can't manage to continue for some reason you are to tell me.

Now I've got it off my chest. Yours ever MARK GERTLER[1]

[1] Marsh's reply to this letter was as follows:

26 May 1915 *The Admiralty, Whitehall*

My dear Mark, I am so glad to have your charming letter, first because it is a great relief to hear that there is nothing really wrong with you, and also because of course it is a pleasure to know that you think I am of use to you.

Of course you know I am very fond of you, and that I have a strong belief in your genius—and for both these reasons I couldn't make a better use of my resources than to help you along as much as I can. Of course I can't expect to like everything you do equally—I know your work is very original, and it is natural that I should want time to take in anything that is very new. Sometimes I take to your things at once and am fascinated and enchanted, as I was by the "Daffodils", but that can't happen every time, and the only thing I ask is that you should not be hurt or depressed if I don't take to everything as immediately as I did to that!

Another thing is that my great sorrow [the death of Rupert Brooke] has so completely absorbed all my power of feeling for the present that I really have nothing left over, even for the greatest masterpiece. Time will cure this, but in the meanwhile I can't take any interest in any pictures at all, except yours, which interest me intensely because they are yours—but not so intensely as they would have if my mind and my feelings had full play. All this only means that you must put up with me at any time when you may feel I am not appreciating your work as keenly as you would like. This need not mean that I had lost my confidence in you in the least. All I want is that you should go ahead on your own lines, and that I should be able to help you and make things easier for you.

To Edward Marsh

May 1915 — *Penn Studio, Hampstead*

My dear Eddie, Thanks for yours. It made me happy, for I know there's nothing to fret about.

I shall come and stay Monday night and see you Tuesday morning unless I hear from you to the contrary.

Professor Brown has bought the portrait of Brett for £20.

MARK GERTLER

To William Rothenstein

[? *1915*] — *Penn Studio, Hampstead*

My Dear Rothenstein, I have been meaning to write to you ever since our conversation at the Grafton Galleries—apropos of the younger generation of artists not writing to their elders. All I want to say on our behalf is that if we do not write it does not mean that we do not appreciate older artists. As you must know, fashions change, and probably the lack of postal appreciation of which you complain is chiefly due to the simple fact that people don't write so many letters nowadays! And as far as my own attitude is concerned, I should like to take this opportunity to tell you how much I always appreciate the help I received from you during the early part of my career. I have never ceased to be grateful to you.

Well, that is all.

If ever you feel like it, I should be very pleased if you would come to tea at the studio—phone or write a day or two before as I should like to have a talk. Yours sincerely MARK GERTLER

To Carrington

Saturday, June 1915 — *Penn Studio, Hampstead*

Dear Carrington, I got your letter this morning and not last night. Of course I am writing at once. Although I may not post it at once.

When the train took you away from me, I was stunned, everything became unreal. I was hardly aware of Gilbert's presence, nor heard his voice.

Brett drove to the station startled as ever. We took her back; still I was dazed and made vague answers to everything that was said to me. Before

---

As far as I can make out, I shall be no worse off in money now than I was before—and I will certainly tell you if it becomes difficult for me to go on with my help—but I hope it won't come to that.

Dr Parkinson is an angel; he said he couldn't take any money for seeing you.

I am going to Cambridge from Saturday to Monday—when will you come instead? Yours EDDIE

tea we weeded, Brett and I. Then I took her for a walk. I woke up then because we talked of you. She also told me more a very little tiny bit more about her relations with the Old Pro![1] Brett has a great deal in her that she doesn't reveal.

I sat her down almost exactly on the same spot that we two sat on only that morning. After supper, of course, Gilbert played the pianola. Brett couldn't hear in the further room so she and I sat in the front room, each occupying a sofa, while Mary[2] sat in the further room as usual doing some work. Of this arrangement I was glad, because then she could not interrupt as she usually does by talking. Gilbert played splendidly. I never wanted it to end. The whole time I was with you, thinking with you, talking with you and listening with you. I dreaded an interruption. I wanted it to go on for ever or if there must be an interruption it should be by you yourself—the reality, which is even always better than my imagination.

It ended and then Brett and Mary went to bed, while Gilbert and I woke up because we talked of you. I told him all. He thought our relations wonderful and worth much and he envied me for knowing you. He appreciates you very much and I love him for liking you.

The next day Friday I was not so dazed and helped Mary decorating her hall. Then Brett and I caught a train after tea.

Now I am in London again and in my studio I feel stunned again and unhappy and lonely. I don't know why you should not be with me always. Such a lot has happened the last two months. Everything has changed so. Especially you. You have completely altered. The day and half that I was with you astounded me. You seemed to have suddenly grown up into a woman. I am almost frightened at the change. I am wondering if it's permanent or only temporary. I could not bear you to go back again and become indifferent again. Oh! I like your present warmth. The fresh scraps you have given me you must not take back again ever! If there must be a change let it be even more happy advancement. Heavens! How near I felt to you! Nearly, nearly, all there! But my head is too full. I must spend the next few days just thinking. I am not ready for work yet. I shall go about the parks and just try and think it out. I am very, very bewildered. If only I could express to you the complexities of my mind. How my love for you grows and grows! The great difficulty is to live without you. We only parted two days ago and I miss you horribly, dearest girl.

MARK GERTLER

To Carrington

[*June 1915*] *Penn Studio, Hampstead*

Dear Carrington, I hope you got home all right. It was a great pleasure having you here. . .

[1] Professor Brown.

[2] Mary Cannan, formerly married to Sir James Barrie.

Today Strachey came, but I peeped through the hole in the door and didn't let him in!

Last night I went home to see my people; they are all in a bad state. Ill and poor. My mother was in bed and my father was very angry with me, accusing me of not caring what becomes of them all. It depressed me very much. I owe them also £8!!

Every day another poor little old Jew is being sent back to Austria. These poor little people are quite unaware of the war and are no more Austrian in spirit than Hottentot.

How is your brother? Where was he wounded?

I saw your landscape at Brett's and I like it. Nash is a fool for not liking it. This evening I spent with Brett in her studio. We had eggs and cherries and strawberries. Brett thinks you are too Puritanical and she can see it she says, in your work.

Afterwards we walked in the Park. It was a splendid evening, the trees were magnificent. Brett received a letter of apology from Lady Tree, who has now found out that Brett was the only "angel" in the case. Am I the villain? Best wishes MARK GERTLER[1]

To Carrington

1 July 1915 *Penn Studio, Hampstead*

Dear Carrington, Yesterday, quite suddenly, I finished my picture. So on Saturday I am going off to my cottage in the country. It will be a great relief to get away and a pleasure to see dear Gilbert and listen to his pianola.

Last night I stayed at Marsh's. Every time I see him I get depressed. I hate having to take this money from him. Today he didn't give me the cheque—this was a great blow to me as I was waiting for it. I don't know whether he merely forgot or whether he doesn't intend giving it me because I sold a picture. At present I haven't a penny in the world and I owe my people £8. When the N.E.A.C. closes, however, I shall get the money for Brett's portrait. It closes on the 10th I believe.

You are certainly lucky that your brother is only wounded and now you

[1] The following letter from Carrington to Gertler may be inserted at this point:

Tuesday, June 1915 *Carlisle Road, Hove, Sussex*

Dear Mark, It seems so like a dream last night and seeing you again that I find it is hard to believe it is quite true. I almost came round this morning to see if you had changed or were still, still there.

But have I been rather stupid and selfish? I did like your work *so much*, and I never tell you lies now. How good "The Mill" is, and although you do not believe me I *do* appreciate the "Still-Life" and the "Swing Boats" very much indeed. Only you must help me. It is no good telling Gilbert and Lawrence my faults. If we are absolutely candid then it cannot help being a fine relationship. But if you nurse your wrath how can you help me? You can correct me without quarrelling, we have at least arrived at that point. . . . CARRINGTON will have a companion. I expect I shall be dragged into this wretched war, before it's over, but I shall keep out of it as long as I possibly can. How hateful it all is. How I shall hate it if it spoils my life and prevents me from carrying on my work. How hateful it would be to lose one's life, or even be maimed for life, through a purpose in which one has no sort of belief. How unfortunate it is to have been born just in a time of war and such a war. There were so many years of peace, why couldn't one have been born then? All I have in life is my work. I have, underneath all, a certain undying impetus to paint and paint. It is inexplicable, yet the most living thing about me. At bottom I know that the most satisfactory thing in life is work—to work regardless of achievement or failure. Now, therefore, all I want is to be allowed to carry on my work; surely that is not much to ask for and quite harmless, yet I daresay this beastly War will succeed in disturbing me.

Of course I never for a moment thought it was Ruth's fault your coming late last Saturday. I hated you very much for it, but with extreme control I managed to be fairly amiable. But how dreadfully disappointing and inconsiderate you are very often. You are a sort of person with whom one never gets beyond a certain point of intimacy, or if one for a moment oversteps the boundary line, one finds that you have immediately rushed back, leaving one alone gaping. You are in some ways amazingly inhuman. I am not lecturing you or quarrelling. Frankly I am tired of it all—I've tried and tried to get something out of you. I've tried now for four years. But now I have given up hoping now. I know that, if I am to get something satisfactory out of life, it's to be from my work and not from you.

That night on the bus did for me. When I left you that night something went out of me. I saw you for a moment in a clear light.

Yet, for your friendship I thank you. It means a tremendous amount to me at present. And considering that you do not love me, I must say, you are extremely kind to put up with all that you do. Do not think I'm not thankful. I will try my best to be equally considerate to you. But I do not know why I've written all this. There is no cause for it. . . .

Best wishes MARK GERTLER

To Carrington

1 July 1915 *Penn Studio, Hampstead*

Second Letter

I have just posted a meaningless letter to you. It was meaningless because though I was full of certain feelings and things I wanted to tell you, I kept them out of the letter and was trying to sulk away all those feelings to myself. Now, here, I am going to tell you all.

The last few days a reaction has set in, after being so happy with you. The old feelings have returned again. I mean again I want *all* of you or nothing. I want you to love me. To love me properly, or not at all. Like

Ruth loves John. Now as these feelings invariably turn up and as, when they come, they come with terrible pain to me, I have decided now that we cannot go on as we have been doing and therefore we must come to some definite arrangement.

You see I love you, as you know, and in return for this love you have only given me friendship. Now friendship feels for the most part not only insufficient but terribly painful. I want your love. I want your body as well as your mind. Whenever I've said anything else, I've been insincere or hysterical. Now before I go any further I am going to prove to you that the desire for the body in the case of real love is not low, but beautiful, and something quite different from the ordinary desire one has for a well-made person physical contact in the case of real love is the *expression of that love* and therefore indispensable. Words cannot express love, just as words cannot express painting. Each is its own medium. Painting expresses art and physical contact love. Therefore my physical desire for you is not merely sexual, but a tremendous desire to *express my love* for you. Do you think that in that wood at Cholesbury I wanted to kiss you because you are a pretty girl? Don't you see that I was full of love for you and that words were useless and that I *had* to kiss you at that moment?! Don't you see also how stupid it was for me at such a moment to have to first ask your permission?! Don't you see how awful it was for me afterwards when I felt that this expression of my love should make you unhappy?! Every now and then when I am with you I feel this. I want to express my love and I mustn't, always I mustn't! Don't you see that this is awful for me? To control an ordinary sexual feeling is easy, but this! Really it makes me hate you. Really I've hated you sometimes. Think about it and you will understand. When you realise that physical contact is the expression of love, you will then understand how people can marry people who seem to others so physically ugly. Because it is not the outward form that they are embracing, but all that goes to make up that which they love. The ordinary sexual affair is quite different. One is then only excited by the flesh. Now if only you could give me all yourself we could have the most tremendous friendship that ever was. If you really can't you must tell me and I must do altogether without you.

You have never really told me why you don't want physical contact. Why is it? Write to me plainly. Am I repulsive to you? But surely in that case you can't love me and yet sometimes you say you do. Is it simply perhaps because you don't want children? Then we should not have them, like many other couples. I would not want you to marry me or live with me, but when I have those feelings for you I should want you to allow me to express them, or else it is too painful a relationship. Oh! why should you spoil such a friendship? What can you lose?

However I shall not try and persuade you. Only you must write and tell me everything *frankly and plainly* as I have done here.

Anyhow it will be something to feel settled. Tell me yes or no.

MARK GERTLER

To Edward Marsh

Monday [*July 1915*] *Cholesbury, Herts.*

Dear Eddie, Thanks very much for the cheque and the *Who's Who* form. All here in my cottage is going well, but as yet I've not commenced work.

You bought the "Agapanthus" for £25, "Drawing of Old Jew" £6, "Daffodils" for £20. That makes £51—£51 away from £85 leaves £34. Therefore I owe you £34.

Please will you tell Mrs Elgy to send me my slippers.

Best wishes MARK GERTLER

To Edward Marsh

[*August 1915*] *Cholesbury, Herts.*

My dear Eddie, Thank you for your letter and cheque. I am glad the work on Rupert[1] has gone well and I hope you enjoyed your stay with the Gibsons.

I have until a few days ago been working on my "Mill".[2] But the last few days I had to leave in order to do some studies for it, direct from nature. At present I am working on a small oil study of a chestnut tree, as I have a chestnut tree in my Mill. I think the picture is going well. I am now working in Gilbert's old motor shed, which is somewhat more comfortable than this cottage as a studio.

I have today had a letter from an old friend of mine, Mr Edmund Harvey, M.P., who is now doing war-work in France, to say that Professor Sadler wants his portrait painted by me and wishes to pay £50 and that I should have to go to Leeds to do it in August and that I should write an answer to Mr Harvey's father in Leeds. The Harveys are cousins of Professor Sadler. I have written to accept, so I may any minute be dragged off to Leeds! In which case I should have to go to London. If this happens I shall make a point of stopping in London a day or two and stay one night with you. I shall let you know.

Best wishes MARK GERTLER

I have never in my life heard of the artist who is going to draw you. Hope you'll sit still.

To Edward Marsh

15 August 1915 *9 Hartley Avenue, Hyde Park, Leeds*

My dear Eddie, I am having a difficult time here. Professor Sadler can

[1] Marsh's edition of the Poems with his Memoir. Owing to difficulties with Rupert Brooke's mother the book was not published until 1918.

[2] "Gilbert Cannan at his Mill, Cholesbury" (Plate 8, facing page 81).

only sit while at work in his office at the University. All day long, he is being interviewed by different people and I have to try and catch him whilst all this is going on! Amidst all this hubbub! He is so busy with war-work; the people that interview him are mostly officers.

Really, commissioned portrait painting is a dreadful occupation. You can't think how this portrait is depressing me! Here I am, dragged away from the work that really means something to me, to paint a man whom I should never dream of choosing to paint. Just because I am paid a certain sum I do it. Never again will I accept a portrait *unless* the sitter interests or inspires me to paint him or her. I would rather starve.

However, now I am in for it, I am doing my very best and I shall not leave it until I paint an honest likeness of the man and make as good a picture of it as I can. I expect it to be finished in about a week. In my spare time I am painting a small oil study for my swing boat picture which I shall paint, I hope, as soon as I am settled in London. After this I am going to Cholesbury again until about the 10th September. Then I shall be in London. Do please write to me very soon. I would like to get a letter from you here. I hope you are well and progressing with Rupert's book.

MARK GERTLER

To Edward Marsh

17 August 1915 *Leeds*

My dear Eddie, I was glad to hear from you. I have today finished the portrait![1] I think it is good, but I don't think Mr Harvey will think so; in fact I am sure he won't. Well, I've done my best. If he doesn't like it, I shall be quite contented if he just pays me my expenses. I shall write and tell him this. In the future, I shall be very careful how I let myself in for such a thing again. Frankly, I am no good at all at any *commissioned* work. I simply can't do it—it is just a terrible pain to me to do. Since I have been here, I have appreciated even more your help to me. Your help is invaluable to me—you just let me paint that which I want to paint. But the future looks very black to me, because the more I go on the less I can paint that which does not very forcibly move me to paint. It is *the idea, the idea* that matters to me. It is torture to me now to touch a canvas without a definite idea or conception, and my ideas are becoming more and more mystical. What I am driving at is that I shall not be able to do commissions and yet not sell my pictures! Ideas for future pictures come to me very often, and these ideas are so mysterious and wonderful that when they come over me—they come in waves—I get so excited and feel so physically weak that I can scarcely stand. It is almost too much to bear. I think when I get to London I might try and get a teaching job in some art school—that would be better than commissions and I would not have to lean so heavily and constantly on you. I must above all try and arrange

[1] This portrait of Professor Sadler was left by Mr Harvey to Leeds University.

my life so that I can give birth one after the other to these pictures which are fighting in me to come out. I have to do a couple of drawings for Sadler of the University buildings. Then I shall come to London on my way to Cholesbury. Then also I must try and fix a night and breakfast with you. I shall write again and tell you exactly when I return. Anyhow I don't expect before the end of this week, Saturday the earliest.

Professor Sadler is going to be in London and wants very much to see you. I believe he has wired you about it. Please do not tell him how much I suffered in painting his portrait, as he would be unhappy and he was so kind to me and tried to make me as comfortable as possible, for which I like him very much.

I wonder why exactly Mrs Brooke objected to the memoirs being published?

Well, best wishes MARK GERTLER[1]

To Edward Marsh

[? *September 1915*] *32 Elder Street, E.*

Dear Eddie, I have just returned to London, I think now for the winter.

We had beautiful weather. Mrs Lawrence tells me that she has written

[1] Marsh's answer to this letter was as follows:

8 August 1915 *5 Raymond Buildings, Gray's Inn*

My dear Mark, Your birth-pains over your pictures are quite torture enough for you. Don't worry yourself additionally about how you are to live, so long as you can manage on what I can do for you, and the extras that are quite certain to come in.

Since the war, and still more since my friends died, I don't care to spend money on myself, beyond just keeping up my life here. You know I believe you were born to be a great painter, and if that is true it will have been a proud thing in my life to have been able to help you, and leave you more or less free to develop yourself unhampered—I can't imagine a worthier use of any money—and even suppose we were wrong about your painting! you are still my friend, and I should hate to be "rolling" while you were in straits. I should be ashamed of being comparatively well-off, if I don't take advantage of it to help my friends who are younger, and poorer and cleverer and better than I am.

Besides, I get your pictures.

And also, since my father died I have still more money (about £300 a year extra, I think it comes to). So please, dear Mark, don't talk any more about not wanting to "lean" on me, and put all *that* sort of bother out of your head.

I'm glad to hear what you say about the way ideas crowd on you and turn you inside-out—fertility, if it doesn't water-down intensity, is a fine promising thing in a young artist. You should take courage and not alarm when you find yourself tormented by inspiration. All great artists have the hell of a bad time like that, now and then. "I am glad you say every man of great views is at times tormented as I am," says Keats in a letter to Haydon that I read this morning.

The Professor is coming here tomorrow evening—of course I won't say anything indiscreet. I'll show him the "Daffodils" etc.

Don't come Saturday or Sunday, as I shall be away—but any other night. From EDDIE

to you about your attitude towards the war.[1] She seemed quite upset.

Well, I hope you will soon give me one of your hours in the evening. Yours sincerely MARK GERTLER

To Edward Marsh

19 October 1915 *Penn Studio, Hampstead*

Dear Eddie, I have come to the conclusion that we two are too fundamentally different to continue to be friends. Since the war, you have gone in one direction and I in another. All the time I have been stifling my feelings. Firstly because of your kindness to me and secondly I did not want to hurt you. I am I believe what you call a "Passivist". I don't know exactly what that means, but I just hate this war and should really loathe to help in it. I wanted to do some war-work simply because the hateful atmosphere had got into me and seemed difficult to create at such a time. But now I've changed my mind I shall paint as long as I can. As long as I am not forced into this horrible atmosphere I shall work away. Of course from this you will understand that we had not better meet any more and that I cannot any longer accept your help. Forgive me for having been dishonest with you and for having under such conditions accepted your money. I have been punished enough for it and have suffered terribly. I stuck it so long, because it seemed hard to have to give up this studio which I love. But now rather than be dishonest I shall give it up and go to my cottage in the country. I have still a little money of my own from the Sadler portrait. On this I shall live. In the country I can live on £1 a week. I shall live there until there is conscription or until my money is used up.[2]

Your kindness has been an extraordinary help to me. Since your help I have done work far, far better than before. I shall therefore never cease to be thankful to you. Also if ever I earn any money by painting I shall return you what I owe you.

I shall send you the latchkey and please would you get Mrs Elgy to send me my pyjamas and slippers. Yours sincerely MARK GERTLER

To Carrington

14 November 1915 *Penn Studio, Hampstead*

Dear Carrington, Thank you dear for writing to me so soon. It was a tremendous evening for me and what a good party and how well you acted! I kept on hearing Katherine telling Murry, "How well she does it."

[1] This may have been to prepare Marsh for the next letter.

[2] Christopher Hassall records in his *Edward Marsh* that in April 1916 Gertler, "destitute", brought himself to accept again Marsh's subsidy.

Three weeks seems a long time to wait for you; couldn't you come up just for a day or two next week? I could send you some money for fares—let me know.

How extraordinary you looked in that make-up. The black eyebrows seemed to completely change your personality. I don't think I could love you if you had dark eyebrows. On those occasions one sees how expressive of the personality the outward appearance is. Were your eyebrows black for instance I am sure that a large part of your personality would be different.

I do not feel inclined to tell you your "faults" just now, but when you come up again I shall tell you all and also my adventures since last summer. We shall have a quiet evening together. Perhaps we could manage a week-end in my cottage? If we did this I should like *you* to cook the food so that we don't trouble Mary.[1] We could look after the cottage ourselves. I also want to have reading evenings—when we could read to one another—and also French[2] evenings.

If you really come up to London to live *do* try and live in Hampstead. You can't think how I enjoy my walk in the morning. If you lived here too we could walk together every morning after breakfast.

The last few mornings it has been particularly beautiful on the Heath. The snow on the ground and very fresh and crisp. How you would love it! How good it would have been if you could have taken the Lawrences' flat!

Last night I went to Brett's studio. The Ranee Muda was there. I must say I don't like her. At this moment also she is pregnant—pregnant to her very nose! Brett also irritates me sometimes. I think she is even colder and more passionless than you!

I am somehow off painting for the present. I am busy thinking out many problems in my mind, also very excited and restless. I am terrified lest I have to give this studio up through lack of money. In about two months unless something happens I shall be penniless! But something may come of this Beecham affair.[3] The works for the London Group are going in on Friday. What is this picture you are painting? . . .

Love MARK GERTLER

To Carrington

21 November 1915 *Garsington Manor, Oxford*

Dear Carrington, I was sorry that you couldn't come. I suppose however you couldn't help it. I know you would have come if you could. Never mind, between ourselves—hush!—you have not missed much.

[1] Mary Cannan.

[2] Lytton Strachey had encouraged him to learn French.

[3] Sir Thomas Beecham's plan for theatrical decoration by Gertler which did not come off.

As for myself, as usual when I go for week-ends, I am constipated—that of course spoils half the fun. Apples or pills or salts are of no avail here. Only in my studio do these things work!

However it's not so bad; we have just finished dancing and acting. I am writing in the drawing-room. Brett is a yard away looking at the Van Gogh book. The company consists this time of Clive Bell, who hasn't stopped speaking once, an old and thin virgin—Miss Sands[1]—Brett and myself—that's all. Not very appetising, you must admit. However most of the day I've spent with the children in the nursery. That I enjoyed.

On Saturday Beecham and Lady Cunard came to see me and practically engaged me to do the scenery! And also bought that little picture "Rabbi and Rabbitzin"[2] for £10!! the day before I sold a drawing for £5 to a poet called Drinkwater!!! What do you think of that, my dear little Friend?!

I will ask Brett to send you the photos of my picture you asked for—I am glad you had a nice day with "Harry Tate".

I have still not done a stroke of work—still I do not feel that I want to! Heavens! supposing I never paint again, but never mind. There are extraordinary things going on in my mind.

I asked you to tell me what you are painting, but you never did, nor do you ever in your letters tell me a word of what goes on in your mind, what you think or how you think! Why is that, I wonder? Do you have mental experiences? Or is your mind a blank? What a funny little letter your last was! And in answer to such a long and good one from me too! Shame! Oh! you little cold fish! Already you are happy in Brighton and not a moment's desire to see me, I bet! You little tyrant you! If you don't write me a *long loving* letter and immediately, I shall never write you a loving one again! Well, good-bye, my dear little tyrant—my devil—my little fish—my little lump of stolid meat. Good-bye MARK

To Carrington

Friday morning, November 1915 *Penn Studio, Hampstead*

My dear Carrington, I have not yet received the long letter you promised me some days ago when you sent me Gilbert's book! But perhaps you are busy and have forgotten poor me for a while.

Gilbert has been in town, these last days. He and the Jowitts[3] and I went to the private view of the London Group yesterday. What a rubbishy show! All the pictures, except my own, were composed of washed out purples and greens, and they matched so well that it seemed almost as if the artists all collaborated in order to create harmony at the show. In reality it means simply that they all paint alike and equally badly!

[1] Ethel Sands, painter and collector.

[2] Plate 6, facing page 65.

[3] William and Lesley Jowitt. Jowitt afterwards became Lord Chancellor and was created an earl in 1951.

Wadsworth sent me a card to say that he liked very much my "Fruit Stall" and thought it the best thing I'd done. This rather pleased me, as I am myself still thrilled about the "Fruit Stall" and am *convinced* of its value. Some day people will recognise its value; at present it's too "hot from the oven". To the N.E.A.C. I sent the "Still-Life" and "Abraham and Angels". This morning I hear that only one of these was accepted! I don't know which yet. Aren't they an absurd crew?! It's unbelievable really!

I am feeling rather ill and very, very depressed. God! How I suffer. I wonder if life will get just a little bit easier for me later on. At present it is so very, very hard to bear. It's funny that people who strive most after truth and bigness should suffer most. You don't know, dear Friend, how hard and difficult my life is!

And how I miss you! This last year I suppose I have seen you for about three weeks in all! You are always so very far away. If it is not too much trouble, please write to me, Carrington. I am sure you will never regret any kindness you show towards me. You can never know how happy you can make me by just a little kindness. Is it not fine to make another happy? Your loving friend MARK GERTLER

To Carrington

30 November 1915 *Penn Studio, Hampstead*

Dear Carrington, The long letter you wrote me, in answer to mine from Lady Ottoline, has gone through much adventure. It was *stolen* by a dishonest postman from the Hampstead Post Office!!!

All last week I waited and waited for it, until I got quite ill with anxiety. Literally, it made me really ill! I shall *never* forgive that postman as long as I live. Now I will tell you how I found out. Yesterday (Monday) lunch-time I was summoned to the door by a police officer in plain clothes, who said that he came from the post office to inform me that a letter addressed to me had been stolen by a dishonest postman, who is now under arrest, and who has been lately in the habit of stealing letters with money in them. Your letter being a fat one, he thought therefore must contain lots of money. This police officer caught him and while taking him to the Police Station, the thief escaped and while running threw three letters into the street—Tottenham Court Road. One of these was yours!

Then he drew forth your letter from his pocket and said that I can read it, but must hand it back to him there and then as it must be used as evidence on the trial against the thief, but that after the trial I shall have it!

Of course with the policeman standing in front of me it was difficult to read the letter, so now I hardly know what was in it. How unfortunate, because it seemed one of the most interesting letters you've ever written! Just my luck! When you do write me a long letter with something of yourself in it I don't get it! Never mind, I will answer your last letter,

which I got yesterday morning, which was rather a good one too. . . .
Your loving friend MARK

To Carrington

Sunday, December 1915 *Penn Studio, Hampstead*

Dear Carrington, I was surprised to hear that you had stayed with the Clive Bells and that crew. I am glad however that you managed to enjoy it. I here am having an exciting time. My pictures, apparently, have created a tremendous uproar! The critics are quite mad with rage. God knows what they are wild about. One paper said that I had done them simply to shock and create a sensation!

However, those criticisms seem to have done me more good than harm, for I have had several offers for both the "Eve" and the "Fruit Stall"!!![1] This is to me very encouraging. Some people in a rage stuck a label on the belly of my poor little "Eve" with "Made in Germany" written on it! Can you understand all this?! Lady Cunard in the meantime is furiously excited, says she "*loves*" my pictures, and carts me about in her motor car to Lords, Ladies and Baronesses who want to meet me, and would you believe it all these people pretend that they like my pictures!

On Friday I lunched with a Baroness and this Baroness is coming here this afternoon for tea!

So you see for the moment I am famous! I expect my fame to last quite four days, but these four days may be long enough for me to get some money out of these titled wretches, so that I can go on quietly again for a

[1] Concerning this picture, Duncan Grant and Clive Bell wrote Gertler the following letters:

Wednesday, December 1915 *46 Gordon Square, Bloomsbury*

Dear Gertler, I must write to tell you that I think your big picture at the London Group very remarkably good. It is much the most serious picture there and to my mind much the best work of yours I have seen. I should like to talk to you about it one day—perhaps I can come to tea one day soon? Yours sincerely DUNCAN GRANT

Friday *46 Gordon Square, Bloomsbury*

Dear Gertler, I know Duncan Grant has written to you already, but I don't see why I shouldn't write too; particularly as I saw your big picture—the costers and fruit—long before he did, admired it immensely, and meant to write and tell you so. Roger Fry and I had been making a round of the galleries, clockwise, and coming on yours at last were very much impressed. I don't know when I saw an English picture that seemed to me so much the real thing. It was a queer sensation being really fixed and fastened by a picture at Goupil. If I were to try and tell you why it moved me so much I should have to try to rewrite my book. Don't be uneasy. I'll only say that it holds one and so strongly that it puts one's mind at rest, quite preventing the non-aesthetic part from asserting itself and asking silly questions. That, it seems to me, is what really satisfactory works of art do always. If I were still lecturing on Art I could spin out a pleasant half hour explaining why I admire that picture and don't care for the one next to it. But I'm not lecturing. Yours CLIVE BELL

while and paint what I want to. Lady Cunard assures me that I am "the talk of London". Also my little picture the "Black and White Cottage" was given as a wedding present to Violet Asquith[1] by Lady Hamilton. It hung among the presents at Downing Street "where it was much admired". "What Fame! What success!"

After this my people conclude that I am the bosom friend of the Premier and that before long the Queen will kiss me on both cheeks and say, "How do you do Mr Gertler."

The scenery I am pretty certain to get also.

I was disappointed to hear that you will not come to London before you get a job, because this may mean that you won't come for goodness knows how long, as it is not easy to get art jobs now, but why not come and see us more often? I mean if you can't manage or don't want to stay in London, why not make up your mind to come and see us for a few days say once a month? I am sure you would benefit by it—one gets so out of touch with you. In letters it is so difficult to express anything. After all, although you pretend that you can't get away from your people when *I* ask you, you seem to manage all right when other people invite you.

If instead of going to the Clive Bells you would have come to see me you would have really done a good deed. Because my desire to see you is about a thousand times greater than all theirs put together, but you seem to shun London as if it was Hell and me as if I was the Devil! A little while ago I asked you to come to London for a little while, but you quite ignored my invitation. I am not lecturing you, only you are so inconsistent! If you said frankly that "I don't care much to see you," well, I would make up my mind to it, but you do *sometimes* pretend to like me, but once you leave me you seem to settle down quite cosily and never think of coming to see me. God only knows what sort of person you must be to be able to settle down "cosily" in Brighton of all places!

If your desire was only *half* as great to see me as mine is to see you, you would not stay in Brighton!

Please forgive me writing to you like this. I really have no right to lecture you, as you are quite free to act as you feel you want to, only you ought not to tell me that you care for me, as it is *not* true. You do not care for anybody as yet. What keeps the fire burning between us is *my love for you.* On your side there is nothing. I have known this now for some months! And this is what I promised to tell you! So now you know; but in spite of this I have made up my mind *never* to leave you again and to devote myself entirely to you, because my love for you is growing and growing! I love you more than anything or person in the world!!! Without your friendly smile I could not possibly live! Having now got this off my chest I can promise you that from now, I shall never grumble at what you do again and never quarrel with you. I think now that I know your real attitude towards me and having reconciled myself to it, we shall get on more smoothly.

[1] Later Lady Violet Bonham Carter (see page 72 and Plate 5).

You need not be afraid of them reading your letter in court, they will only just produce it. . . .

Yours ever MARK GERTLER

To S. S. Koteliansky

3 February 1916 *Penn Studio, Hampstead*

Dear Koteliansky, . . . I am working hard at my picture. It helps me to forget my troubles. I have never felt more passionately a desire to paint than now. You can't think how many wonderful ideas I have for future work. Yet at any moment I may be dragged away into this war. What a nightmare it is to me! Also I've written to Lady Cunard about selling that picture and she has not answered me yet. This frightens me very much also, as I am placing all my hopes on selling my "Eve" to that woman.

What frightens me most is the possibility of having to give up my studio. Shall I confess a weakness to you? Well, I feel *almost* sorry that I gave up Eddie Marsh! for after all his money was such a help. And isn't it after all worth undergoing any trouble and humiliation to be enabled to paint? To paint and paint is what I want. . . . MARK GERTLER

To Carrington

27 February 1916 *Penn Studio, Hampstead*

My dear Carrington, Your talk last night was most inspiring. It was like a revelation to me. For the second time I realised the beauty of your nature. The other time was in that wood last summer. It seems almost worth while to quarrel and have misunderstandings if they are going to end up so wonderfully and enlightening. Really, I think that is what they are for. But you can't think how much you helped me last night. If only you would talk more often to me like that how thankful I should be. You must try more to help me out of myself, out of my petty vulgar mean little self.

The tragic part is that we shall never reach to that state of spiritual friendship both you and I desire so much. The reason is that we both have different ways of reaching it. And the two ways are so different that they clash and fight and they always will clash and fight so that we shall therefore never be able to succeed together. Your way of reaching that state of spirituality is by *leaving out sex*. My way is *through sex*. Apparently we neither of us can change our ways, because they are ingrained in our natures. Therefore there will always be strife between us and I shall always suffer.

Try and come to the Campbells'[1] on Sunday evening at 8.30. Their number is 24 Norfolk Road. And remember Tuesday and Wednesday.

[1] Gordon and Beatrice Campbell, later Lord and Lady Glenavy, had regular "Sunday evenings".

I shall especially look forward to Wednesday when we shall be alone and be able to talk.

How well Brett is getting along with her work. I found looking at her work so inspiring and helpful.[1] MARK GERTLER

To William Rothenstein

4 April 1916 *Penn Studio, Hampstead*

My Dear Rothenstein, Thank you very much for your letter.[2] I am so glad that you like my drawing and that you are still interested in my work. But

[1] Gertler, as appears in other parts of this correspondence, was ready to confide in most of his more intimate friends concerning the problems of his love affair. Two letters on the subject, neither as far as I know previously published, seem worth quoting, if only to show how others viewed the situation.

20 January 1916 *Porthcothan, St Merryn, Padstow, Cornwall*

Dear Gertler, . . . I don't know how long we are to be here—not very long, I feel. Yet I don't know what the next move will be. Out of England, I hope: We hear from Murry and Katherine that they are both exceedingly happy. They have both found themselves, and each other and the blessed sun also, at last. I am very glad. I hope the spring is going to blossom now for you and Carrington as well.

I liked her very much at the party. If you could only really give yourself up in love, she would be much happier. You always want to dominate her, which is no good. One must learn to relinquish oneself, not to bother about oneself, but to love the other person. You hold too closely to yourself, for her to be free to love you. . . .

Tell me all your news, when you write. Warm greetings to Brett and Carrington. Frieda sends her love, and says she is happy down here. I hope your work goes well: are you reconciled to Eddie? Yours D. H. LAWRENCE

Saturday, 9 April 1916 *2 Tilney Street, Mayfair, W.*

Dear Gertler, . . . Do try and not worry or rather brood over your troubles. I had a long talk with Carrington and I have now a much clearer conception of what she thinks than before. I think when one is in for a strong bout of introspection one should remember to peer into all parts of one's self, not only into the part that is hurting one, and then try and reason out how far one is justified in one's gloom. Will you ever be happy? Is happiness a real thing to possess? I don't think so. Directly one *thinks*, mental misery is added to physical misery; personal things, such as a desire for the possession of things and people, is not only a source of misery, but impossible to obtain. Material things you can possess but you cannot possess for ever or even for a bit the entire body and soul of another person who is in anyway worth possessing. This is my experience and, until I grasped the hopeless truth of it, I was thoroughly miserable and made others miserable too, but since then I find people far more wonderful, far more lasting and, if desire comes in the way, it can either be accepted or controlled. The physical side of all this trouble of yours is far more solvable than the more delicate intricate temperamental side, but don't rush off with the idea that I don't and can't understand. I understand, but the difficulty is to know how to help you most. . . . Yours BRETT

[2] Rothenstein had written as follows:

31 March 1916 *Ashburnham Grove, Bradford*

My dear Gertler, I think you have forgotten me. I have not forgotten you, and I watch your work with interest. You have been developing all sorts of qualities

you are very mistaken to think that I had forgotten you! I shall never forget your help in those "E.A.S." days. That first day when I came to you was enough to make me always grateful to you.

I feel this last year or so much surer with my work. I have never felt quite like it before. I live in a constant state of over-excitement, so much do my work and conception thrill me. It is almost too much for me and I am always feeling rather ill. Sometimes after a day's work I can hardly walk! One seems to work at the expense of one's body and there is no other way, apparently, of doing it. At any rate I can't find an easy way of working. However it is worth the sacrifice. Do come and see me when you are in London and then we shall talk.

Best wishes to you and your family. MARK GERTLER

P.S. My people are pretty well thanks, but they have their struggle to exist as usual. They will be awfully pleased when I tell them that you have written and enquired after them, they are always asking about you.

You ask whether I find enough admirers to live on. Well, I have a few people who believe in me, but they are not buyers, so that I always have difficulty about money. However at the last moment I always seem to sell a little picture which keeps the "wolf from the door". But I am doing large work just now, and that is so difficult to make any money out of.

To Lytton Strachey

[*May 1916*] *Penn Studio, Hampstead*

My dear Strachey, Thanks for your letter. I knew you had been in London, from a certain friend of mine—Campbell—who saw you collide with a woman outside an escalator "somewhere" in London. Really I was hurt that you had not called on me. So you are now back in Garsington. I am sorry you have been so wretched again. As for me, my biggest worry just now is the lack of money. But it is by not any means a new trouble; fortunately I am used to it. Yesterday I drew my last £2; in about a week I shall be penniless.

---

of late, and I feel your work is beginning to take shape. There was a nude of yours at the Friday Club I much wanted to possess, and when my brother comes back I want him to look at it. Your work shows a fine sense of weight and a new element of drama I am delighted to find developing. You are of course still searching, and the spirit of the day tends to a certain self-consciousness which I am sure is of use for the moment—in days to come I believe you will be less affected by it, and will doubtless find your vision and improve it on others. The still-life at the Friday Club was strong and vital in colour but I liked some work I saw in a recent N.E.A.C. still better in form. I hope you are finding enough appreciations to live and work without too much worry. Some day perhaps I may see you and something more of your work. We have left Hampstead for good, having given up our rooms there. Write and tell me of yourself one of these days.

Sincerely yours W. ROTHENSTEIN

I hope your people are well—please remember me to them.

I hate with all my being the idea that money should so be able to influence my freedom. It is terrible to think that the more interesting my work becomes, the more difficult it becomes to sell it and to live! If it was not for money really I should be happy, because I only ask of life to be allowed to paint, to be allowed to dip deeper and deeper into the wonderful mysteries of art. But if one has no money the purity of one's art studies are spoilt, because one can't help thinking sometimes of what the *stupid* buyers would like, as one *must* live. That is *my* trouble. To be a good artist one must have an income. Believe me that is true. The starving artist in the garret is a thing of the past. To paint good pictures one must have a comfortable studio and *good* food—a garret and crust of bread isn't good enough. Let no person come and tell me that poverty is good for an artist! If an artist is poor he simply has to please, if not always then sometimes, the public, and the public doesn't know a picture from a broomstick! That's my experience anyhow.

Please forgive me for thrusting my troubles at you and please don't be sorry for me. I shall get along somehow and what's more paint my pictures too! I shall paint what *I* like.

Yes, aren't the colours of the spring marvellous! Really it is too much for me! I get almost wretched with the beauty of it. There is one tree in blossom in Golder's Hill Park that I fell in love with, but as usual my love was not returned! Pale pink blossom against the blue of the sky—the whole thing seemed sweating with love. I can't describe how wonderful my feelings were when every morning I stood sick with love in front of my tree. I was so jealous of the other people who looked also at her. Please do not think me silly, but I loved that tree for a week!

Gilbert is *not* writing, but *has* written a book[1] (it took two months) about a young man who, I believe, is supposed to resemble me, but I don't know.

I agree with you about the dullness of books, but I am now reading Nietzsche!! I can only just understand it, but somehow I think I shall like it. Do you know, I read a book called *Green Mansions* by Hudson and I liked it immensely!

My French is getting on better. I do a half-an-hour a day!

I am working hard on a large and *very unsaleable* picture of "Merry-Go-Rounds".[2] I am *so* excited about it. It will be finished in a few weeks.

Please remember me to: Lady Ottoline, Philip Morrell, Julian,[3] Lalage, M'moiselle,[4] Maria,[5] the Pugs, the Pigs, the Houses, the Cows, Yourself.

Yours ever MARK GERTLER

[1] The novel *Mendel*, published in 1916 by T. Fisher Unwin (see Appendix, page 253).

[2] Plate 10, facing page 129. For letters from St John Hutchinson and D. H. Lawrence on this picture see pages 128–129.

[3] The Morrell's daughter, later Mrs Igor Vinogradoff.

[4] Juliette Baillot, afterwards married Julian Huxley.

[5] Maria Nys, afterwards married Aldous Huxley.

To Richard Carline

3 May 1916 — *Penn Studio, Hampstead*

Dear Carline, . . . However, yesterday, after a fortnight's delay I managed to start a picture of Daffodils and have got really interested in it, which means, probably, that it will be too good to sell!

It is an experiment. This lovely spring sunshine has given me new notions for colour, and in this flower picture I shall be able to try them. Nevertheless I shall be glad to get back to my "Merry-Go-Round".

I have also been suffering from headaches. I had them every day for about a week! But I am better now. Then I have been miserable. This first lovely spring weather always depresses me! It is too beautiful! I fall painfully in love with the world! I long and long for vague and impossible things. One marvellously beautiful tree in blossom at Golder's Hill Park absolutely bowled me over with its beauty.

Yours ever — MARK GERTLER

To Carrington

20 May 1916 — *Penn Studio, Hampstead*

Dear Carrington, I have just got your letter. I am answering it at once because you asked me to do so and because I feel this morning that I have much to write you. When I first got your letter I was terribly disappointed and furious with you for not coming back today. However, now I have got over my fury but still not my disappointment, I was looking forward to seeing you today very much as I am not particularly happy—yes, in spite of my having money now!—spring sunshine always has a depressing effect on me! It always makes me feel, oh! yes, beautiful, but how much more beautiful it all could be if this or that was so and so. It always in fact seems to point out how wretched and unsatisfactory my life is and yet I don't know what is missing in it to make it perfect and beautiful. In the summer I get used to the sun and enjoy it like other people.

Your letter gave out an odour of simple pure-hearted enjoyment. The capacity of simple enjoyment on your part usually irritates me beyond words, but really it is mostly envy on my part, simply because I am too sophisticated, too critical, too reactionary, too egoistic, too conscious and too old and at the same time too young in spirit to be able to enjoy myself as simply and pure-heartedly as you! Nevertheless I would not change places with you!!—or anybody else in the world!!!

I am depressed just now because I am feeling all over again the isolation of my spirit. I cannot make people understand me or my work, neither can I understand them. The best thing that happens is between us and that is *not* because we understand one another or because we are the same. Oh no! at the best it is a flight of two very different souls to Heaven arm-in-arm in harmonious discord, but occupy the same plot of ground we never can. We are two distinct beings—I stand alone. The best that happens is that you are close by my side. You ask me if I am happy now you love. Well, firstly, nothing can make me absolutely happy and secondly I have such a mistrust of human nature that I sometimes mistrust your love for me! Forgive me, I can't help it! Besides your love is so unusual and difficult to understand; some moments however I believe in it and then I must say I am happy. But I never know whether or not those moments are concoctions merely of my own feelings and imagination. God! how is one to climb into another person's soul and find out what is really there! Oh! How I suffer from doubt! If only I was sure your love for me was real and permanent and that your soul was really capable of profound and single-hearted love like mine. You ask me how I feel towards you. Well, I will tell you. As always I love you, and I will tell you more, *My* soul *can* love. My love is such that you or anybody else will never understand its depth! You are not able to return me an equal love and for that I hate life. What is the good of having this depth of feeling it no one wants or understands it! I paint pictures that seem to me wonderful but no one understands them; I love with a wonderful love but no one wants my love! Forgive me again please; perhaps I exaggerate in your case. Well, excuse me for writing all this heavy stuff to you, but I had to write it —don't let it spoil your enjoyment.

You ask me to read Keats. I have no use for Keats in my present mood.

Why be sorry that you don't look like the children in body?! You are a woman and have womanly beauties and they are children and have childish beauties. On the whole I prefer yours and certainly have more use for yours.

Don't write and congratulate me on having money; I hate money and the people I get it from. Well then, I will see you on Tuesday at Brett's.

Please don't stay on any longer; it seems to me that you will go on staying there forever. At least you might, if you love me, have come home on Monday so as that we could have had our Monday evening together.

As we are not having Monday together and "you love me now" could not we have another night alone instead next week? Say Wednesday or Friday. If you love me enough for this will you please write me a note from Garsington immediately you get this and tell me which day would suit you? Or are you engaged every night next week? If you could give me one night do, as you would make your unhappy friend happier!

Are you bathing all day and drying all day on the roof? How pretty, how good I am not there. What a lot of "Barbara" you have in you! *Again forgive me!* I didn't altogether mean it! Tell Brett that I send her my love and that on my knees I implore her just this one Tuesday *not* to have Nash and Binkie.[1]

Well, I must finish as the nib has begun to splash and splutter and to dig.

Your very critical and unhappy friend MARK GERTLER

[1] Paul Nash and his wife.

To Carrington

30 May 1916

Dear Carrington, I would rather not see you tomorrow, Saturday. I am still not certain of you. Better let us leave things as they are. I do not think we can go further. I believe we are too fundamentally different to become lovers. For me to love a woman without hatred she must be above the average, not like the average woman—casual. I am unusual myself—*painfully* unusual. I am a tormented suffering creature.

I am like the boy in *Jude the Obscure*. I cannot enjoy the beauty of a rose because I know it must fade! Forgive me, you will do far better without me. I can only be like a heavy weight on your life.

If only I could believe in you more, all would be different, but I can't. You do and say things which disprove the whole. One small detail can upset the whole for me. Besides, physically I am no use to you—you would hate me. I have a small wretched skinny knotty stringy body, worn out by continual nervous strain. All my limbs speak of my wretched life. On my body, more than on my face, my unhappy life has told. You alone have tormented me for five years and now after all that time I find you unsatisfactory. Please leave me, I cannot bear any more. *I have a reason for writing this letter*. It is not just out of my head. I feel now so tired and ill that I can't think how I will go on living. MARK GERTLER[1]

To S. S. Koteliansky

20 June 1916 *Garsington Manor, Oxford*

My dear Kot, Well, I hardly know how to write to you because I have been so wretched here. When I arrived I found Katherine had already left. She left Monday morning apparently in order to catch a train to Murry in Cornwall! If this is true, and I believe it is, I was not very far

[1] Carrington wrote the following answer to this letter:

31 May 1916 *Garsington Manor, Oxford*

Dearest Mark, Your letter came this morning and filled me with the uttermost sorrow because I know how miserable you have been. It makes such a big gap and makes me realise how little you believe in me. Do you not see an island in the middle of a big lake? Many islands of adventures which one must swim across to? But one will always return to the mainland. You are that mainland to me. I will leave you sometimes perhaps, but always I shall come back, and when the best state of our friendship is arrived at you will love my adventures as you do your own. Mental and physical adventures perhaps, perhaps none. This world is so big and full of surprises but the great thing is an implicit faith in you, and a greater love for you than mankind. Do you never feel the excitement of this big world, and ships, and many people? . . .

I will not fail you. Do not fear. But I am human also. You have had phases and moods. I also am mortal and am like unto you. I may have had phases also. You must never be surprised or distressed because you know I shall come through and we are in the whole part together. CARRINGTON

wrong when I told you that night that she would go back. But she went back even sooner than I thought.

About myself I hardly know what to tell you. I am desperately miserable, not so much because of the Lady Ottoline and the household, but because of more intimate reasons. But I am tired, tired of speaking of my eternal worry. You know what it is. It gets more and more complicated with C. I get so tired and worn out some moments I can scarcely stand. And I have to pretend I am happy here. If only the torment would end. It is like some terrible disease and incurable. We both put our heads together to try and end it, but we can't. It goes on in spite of our both being tired and worn out. But I will not write about it any more, because it has neither beginning nor end.

I am happier since yesterday afternoon because I have started a picture, a landscape, from the lawn looking on to the fatal[1] pond. If all goes well, it will be a good thing and keep me busy. The best thing in life I have found so far is *work*. I can bear almost anything as long as I am working. It is wonderful to create and feel, as I do, able to create wonderful things. You can't imagine how wonderful I feel sometimes. I wish I could tell you my inner experiences. I would like you to know. On Monday night I thought of you all night. But I wish you could feel my painting more than you do, because you are so necessary to me. Your friendship is simply invaluable. But why did you say on Sunday that after the war I must travel? That is what depressed me because I wanted you to understand that I am at present far too full of things to express to travel. Travelling would only throw me into a chaos. I don't want to travel. I could write three volumes on how travelling would be destructive to my temperament and to my art. I see more and feel more in a lavatory than the average person sees and feels travelling round the world. The greatest travel is mental travel, and the mental traveller travels round the world in a back yard. Anyhow I shan't budge till I feel mentally exhausted. For the present I am too full and you must know this.

Don't be annoyed or put out by what I have written. My intention is merely to keep as near to you as possible; you are so necessary to me.

Write to me at once. MARK GERTLER[2]

[1] Curiously enough Gertler did nearly drown in it later, see page 173.

[2] Koteliansky's answer to this letter was as follows:

My dear Gertler, The news about Katherine having left so abruptly for Cornwall would have simply staggered me this morning, when I received your letter, had I not had a letter from Lawrence yesterday to the same effect. I must say, it sounds terribly strange. Well, your maxim about couples came once more true. But we will better campbell about it when you are here. Yes, I was so surprised at the news that I could not help going to see the Campbells yesterday evening and impart it to them. They too had a letter from K. saying that she had left for Cornwall.

Now, I really must deliver you a lecture. Why have you misunderstood my "travelling" proposition? Is it that you are not perfectly sure of my real attitude to you? You know what great value I attribute to your work though I am a profane. This is only because I know you and I believe in you. What I meant was simply this. When I heard from Farbman in your studio that there was in

To Carrington

14 August 1916 *The Mill House, Cholesbury*

My dear Carrington, Thanks very much for your letter. I was glad to get it this morning. I was getting impatient. I am answering it at once. After you left on Wednesday evening, we had an exciting talk. We arranged between us to artfully get Gilbert, when he would arrive the next day, to tell us his life story, from beginning to end, and *above all* we were *not* to let him be vague. We *would* have every detail, or at any rate *precision*, this time, and so at last we thought we'd find something out about him. All this was very exciting and we awaited his arrival impatiently.

He arrived, just as usual, apathetic. However, we were determined to tackle him. After dinner we sat in the shed. It was a fitting night, moonlight—romantic.

Well, we artfully led up to the point and at last—oh! how my heart beat!—Mary said, "Gilbert do tell us your life tonight. But tell us all—every detail." A dreadful pause and then Gilbert drawled out "All right" and commenced.

Well, it would take too long to write it all here. I will tell more when we meet, but really as a life it was very dull and he told it in a dull dreary voice, all even, but nevertheless it was very important to help us to understand him. You see, it is just as I thought, nothing ever *really* stirred him, nothing ever made a real impression. When he came, for instance, to the part of his life where a rich cousin comes as if from nowhere and adopts him, puts him into a rich home suddenly after his own sordid environments and then to Cambridge, he did not seem at all im-

---

Russia an interesting painter, and you seemed to be interested in him, I thought that it would be interesting for you to acquaint yourself with the new people, with the new things; to see for yourself the various efforts made by others. You know perfectly well that I did not mean travelling in the sense in which you describe R. Fry's and Bell's arriving just from Paris with traces of paint and handshakes of the illustrious ones. I meant going for a short time—for two or three months—do you remember that?—to Russia, France, Germany, Italy, Austria, Spain. And from the point of view of time, i.e. that your time may be better spent in work than in travel, why not look upon such a travel as a holiday, like other people going to the seaside or country for a couple of months? I still think that it is always interesting to know what is being done (if not achieved) by other seekers. I do not doubt for a second that you have your own way, which is only yours. But, take this instance. Do you not think that Thomas Hardy, who is a real good writer, would be more interesting if he knew intimately what had been achieved by the Russian and French literature?

But the lecture really seems to be too long. And what I wanted to say is only that I believe in you, and would like you as speedily as possible to gather the outside information which—in your case—will do you good. But more about it when you come back.

Do not be miserable about C., do not be too impatient. Did you not tell me yourself that—in your work—you felt sometimes that it seemed as if you had still hundreds of years before you? Apply it to life—which is also art.

I have no news, and am now less depressed. Thank you very much for certain things you say in your letter; it made me really happy.

Write to me if you feel in a mood.

My kindest regards to Carrington. Yours S.K.

pressed or excited. He did not seem to feel the change, and was not surprised. He told it all in the same even bored voice! And so on and so on. There were many more instances of the same sort. I will tell them you when we meet.

Of course many, many times we had to pull him up to prevent him from becoming vague and abstract. We would ask him "What do you mean exactly?" or "Tell us the details."

When it was over we all—Jack, Mary[1] and myself—gathered in Mary's bedroom—Gilbert slept in the shed—and talked and talked, in excited whispers, all of us half naked, as we had commenced to go to bed, Gilbert having come back to the house with us to have a drink, so we had to pretend we were going to bed in order to get him to his bed in the shed.

Oh! How exciting and intriguing it all was! But we felt very happy with our artfulness and really felt that we now understood Gilbert much more.

Well, enough about Gilbert; we'll continue that when we meet. But one thing more: the Tribunal let him off from General Service; he is to find work of national importance in a month's time.

Friday, we bathed and dried on the sands.

In the evening I went for a long walk myself and as usual thought lovingly of you and was very happy. Got a long letter from Ottoline,[2] in which she likens you to a "wild beast, greedy of life and perhaps *never* to be mated!" There's a nice thing to write to *me*! *Never* to be mated! She meant well, however. Brett is still at Garsington! . . .

Kot is in an extremely depressed state. His life and future outlook is certainly most dreary and there seems no way out of it for him, because it is not so much the circumstances of his life, but the way he is made. Some moments his life oppresses me terribly, and God knows I am not a very happy person myself.

I went to see my people, but that was also oppressive. . . .

I am sure you do not understand my "love for the masses" or you would not jeer at it. Some day I will explain it to you and you will then see how I mean and how important it is—believe me, don't be sarcastic.

I am sure Mary and Jack liked you.

Yes, we had fine moments at Wittering.[3] *Thank you very much for them. Write soon*, my dear MARK GERTLER

[1] Jack and Mary Hutchinson.

[2] The relevant parts of this letter are as follows:

8 August [*1916*] *Garsington Manor, Oxford*

My dear Gertler, . . . Carrington is like some strange wild beast—greedy of life and of tasting all the different "worms" that she can find without giving herself to any mate. Sometimes I wonder if she ever will find a mate that fulfils all she desires. I wish she would concentrate more on her work. But I hope she will soon—for after all nothing is so important as that. It would get her proportions straight. . . .

Brett and I are alone here. I have persuaded her to stay on, as I hope she is happy and I think it is good for her here. I love her and I love Carrington too and you. I hope you will always tell me anything you feel like and when you feel like it. . . . Sincerely O.M.

[3] Eleanor House, West Wittering, near Chichester was the country home of the Hutchinsons.

To Carrington

15 August 1916 *The Mill House, Cholesbury*

My dear Carrington, It was really kind of you to write to me so soon again, even before you got my answer to your first letter. Imagine my delight when on the tray with tea that Grinnel brought me up in bed this morning I found a letter from you!! Oh what joy. How I loved you for it! And I didn't expect one from you for ever so long. Wales seems so far off. Thank you, dear friend, for it. It was such a good letter too.

I hope this morning you will have got my letter to you that I wrote yesterday. I am glad you are so happy. The country sounds wonderful. The only sort of country like it I've ever seen was up in Yorkshire. There also there seemed no order, but all vast and chaotic, endlessly spreading and up and down. It used to frighten me when I came home at dusk from a lonely walk—it terrified me. But Wales I suppose is still more so.

What you say is so true, about how all other relationships beside our own intimacy seem lifeless. How well I feel that. But you must be happy and enjoy yourself where you are, as I am always with you in spirit—I never leave you for a moment. I am always talking to you and I have never loved you more and felt more thankful to you or more happy. I daren't say how happy I am and my happiness is solely due to our wonderful friendship. Nothing else matters, everything else is subsidiary to it and could not exist without it.

I am sure I shall like Donne very much although I must confess I don't understand the art of literature or poetry as I should like to. I feel everything more and more through form and colour. Although I understand and feel music quite as much as my own art, when I come to literature I immediately feel it *not* as art but as *thought*. It's the *thought*, the *idea* that matters to me, but I don't feel satisfied because I know there *must* be something else—*the* "something" that I feel so well in plastic art and in music. The *only* time I've ever felt it in literature was in the Song of Solomon and even in other parts of the Old Testament, but in no other literature. You see, I can't even feel the art of Shakespeare. But I suppose it is difficult, too much to expect almost, to understand all three arts.

Of course I get a *great*, *great* deal from literature and poetry, but as I say, only for what it *means*. The *thought*, the psychology of the people in Dostoevsky's book interest and excite me enormously. Have I explained myself, I wonder? I may yet get hold of the *art* of literature and as you know I have great desire to write myself, but I shan't do so until I discover for myself the art of it.

As for my philosophy, I am excited about it and believe what I have written absolutely. But what I've written is *not* art, only *thought*, and to me there is a great difference between the two. No, I've not written any more yet. I would like to tell you now that I feel, if I live long enough, I shall do not only important painting but also sculpture and writing! I even sometimes get ideas in sound!!!

I am terribly, terribly rich in spirit just now. I can't tell you all, I am afraid, but I live in a world of wonder from morning to night! Every now and then a vision of a huge and wonderfully coloured piece of sculpture comes before me. It dazzles me and makes my blood run cold. It is so wonderful. I find it difficult to hide my joy from everybody and I want to hide it, because my inspirations are dear to me, though painful!

I must stop. I can't write any more—I am full to a bursting point. I must control myself or I shall destroy myself, through mere abundance of feeling.

I came here yesterday. I am liking it. It is quiet, peaceful. I am happy. There is no interference, my spirit can travel at ease without disturbance. It flies high; let it fly. I sit here below pretending I am normal and no one knows of the magic inside me. I eat, I drink, like everybody else—what a joke!

Write at once to me, dear Friend. Let me often have a great joy like I had this morning.

My love to you. Yours ever MARK GERTLER

P.S. Remember me to Barbara and my *love* to Lytton.[1]

To S. S. Koteliansky

16 August 1916 *The Mill House, Cholesbury*

My dear Kot, Well, here I am. It is quiet, uneventful and I like it therefore. Every now and then I get swept off my feet by terrific ideas for future work. These moments are almost painful, so wonderful are they. But externally all is, as I say, peaceful and restful, and I am happy.

I would like you to be happier but your case seems beyond comprehension to me. You hate the Bureau,[2] yet you make no effort to get out of it. If you had a certain thing in view, you could then fight for it and the fight itself would mean a great deal to you. But no; apparently you want nothing.

Don't forget your promise to come here on Sunday. MARK GERTLER

To Carrington

20 August 1916 *The Mill House, Cholesbury*

My dear Carrington, . . . I hardly know what to write you about myself. My feelings have been so mixed here. The inspiration inside me still

[1] Lytton, Carrington and Barbara Hiles were having a holiday at the Hiles' cottage in North Wales.

[2] The Law Bureau where he worked.

goes on—nothing now can harm that world of wonder that I contain inside me and which has now become as if fixed there. Nevertheless, I have suffered a good deal lately—these last few days. I have been unable to start any sort of work here yet, somehow the atmosphere is against it. I don't think I shall do any work here now. I shall start in my studio, when I get back to London. Mrs Sanger[1] cannot have me the time I chose, so I shall stay here until September and then go back to London and start my real work there.

Some moments I long for London and work. I find it very hard to go idle. When I am not working hard at my art, I begin to be critical about life and sure enough there is much to be critical about. I then get very, very miserable. There have been times here even when I have been unutterably bored! If I hadn't my art, I could not possibly go on living. However, I have it and therefore I must not grumble. Also I have your friendship and that is a great deal.

My feelings for Dostoevsky grow stronger and stronger. I have taken up *The Idiot* again. Heavens, how wonderful it is. What a great man he was to write such books. I get so excited when reading him that my heart beats with a thud and I feel my flesh fall away from my bones. I can read nothing after him. He is my Shakespeare. I worship him.

I read my philosophy to Gilbert. He liked it very much and also a poem[2] I've written—some time ago—in a light-hearted mood.

MARK GERTLER

To Carrington

24 August 1916 *The Mill House, Cholesbury*

My dear Carrington, I was very glad to get your letter,[3] and more so as it

[1] Dora, the wife of Charles Sanger, barrister, who became a helpful friend of Gertler's. The Sangers had a wide circle of intellectual friends from Cambridge and Bloomsbury.

[2] One or two draft poems were amongst Gertler's papers but not dated.

[3] Extracts from this letter may be quoted here:

c/o Mrs Hiles, Llanbedr, Taly-Cafn, S.O., N. Wales

Dear Mark, . . . I cannot write to you about my inner self because it is all confused and very agonising to pull out.

If you cast your mind back to the period before you painted your "Fruit-Gatherers" could you have told me then about your future desires? No. You never could have. Besides—may I say so frankly—you asked from two reasons, neither of which were real interest. Be frank with yourself and you will find it was so. One was a kind of curiosity to know what I do not tell you, and the other a mixture of knowing I would like you to be interested in my work as I am in yours. Am I not right? You will never have a passion for another person's point of view and desires, as your own is so great. Don't be vexed and rush at me with protests—it is only truthful, and why not let us both be thus?

Of course you liked Lytton and praised him before I did, because I did not even know him in those days when you did. But I felt at Mary's, and do feel, that you do not appreciate Lytton very much. Probably as you say because that arrived so much sooner than I expected—I loved you more than ever for writing so soon.

I am sorry but I can't send you my poem, I am too sensitive about it. I only read what I have written to Gilbert, because I wanted to see what kind of effect it would have on a literary man. Otherwise what I write is really only for myself, especially this poem, which is only a light sort of thing and not worth troubling about, I assure you. I may read it to you some time in the future.

You can't think how you hurt me by doubting the genuineness of my feelings, when I asked you to write me more about your *inner* self. Why do you distrust me? If you distrust this surely you must also distrust my love! for how could I really love you and not want to know what you think—your point of view and about your work? Is it not natural for me, who loves you as I do, to want to know what you think? How can you doubt such a thing? Oh! how can I make you believe me!?

You say my own point of view is so strong that I cannot, cannot care about anybody else's—or anybody else's desires or passions! Even if this was true, and it is *not* true, wouldn't *you* be to me an exception if only because of my true love for you?!! Don't you see that my love creates a bridge from my heart to yours, over which I can occasionally travel into you and over which I long constantly to travel. Don't you see this? You *must* see this or I shall be miserable.

Dear, dear Carrington, I am as interested in you and your aspirations as in my own if not more. My own aspirations, work, or any other, do *not exist* apart from yours. They have grown together now. *They are one lump.* I do not make a single move without spiritually consulting your mind and heart, can you understand such a thing? But I must not write any more about this or I shall weep with misery.

Dear girl, I can only say that some day if you do not understand this now, you will—apparently, you have not yet realized what kind of love mine is. Some day you will. You think I am an egoist—only thinking of myself, wanting only you physically and that once I have you, I shall throw you aside. That no doubt is what you think. Some day you will discover your mistake and I assure you when you do your remorse will be great. You think because I am an egoist I cannot love in the true sense. In that also you will find out some day how much you are mistaken.

You ask me if I could have spoken of my inner life before I painted my "Fruit-Sorter", when I was all confusion. *Yes*, I could have. But I had nobody to tell, that's the great difference. *You have me*, in whom you can trust *everything*, because I love you more than anything in the world and *I* could help you. Do not think that by keeping away from me you will

---

other objection comes so much always before you. I have altered my views about that, and think one always has to put up with something, pain or discomfort, to get anything from any human being. Some trait in their character will always jar, but when one realises it is there—a part of them and a small part—it is worth while overlooking it for anything bigger and more valuable. . . .

CARRINGTON

find yourself. *Never!* You can *only* find yourself through *me*! Just as I am finding myself through *you*!! You are afraid of telling me all or coming near to me in case you lose yourself. You are *absolutely* wrong. Your mind, if you are not careful, will lead you hopelessly astray. You will make us both miserable, simply by going against the grain. I am frank with you. I open all my heart to you. Why not you do the same? *Don't* for God's sake fight away from me. Believe me there is no reason to. You will gain nothing and certainly lose a great deal. No one can help you like I can. Because no one loves you like I do. Friendship is all right, but it is *not love*. Don't fly to weaker people for refuge; come close to me, you need me. Don't be afraid of my strength. My strength will feed you. It is the most nourishing food for you. You are a terribly strong person yourself and I need your support. I am weak, helpless without your strength. My strength, if severed from yours, turns into weakness.

Let us frankly combine. We can make a splendid unit. Only believe me and trust me. I know more what goes on in your mind than you think. I watch your mind with distress. I see its dangers and I must and will help you for both our sakes.

You are afraid of frankly combining with me, *not* because you do not love me, but because you have an *erroneous* idea that by combining with me you will lose your personality.

I see this plainly going on in your head and it is this which is nearly killing me, because it is so false. We are both suffering through a false idea of yours. It is this idea which makes you go and stay with other people when we, who love each other, might be together. It is this idea which makes our otherwise wonderful relationship almost impossible! It is this false idea of yours which is killing me and if you keep it up for long, will kill me, because I cannot go on living much longer without your full love. I must have it. I am nothing without you. I miss you terribly. I long and long for you.

Dearest, dearest girl, don't be annoyed with this letter; weigh every word of it first, before you deny the truth of it, because it is as if written with my blood.

It is all absolutely true. We both love one another terribly. Let us therefore openly admit it and be frank: I will hate you if your next letter isn't absolutely frank and open. *Trust me in everything.*

Yours ever my dearest love MARK GERTLER

To S. S. Koteliansky

29 August 1916 *The Mill House, Cholesbury*

My dear Kot, . . . I am looking forward to my return to London although I know full well what suffering there awaits me. I know from experience. It's always the same: nervous, anxious, tremulous life. Influenza, eye-aches, indigestion, stomach-ache, love-ache, mental despair every other day and many other sources of abject misery. However I am drawn to it as if by a magnetic power. In London is my true life.

I have finished *The Idiot*. I am writing a poem at present. I can't tell you what an impression it made on me. I now seriously mean to express a great many of my thoughts in writing. Some of my feelings can't be expressed in painting. So I will write also. It is so exciting and relieving. What does it matter after all if I do it badly as long as I express a little of what I feel? . . .

MARK GERTLER

To Carrington

29 August 1916 *The Mill House, Cholesbury*

My dear Carrington, Please write at once, as your silence has made me miserable with apprehension. I am just finishing a poem I have been writing here! It was so exciting and painful to do. Last night it kept me awake all night. At last I had to get out of bed and write a verse of it that kept ringing in my head! But all night it kept going round and round in my head. Today, therefore, I am feeling worn out, but I am pleased to have expressed a thought in writing. In fact I am excited and pleased with my poem! But I dare say it's technically all wrong and bad poetry, but I don't care as long as I have expressed a thought of *my own* and that I know I *have* done.

I have read parts of my diary and the beginning of my "Currie" chapter[1] to Gilbert. He was impressed and of certain bits he said "were very good bits of writing".

But do, do please write to me, I can't bear this silence. Ever yours

MARK GERTLER

To Carrington

1 September 1916 *Penn Studio, Hampstead*

My dear Carrington, I have only just come back to my studio. I am so glad. It is so good to be here once more, between these tall silent walls. Here I can do what I please; no one can interrupt me, or get on my nerves. At Cholesbury I did no actual work, except that poem which I wrote you about in my last letter.

As it seems really impossible for you to tell me more of what you feel, I will trouble you no further about it. But there are one or two things in

[1] There is a description, which was among his notebooks, of Gertler's feelings on hearing that Currie had shot his mistress and then himself. It appears to be only a draft. Currie's death is an important feature in *Mendel*. No trace of Gertler's diary has been found.

your letter against which I really must protest. You say that, were you to tell me your true feelings, I should not be interested because I have a preconceived notion or a fixed idea of your character. This is *absolutely false*! Not only have I *not* got a fixed idea of your character, but I have not even *any* idea of your character: in fact I must confess here that I don't understand you in the least! That, in fact, is why I asked you to tell me your feelings, because I want to understand you. I would like to know what sort of person it is that I love! If anyone were to ask me "What sort of person is Carrington?" I should answer "I haven't the faintest idea, but I love her very much."

Then you say that I also shouldn't be interested in your beliefs, if they didn't directly concern me. Surely that's having a very low opinion of me! However I would rather now drop the subject.

Thanks very much for the Donne poem. I like it very much, but there are some others I like even better. I read all Donne and Marvell at the Mill, also Shakespeare's sonnets. I like them all. But Donne impressed me immensely. But how wonderful Marvell's "To His Coy Mistress" is. It nearly made me weep. It is so much what I feel with you! If you have it by you, you *must* read it *carefully* and imagine yourself to be the "coy mistress" and myself the writer. You will then have all my sufferings in a nutshell. Yes, it hurts me terribly to see your beauty pass by before my very nose. Time passes so quickly. Already I have known you five years. How lovely your body must have been then! It is terrible to see you getting older and older and still be patient and happy. Sometimes I can't bear it. How I could love such beauty as yours and youth is the time for loving. However, I must stop. I didn't mean to grumble like this—forgive me—it was Marvell's poem that made me. Apparently such joy was not meant for me.

You say that we can never be more than "twin souls", always two. That's only too true and that is one of the greatest sorrows of my life. You see, in friendship, that's the most that can happen. It is only given to lovers to experience that most ecstatic of emotions, the *exchange of souls*, or to make two souls into one, for one moment of ecstasy by love! I am a lover myself, so I know that ecstasy from perception. I have never actually felt it myself, because I am a lover without a partner. I, like Moses, have only been shown the "promised land". But that was a torture rather than a pleasure, for having seen that wonderful country, I long to live in it. All else, friendship, seems cold in comparison. *But enough of that!*

Now I am back I really don't know what sort of work I am going to do. My sculptural conceptions have thrown me into a chaos and painting into the background. In the meantime I shall give my studio a thorough cleaning out and perhaps by then I shall know how and what to do. It seems so strange being back here, like starting a new chapter.

Well, write me soon about yourself. And don't let anything in this letter worry you. For although friendship is but a poor return for love, yet you must realise how your friendship is valuable to me; in fact I have told you many times before, I could *not* live without it. I find you such an inspiring person to know. Without you all my life would collapse—like a punctured balloon. And if, in this letter, I have let out to you my troubles, it is after all only right, for to whom shall I confide my love-sick pains if not to my greatest friend?!

Miss Friedlander[1] was in Cholesbury and I had some interesting walks and talks with her. Last night we walked through some wonderful woods. My eyes filled with the beauty. The whole wood was sun-spotted! Green, silver, russet and gold, so beautiful.

Well, write soon to me and don't worry to write anything about your inner feelings as it is difficult. Just write anything you like. Everything from you is welcome. With love MARK GERTLER

P.S. This letter may seem a contradiction because I have told you lately that I believe in your love and here I say "I am a lover without a partner".

I meant that you love me as a friend. There is all the difference in the world between loving a person and being *in love* with a person. You are *not in love* with me or anybody else as far as I can see. So don't please, dear friend, read this letter wrongly.

To Carrington

8 September 1916 *Penn Studio, Hampstead*

My dear Carrington, Thank you for your letter and two cards.

I am sending you here the poems and satires of Marvell. I believe they contain all his poems. If you have not got Donne let me know and I will send you him. "To His Coy Mistress" is indeed a good poem. I tried to underline certain lines for you, but I found it very difficult to know what to underline because *every* line, *every* word is so good and expressive.

The whole meaning is so good. If, it says, we had thousands of years in front of us, all right, we could go on loving in this slow gradual way:

> An hundred years should go to praise
> Thine eyes and on thy forehead gaze;
> Two hundred to adore each breast, . .
>
> For, Lady, you deserve this state,
> Nor would I love at a lower rate.
> But at my back I always hear
> Time's wingèd chariot drawing near; . .
>
> That long-preserved virginity, . .
>
> Now therefore, while the youthful hue
> Sits on thy skin like morning dew, . .

[1] Artist and critic.

Let us roll all our strength and all
Our sweetness into one ball.
etc., etc.

Yes, that's a very fine poem. I also like the "Mower's Song".

When Juliana came, and she
What I do to the grass, does to my thoughts and me.
etc.

I don't know the book well enough to point out other poems to you, but there are many that I like very much.

My life here in London is as usual and exciting.

Iris is back! She came and had tea with me. That was very exciting. She has managed to get thinner! It suits her well.

I had an exciting and adventurous evening also with Katherine and Kot. Another evening I had with Jack Hutchinson, Monty[1] and Gilbert....

[1] Montague Shearman, barrister and a friend of the Hutchinsons. He was also a collector of pictures. He became one of Gertler's most devoted friends and patrons, giving him the free use of his room in the Adelphi. Two of his letters are here quoted.

[*12 October 1916*] *London, W.C.*
Dear Mark, Money is a horrible thing. I should like you to feel however that you can always have what you want from me if you like. But it must be as between friends and there must be no feeling of patronage or obligation whatever. I don't want to be a Conway or an Eddie Marsh—not that I am saying a word against Eddie Marsh, who I am sure meant to be kind. But I am not, as you know, the sort of person who would give money and expect to take pictures instead. If I want a picture I would buy it outright. So if you would like me at any time to guarantee the extra room or rooms out or the studio itself or any other thing you like, let me know. I am sure you would not ask for more than was necessary and I hope you would not mind accepting it if it is necessary. If it isn't, so much the better, but if it is I can easily afford a bit and I think it would help your work if you felt more comfortable. M.S.

P.S. Pianola just arrived!

[*22 November 1916*]
My dear Mark, There are one or two things I should like to say in continuation of our interrupted conversation. I can understand quite clearly what you mean by your repugnance to your past life and the surroundings that suggest it. It is strong and good of you to cut it out and start again. Your absolute independence and contempt of all fleeting and material things in life is always a source of admiration to me. What I was going to say when the rush of people came was this. That life is a development, not a series of disconnected episodes. It would be most ideal not to be affected by the association of old acquaintances and visits to the Café Royal at all. Strong in the knowledge of victory and of your triumph over the false glaring atmosphere of so-called Bohemianism you may some day go through life serenely content and not the prey to fierce animosities or moods. The self-control of Englishmen is a bad or lifeless thing if there is no feeling at all. But if there is feeling or great emotional experience it is a good thing to be able to conquer the desire to succumb to one's feelings. I think you are infinitely greater and deeper in your moods than any Englishman I have met and when there is a contrast I prefer you to them. But I still look to something greater still in you and hence this letter. . . . Yours M.S.

Monty is definitely buying my landscape. I am glad because I am getting short of money. . . .

With love

MARK GERTLER

To Carrington

13 September 1916 *Penn Studio, Hampstead*

My dear Carrington, . . . I have been some time cleaning my studio and putting it into order, but now I have commenced work. I am doing a small model in plasticine for my "Acrobats".[1] So far it goes well, although the technical difficulties are most worrisome. There are hundreds of little things I don't know and ought to know. But I shall find all these out through experience and mistakes. I must have patience and expect many failures at first. But it is all most wonderful and is opening up a new world with immense possibilities, but I must have *patience, patience* and control my excitement. There are also many things I must write. . . .

With best wishes, yours ever

MARK GERTLER

To Carrington

16 September 1916 *Penn Studio, Hampstead*

Dear Carrington, . . . I have done my small model and am now about to start the full-sized one in clay. In the meantime I am just finishing a study of the flowers you sent me! They looked so irresistible the other day that I left everything to paint them. Now I am pleased because I have turned out a little thing which I like very much. It is very realistic—imitative almost—but one of the best studies I've done!

Today or tomorrow however I return to my wonderful and most exciting world of sculpture. I am ill with over-excitement.

Frieda Lawrence was here to tea yesterday! She is for the moment in town. . . .

Yours

MARK GERTLER

To Carrington

25 September 1916 *Penn Studio, Hampstead*

Dear Carrington, . . . I hope to see you before Friday—it is so long to wait. I thought it was all so beautiful on Saturday night—talking to you. You are so interesting both to listen to and to talk to. What wonderful times we shall have later! When we are freer with one another. Until

[1] Now in the Tate Gallery (Plate 12, facing page 145).

now we have really been constrained with each other because of our "difficulty", but Saturday night was an example of the sort of time we shall have when the "difficulty" has completely dissolved itself—such interesting intimate times, close moments—moments of ecstasy! But above all it will enable us to be entirely free and open together and what heights we shall reach! Oh! Love is a good thing! But it's that *freedom* that I shall love above all things. There will be no dreadful difficulty to prevent me telling you all I want to and can and nothing to prevent me listening to you. There will be no "but" or "if"—no hatred to destroy our freedom. That which we have to give, we shall give freely, and with joy, and giving we shall receive in more in return. Yes, it will be good—already the difficulty is dissolving, already I am happier! Never have I looked forward more to the future of our friendship because the present promises so much.

Your loving Friend, MARK GERTLER

NOTE ON "THE MERRY-GO-ROUND"

(*Plate* 10, *facing page* 129)

Gertler's painting of the merry-go-round at the London Group in the autumn of 1916 caused a stir which may now seem rather difficult to comprehend. St John Hutchinson had befriended and legally represented several writers who had conscientious objections and was no doubt concerned for Gertler's liability for national service. It needs to be remembered that the latter part of 1916, after the Somme, was one of the darkest periods of the First World War. Gertler's soldiers on the roundabout are certainly not cast in a heroic mood. D. H. Lawrence may have read more into the painting than Gertler himself intended. It was included in the London Group Retrospective Exhibition at the Tate in 1964.

From St John Hutchinson

River House, Hammersmith

My dear Mark, I have been thinking over matters and I want to ask you whether you think you are quite wise in exhibiting the "Merry-Go-Round" at the London Group? It will of cause raise a tremendous outcry—the old, the wise, the professional critic will go mad with anger and righteous indignation—and what strikes me is that these symptoms may drive them to write all sorts of rubbish about German art and German artists in their papers and may raise the question acutely and publicly as to your position.

I think, if matters remained quiet, you are quite safe, but I am rather afraid of what might happen if the matter got into the papers and was taken up by the public at large. I don't want to advise you; that would be impudent on my part, and of course nothing of what I imagine may take place, but I thought I might draw your attention to the question as it strikes me, so that whatever you may decide you will do after full judgement. I thought that perhaps it would be rather fun to have a sort of little exhibition of your work including the sculpture at his [Shearman's] rooms. We would of course ask all sorts and conditions of people. It might be worth thinking of?

I am so delighted, more than I could tell you, at your selling "The Fruit Stall", tho' I know that you will hate parting with it. I sat all last night in Monty's room looking at "The Mill" and liked it even better than before. It is splendid.

The Dutch Doll

Oil painting (30 × 30 in.) 1915

Reproduced by permission of the Brighton Art Gallery

(Gertler painted several versions of this doll, the first being in 1915)

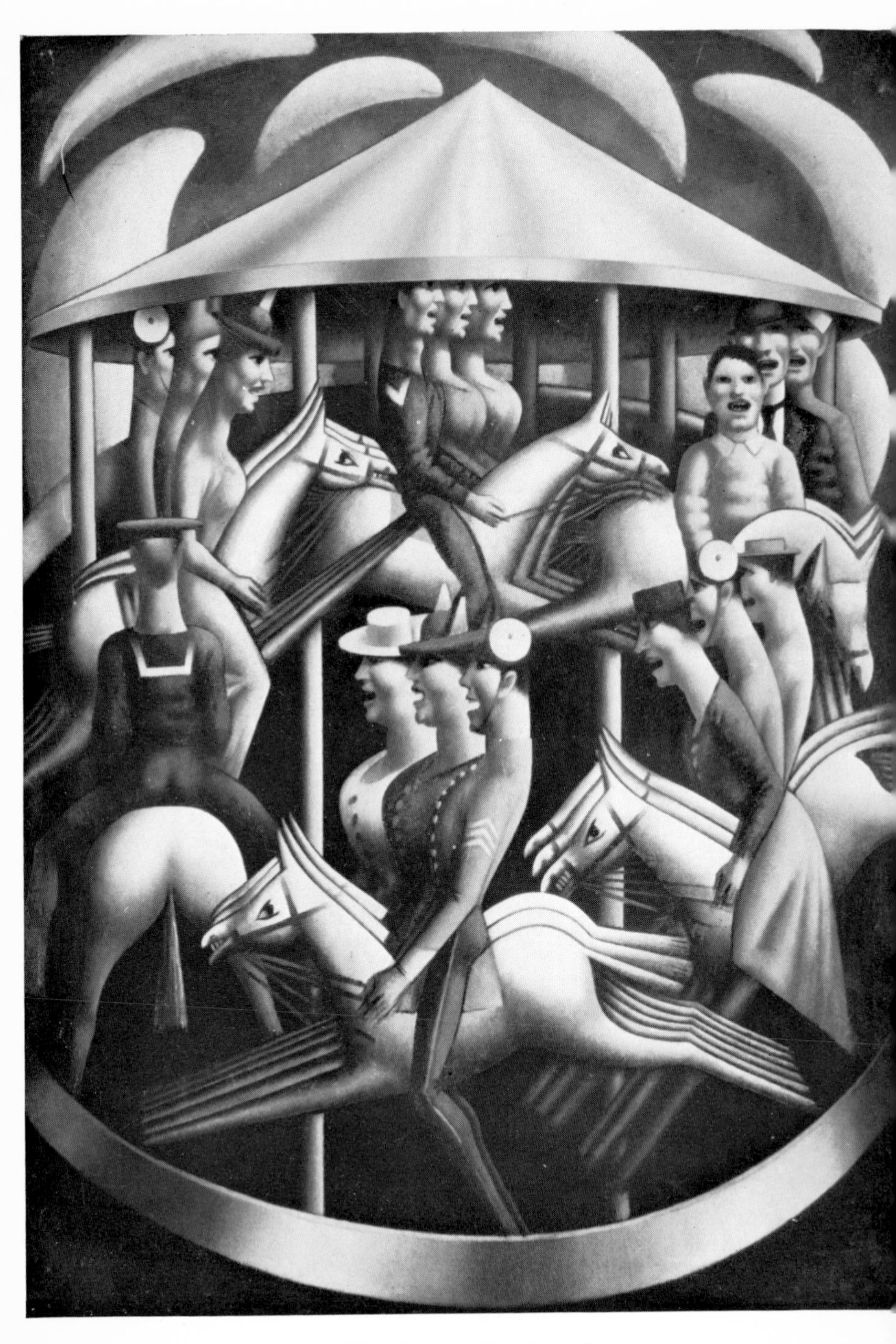

The Merry-Go-Round

Oil painting (75 × 56 in.) 1916

Reproduced by permission of the Ben-Uri Gallery, London

I hear possibly we may meet on Thursday latish if you can drag yourself from the arms of the blackberry—I hope you will. Excuse my writing. Yours JACK H.

From D. H. Lawrence

27 September 1916 *Higher Tregerthen, Zennor, St Ives, Cornwall*

Dear Gertler, I would write, but there seems so much noise, one is afraid to open one's mouth. I was glad to hear such good news of the "Roundabout". I want very much to see it, and look forward to having a photograph copy. It seems to me, the stark truth is all that matters, whether it is paint or books or life: the truth one has inside one; and away with their old lies, whether they are of vision or ideas.

I saw the *Daily Mirror* today—the Zeppelin wrecks, etc. How exhausted one is by all this fury of strident lies and foul death. But less and less does the world matter to one—people, and all they say or do, life, all that is out there in the world—it ceases to have any significance. Nothing matters, in the end, but the little hard flame of truth one has inside oneself, and which does not blow about in the draught of blasphemous living. It seems to me, things matter to one less and less and less, till little remains to one but the pure abstraction within one, and that is inviolable.

Still, I know that there are some other people who have the same abstraction, who live finally by the central truth, and by nothing of the loathsome outer world. And in the end, I hope we can add our spirit together, unite in essential truthfulness, in the end, and create a new ell-shapen life out of the smashed mess of the old order—I do believe we can, in time. But we have to give ourselves time—heaven knows how long.

This is to tell you—and Kot—that the essential thing is not gone, that is in our relationship. It is only purifying itself and ridding itself of externalities and extraneous things. I will write the same to Gilbert, soon. Our hope is in the central truth, and then in each other. And then we can create a new order of life, in the times after these. Yours D. H. LAWRENCE

From D. H. Lawrence

9 October 1916 *Higher Tregerthen, Zennor, St Ives, Cornwall*

My dear Gertler, Your terrible and dreadful picture ["The Merry-Go-Round"] has just come. This is the first picture you have ever painted: it is the best *modern* picture I have seen: I think it is great, and true. But it is horrible and terrifying. I'm not sure I wouldn't be too frightened to come and look at the original.

If they tell you it is obscene, they will say truly. I believe there was something in Pompeian art, of this terrible and soul-tearing obscenity. But then, since obscenity is the truth of our passion today, it is the only stuff of art—or almost the only stuff. I won't say what I, as a man of words and ideas, read in this picture. But I *do* think that in this combination of blaze, and violent mechanised rotation and complex involution, and ghastly, utterly mindless human intensity of sensational extremity, you have made a real and ultimate revelation. I think this picture is your arrival—it marks a great arrival. Also I could sit down and howl beneath it like Kot's dog, in soul-lacerating despair. I realise how superficial your human relationships must be, what a violent maelstrom of destruction and horror your inner soul must be. It is true, the outer life means nothing to you, really. You are all absorbed in the violent and lurid process of inner decomposition: the same thing that makes leaves go scarlet and copper-green at this time of year. It is a terrifying coloured flame of decomposition, your inner flame. But dear God, it is a real flame enough, undeniable in heaven and earth—

it would take a Jew to paint this picture. It would need your national history to get you here, without disintegrating you first. You are of an older race than I, and in these ultimate processes, you are beyond me, older than I am. But I think I am sufficiently the same, to be able to understand.

This all reads awkward—but I feel there ought to be some other language than English, to say it in. And I don't want to translate you into ideas, because I can see, you must, in your art, be mindless and in an ecstasy of destructive sensation. It is wrong to be conscious, for you: at any rate, to be too conscious. "By the waters of Babylon I sat me down and wept, remembering Jerusalem." At last your race is at an end—these pictures are its death-cry. And it will be left for the Jews to utter the final and great death-cry of this epoch: the Christians are not reduced sufficiently. I must say, I have, for you, in your work, reverence, the reverence for the great articulate extremity of art.

Perhaps you are right about sculpture—I don't know—probably you are, since you feel so strongly. Only, somehow, it seems to me to be going *too far*—over the edge of endurance into a form of incoherent, less poignant shouting. I say this, trying to imagine what this picture will be like, in sculpture. But you know best. Only take care, or you will burn your flame so fast, it will suddenly go out. It is all spending and no getting of strength. And yet some of us must fling ourselves in the fire of ultimate expression, like an immolation. Yet one cannot assist at this *auto-da-fe* without suffering. But do try to save yourself as well. You must have periods of proper rest also. Come down here and stay with us, when you want a change. You seem to me to be flying like a moth into a fire. I beg you, don't let the current of work carry you on so strongly that it will destroy you oversoon.

You are twenty-five, and have painted this picture—I tell you, it takes three thousand years to get where this picture is—and we Christians haven't got two thousand years behind us yet.

I feel I write stupidly and stiltedly, but I am upset, and language is no medium between us.

With love from Frieda and me D. H. LAWRENCE

I am amazed how the picture exceeds anything I had expected. Tell me what people *say*—Epstein, for instance.

Get somebody to suggest that the picture be bought *by the nation*—it ought to be—I'd buy it if I had any money. How much is it? I want to know—how much you want for it.

PART FIVE

Creative Ferment

By the end of 1916 Gertler could be considered to have arrived as an artist. He was taken seriously by some of the leading critics of the day, notably Roger Fry. He was receiving the support of a number of discerning collectors, and—more important to him financially—art dealers were beginning to interest themselves in him. If the Philistines made him a target from time to time that seldom damages a young artist.

Increasingly his letters reveal the state of mental ferment in which he lived. Everything that he has hitherto achieved is questioned. New ideas keep bubbling up and he is tormented to give them expression in his art. His creative activity overflows into sculpture, rather to the dismay of some of his friends, and into writing. Periods of harrowing depression recur with greater frequency, but they alternate with moments of exaltation of such intensity as to leave him physically exhausted. Even Lawrence, no quietist himself, begs him to take his work less seriously.

His love for Carrington at last finds fulfilment and for a brief space it seems as if all barriers between them were to dissolve. No sooner, however, does he demand the complete sharing of their minds than she again eludes him. In part this was because she was making other friendships which were too important for her to sacrifice. She had always had something like a genius for friendship and ironically enough it was Lytton Strachey, whose intellectual virtues Gertler himself had extolled, who was to replace him in her affections. She was at first inclined to regard with suspicion the peculiar Strachey air of amused detachment—"he is better when you get to know him"—while Lytton found her intellectual naïveté mildly entertaining. However not only had Lytton learning, wit and charm, he was also a natural teacher. He delighted in reading his favourite authors—among them Shakespeare, Voltaire and Gibbon—to a small congenial group. He found in Carrington an insatiable listener and, perhaps unexpectedly, a companion for life.

That Gertler should become jealous of Strachey's influence was to be expected. Apart from this a rift was developing between various groups of intellectuals who had been brought together on the common ground of pacifism. This was particularly so between the group already nicknamed Bloomsbury, which included the Stracheys, Clive Bell and Duncan Grant, and those outside it, the Lawrences, Murrys and Gertler. If they still met at Garsington, the atmosphere can no longer have been one of ease.

To Carrington

2 November 1916 *Penn Studio, Hampstead*

My dear Carrington, Thank you for your friendly letter. No, I am not at all unhappy. I am very happy. As you say, we have been talking too much, yet what wonderful times we've had, more wonderful than ever! Our former wonderful times in comparison to these last are like my early work compared to my latest. The early were beautiful, childish, almost more beautiful than these last. But what are they in comparison to these last! Our love has been and is nothing less than a classic, so wonderful is it. What a book it really could make! How can people ever know what goes on between us on Mondays! Heavens! how wonderful it all is!!

Really we have no reason to be unhappy, we ought in fact rejoice in having found each other. I suffer simply because I love so much that I can't express—like the people in my "Paradise". Do you remember their only suffering was that they could not express their infinite love! Do not think you will make me suffer afterwards—you cannot. I have changed. I am your greatest friend. I love your freedom—my love is of too good a quality to desire to imprison you. Through my love you become entirely free! This is the truth—not mere words. Therefore be happy. *I* am very happy. I thank *that* which created *you.*

But above all do not be afraid of hurting me. You cannot now—I love you too much. So let yourself be free—do everything you want to. What we have between us no person or thing can touch.

It does not matter when we start—tomorrow or next year—or never! It does not interest me! What a fool I was to think all these years that that was what I wanted! I have lost all interest in it except as a natural physical necessity. Well, I can say no more here. But I have never loved you higher than now. I am too upset to write more, but thank you for your letter. It was somehow a necessity with me to get a letter from you this morning.

My best wishes go with your work, and I hope it will be all right about your brother.[1]

MARK GERTLER

To Carrington

30 November 1916 *Penn Studio, Hampstead*

Dear Carrington, I went yesterday with the brothers Carline[2] to the South Kensington Museum. I was very much struck with the great beauty of some of the things in Indian Museum.

Sculpture is certainly a great art—but it needs almost more patience than we "moderns" have got and a badly finished statue is much worse than a sketchy painting.

[1] Carrington's second brother was missing on the Somme.

[2] Sidney and Richard Carline, artists who lived in Hampstead.

I am now working on my carving of the "Merry-Go-Round"—if it goes well it will be a beautiful thing, but it is a greater job than I thought and will take a long time.[1]

But I *do* want to see more of *you—you alone*—because you inspire me as nothing else does.

With much love your friend MARK GERTLER

[1] This carving does not seem to have survived. A good many of Gertler's friends were dubious about his sudden enthusiasm for sculpture. D. H. Lawrence wrote:

13 November 1916 *Higher Tregerthen, Zennor, St Ives, Cornwall*

Dear Gertler, Kot told me you had done your first sculpture—"The Acrobats". I wonder how you like it, what you think of it. We had an American woman here the other day, an artist. She admired the "Roundabout"—the "Merry-Go-Round"—immensely. We liked her very much. Do you think you might ask her up to see the picture one day? I wish you would. She is Miss Esther Andrews, 131 Cheyne Walk, Chelsea, S.W. Ask her and Mr Mountsier together, will you? He is a journalist for the New York papers. He wants to interview Gilbert. I am sure Gilbert would be delighted. So you might arrange things. Miss Andrews and Mountsier were staying in Penzance and in St Ives last week. They came up here several times. I think you will like them. Have Kot with you when they come.

Oh, and do send me Gilbert's address, will you? I will surely write him. Thank heaven I shall not be expected to condole with him for the loss of Sammy and Soofie—not at this late hour.

I think the Murrys must have heard what Frieda said to you and Kot when she was in London, for they have utterly dropped communication. This is just as well, for I don't want it to go on. One gets too sick of all these twists and falsities.

Tell me the news of everybody when you write—I like to hear it. Of ourselves there is nothing to say, it is so quiet and remote down here, there is nobody to quarrel with. I hope the accursed army still ignores you.

My health is not particularly good just now: and we are very hard up: all of which isn't worth the telling.

Frieda sends her greetings. D. H. LAWRENCE

5 December 1916 *Zennor, St Ives, Cornwall*

My dear Gertler, . . . One ought, like the fields, to lie fallow during the winter and neither work nor think, but only, in one's soul, sleep. Can't you put your soul to sleep, and remain just superficially awake, drifting and taking no real notice, just amuse yourself like a child with some sort of play work? I have just made a *pouffe*—a sort of floor cushion, square, and like a mound—and on the black cover, all round, I have stitched a green field, then house, barns, haystacks, animals, man and woman, all in bright-coloured stuffs—it looks very jolly and bright. That is a kind of play, which makes one busy and happy while one's soul of contention sleeps. I wish you could take some of your sculpture rather like that.

Looking in a dictionary the other day I saw, "*Sculpture*: the lowest of the arts". That surprised me very much—but I think perhaps it is true. Sculpture, it seems to me, is truly a part of architecture. In my novel there is a man—not you, I reassure you—who does a great granite frieze for the top of a factory, and the frieze is a fair, of which your whirligig, for example, is part. (We knew a man, a German, who did these big reliefs for great, fine factories in Cologne.) Painting is so much subtler than sculpture, that I am sure it is a finer medium. But one wants the unsubtle, the obvious, like sculpture, as well as the subtle. . . .

D. H. LAWRENCE

To Carrington

December 1916 *Penn Studio, Hampstead*

My dearest and most beautiful girl, How happy I was to get your letter this morning! Since I left you I have been suffering dreadfully—I missed you so terribly. I can't work—I can't do anything but think of you. Some moments I have been hating you, because I thought you can't love me if you could go home for the week-end. It is still terrible for me, as I shall not see you until tomorrow evening and then perhaps you will put me off! My love has now reached to such a point that I can hardly bear it. I never quite knew how very beautiful you were! For God's sake don't torture me by not letting me see much of you—I must see you *very* often. I shan't worry you for much "sugar" if only I can see you and talk—I must, I must. And if any other man touches any part of your beautiful body I shall kill myself—don't forget that! I could not bear such a thing. Give me time—give me at any rate a year or so of happiness. I deserve it—you have tortured me enough in the past. Perhaps later I shall be able to be "advanced" and reasonable about your other friends. Then you can have other ships. Not now—at present I am too much in love to be advanced or to reason. You are by nature cruel, but you must not be too cruel where I am concerned. Don't believe those "advanced" fools who tell you that love is free. *It is not*—it is a *bondage*, a beautiful bondage. We are bound to one another—you must love the bondage. How I hate your "advanced" philosopher self! Yes I hate that part of you—you have lately added hateful parts to yourself. If you really loved me you could not be so advanced. A person really in love is *not* advanced. I loathe your many ships idea. I may yet tear myself away from you—then you can have your beastly ships. I wish to curse you, I would curse you with love—may you one day [*letter torn*] then you could not air those ideas of yours—got from people who never loved. Then you would know what it is to desire and to suffer. Some moments I wish one of us dead! Also you would not call love-making "vulgar" if you were in love. You would not arrange for it only to happen three times a month. You would want to see me more. But all these things—my undisturbed beauty—you don't understand.

I hate you for three things:

1. Because you can't love passionately.
2. Because of your advanced ideas.
3. I hate you because I love you and am therefore in the power of your cruel, advanced and unpassionate self!

But please remember dearest that I love you far more now than before. Therefore you must be kinder to me, you must let me see you—*only* see you often and don't make me jealous. If you do this for me I shall do my best to deserve it.

Well good-bye until tomorrow my dear, dear beautiful friend. Yours ever

MARK GERTLER

To Carrington

29 December 1916 *Peveril House, Swanage, Dorset*[1]

Dear Carrington, This drawing is a view from one of the glass doors. From every window one gets a good enough view for painting. I wish I had my paints with me. The sea surrounds the house on two sides. There is just a bit of garden and then cliff, below which is the open sea!—It must be marvellous here in warmer weather.

This morning we went for a long walk by the sea. Huge rocks and quarries, chunks of beautiful stone everywhere. I wish I could carry a lump of stone home with me for carving in.

There was a terrific wind—also rain and I never had a wilder walk. We have just come in and I've had a hot bath. On my walk, I lost my old black hat—my hair got soaked.

Since I have seen you I have commenced to write a play. Also I am doing at home a drawing for a wood carving which, if I am not hindered by lack of craft from carrying out, ought to be very wonderful.

I hope you will see me on Tuesday. Love from Monty and me

MARK GERTLER

To Carrington

31 December 1916 *Peveril House, Swanage, Dorset*

Dear Carrington, Thanks for your two letters—I shall answer the contents of them more when we meet. I am sorry you are worried with money troubles etc. I wish I could help you with money, but nobody wants to buy my sculpture and I have nearly come to the end of my £60! So, soon, I shall be hard up myself and it will be very difficult for me to get money as long as I do sculpture....

Yesterday again we went for a long walk—miles and miles! It was wonderful, it is wonderful country here—one stands on the edge of terrifically high cliffs, looking down on the sea—it is terrifying! But all the different coloured rocks keep suggesting sculpture to me. But how you would love this country! From every window one could paint a splendid picture. I am afraid we walked too far yesterday as I have been very tired ever since.

Among the many conversations I have had with Monty the one on Natural History stands out most clearly in my mind. There is a wonderful book on butterflies here and there are many wonderful kinds of sea birds and different shells and stones and I've seen a kingfisher. Yesterday we saw a flock of birds flying with the regularity of a regiment of soldiers. They were beautiful—in some lights they looked like a shower of silver coins, sometimes gold. We talked of the habits and instincts of birds and fish, etc., and I am filled with the wonder of it all. I have learnt a lot about such things from Monty. He is very refreshing to know.

[1] Home of Monty Shearman.

Well, I shall look forward to seeing you at Gustave's at 7 o'clock on Tuesday. My love MARK GERTLER

To Carrington

Monday morning, January 1917 *Penn Studio, Hampstead*

My dear Friend, . . . I have at last managed to get the wood I want and am just off to the East End to get it cut in a neighbouring sawmill. They will cut off for me all the unnecessary chunks, which will save me time and trouble. In the meantime I have been "overcome" with my "Nude" idea—which has suddenly become clear to me. I have started a small design for it in pencil—it is to be a good old-fashioned "Cézannish" bathing scene,[1] but I am very excited about it. The opportunities are immense for drawing and colour—I shall revel in the drawing of the nudes. The background is to be based on my "Pond" picture[2]—so now I am full of these two things, the carving and the bathing scene. How I should love to make studies of *you* for my picture instead of having models! But you are so busy, aren't you?

Well dear, do write to me and ease my mind. I have been longing to phone you or to come and see you, but I was so nervous and besides I thought you might be irritated if I did. My biggest trouble just now is *money*—I have practically no money!

Ever yours MARK GERTLER

To Carrington

Tuesday, January 1917 *Penn Studio, Hampstead*

Dear Carrington, . . . Yesterday I came tearing back here from the East End with my log of wood, which was so heavy that I nearly collapsed on the way! But I bore the burden bravely! and proudly! I started work on it immediately and worked till bedtime! Oh! the excitement! The muscles of my arms ached so when I finished. I had to saw out middle bits and the plank is four inches thick! Still I don't know if I shall be able to carve it, through ignorance of the craft of wood carving. How I wish I could, because my conception is such a good one—about the best thing I have done. If I fail I shall turn sadly away towards my "Bathing" picture—but I shall feel like a defeated man. But God! you can't think how hard it is to carve a subtle thing out of a large rough square piece of wood![3] Especially when one is ignorant of the craft.

[1] Probably "Bathers", now in the collection of Gwendoline, Lady Melchett.

[2] One of the pond at Garsington Manor.

[3] I cannot trace this wood carving, nor that it was exhibited.

Please write to me every few days if I don't see you, but of course I should prefer *you yourself* to a hundred letters.

Dearest friend, ever yours MARK GERTLER

To Carrington

[*Thursday, January 1917*] *Penn Studio, Hampstead*

Dear Carrington, Thank you for your letter. All right, I'll forget all about it and in future I shall control myself more and not ask you to live with me often, although control is hardly necessary to prevent that often, because what with your moods and our quarrels and country goings, we in any case only meet about once a month on the average. What with one thing and another we hardly ever meet alone—no wonder we get out of touch with each other. I see you less than any of my friends! . . .

Mary came here the other day and told me amazing things about Gilbert which I will tell you when I see you, but it is a secret and please don't even mention that there is a secret or people will worry me. Anyhow in the meantime Gilbert is worse and Mary terribly upset and I am very sorry for both of them.[1]

I am working terribly hard on my carving; words cannot describe what difficulties I am having with it! I get literally physically sick and giddy at the end of each day's work. The last day or two it has gone a bit better, but still I am not certain of it. But I love it in spite of all the difficulties, because it is the only thing that is keeping me going through all this wretched period that I have been passing lately. Also I have a great deal to thank Monty for. He and his room have been a blessing to me and still are—there I can always go and find a friend. He just prevents me from feeling utterly isolated in spirit, but I am beginning to whine and to feel sorry for myself. I must hastily end this letter. Yours ever

MARK GERTLER

[1] Gilbert Cannan had a nervous breakdown and his marriage was also breaking up. Two letters to Gertler are given here:

25 Ferncroft Avenue, Hampstead

My dear old Mark, We do seem to go through things together in this awful mess called life, and I wish I had your toughness. I'm not fit to go out on Thursday and shan't be fit, I'm afraid, for some time, but I am to go out by degrees. I am to see Gwen Wilson tomorrow, and will hobble over to tea with you on Friday. I'm in a very queer condition, terribly weak physically, but with such a mental and spiritual clarity as I never had, and the terrible unceasing effort to get it has produced the growing indifference to anything else which looks to outsiders like sheer madness. However we can talk on Friday. I'll come about 3.0. Poor little Mary has lost her head in her turn, but it will all work itself out in time. Yours GILBERT CANNAN

25 Ferncroft Avenue, Hampstead

My dear Mark, I wish you would come and see me and don't be worried over the bursting of the cloud of insanity that has been growing and growing in me until

To Richard Carline

22 January 1917 *Penn Studio, Hampstead*

My dear Carline, I am working on a carving in wood of those acrobats that I showed you the design for in charcoal. You can't imagine what difficulties I've been through. First of all—for some time—it was almost impossible to get the wood, which nearly drove me mad—I was so anxious to start. At last I got it and then commenced the "Craft" difficulties—which I found enormous! Now at last I have got it well on its way and so far have had only one mishap—in the sawing I broke off a piece, which was to be the hands on the left. That however can be glued on again afterwards. I really think now I shall be able to carry it through. If I do, it will be the best thing I've done. But whether I carry it through or not, it is terribly exciting to do—I have never been more excited about anything!

In the meantime however my money is coming to an end and people, even some of my best friends, think my sculpture only a *phase*, which they would be glad to see the end of! You can't think how this irritates me! "Why doesn't he paint?" they say! They will not understand that it is a *natural* and *necessary* development and that it is *real pleasure* that makes me do it. So in my sculpture I am even more isolated than before in my painting!

You ask me if I ever read the Bible. Then let me tell you it is by far my most favourite book and especially the book of Job!

Yours ever MARK GERTLER

To Carrington

Tuesday, February 1917 *Penn Studio, Hampstead*

Dear Carrington, Thanks for your letter, I am glad you are still having

---

now when I have emerged sane and in my right mind. The facts are appalling but they simply are not open to moral judgement. I have been right through the whole Hell of it and the story is more mysterious and terrible than anyone can guess, and I want to tell it you, for I am only just now in possession of the facts of my life. Yours GILBERT CANNAN

The following letter from Shearman may be quoted here:

[*Wednesday night*] *The Mill House, Hurley, Marlow*

My dear Mark, . . . As for the new picture it opened a new vista for me. As I tried to explain rather awkwardly today on the bus our friendship has come through your art. People sometimes think that if one gets to know and like a person one is hypnotised into liking his art that way. I am not like that. I first saw Jack Hutchinson's picture and was deeply moved, slight though it is compared with your big work. Then the "Mill", the "Merry-Go-Round", and above all (though you don't agree) the "Fruit Stall". Then the landscape, which seems the epitome of your work as a colourist at which I think you are unique—the great skill and dexterity of the design and the depth of soul most of all. You will understand I am speaking as a novice with no great knowledge except what comes from looking at pictures (mostly old masters) steadily for about twelve years. Ever most sincerely MONTAGUE SHEARMAN

such a happy time. Since I last wrote to you, troubles have showered upon my head like Job. . . .

I found a wire waiting for me to say that I must come home at once to see my father. When I got home I found that my father was dying. Oh! if I could only describe to you the suffering that's going on at home and my own wretchedness. Also I am feeling ill through my operations. Lastly when I dragged myself to Monty's last night he told me there was a probability of his being sent to America for the duration of the war any moment!

I cannot write you much today, but I must tell you that I entirely disagree with you when you came to the conclusion that, of all "Good, Evil, Beauty, and Pleasure, Pleasure was the most certain". I think that of all those uncertainties, Pleasure is the *most uncertain*!

Monty has brought the drawing for my statue and the study for "Floating woman" for £20 both. I spent a very inspiring evening with the Hutchinsons last Friday.

Well, I must go home and see my father now. MARK GERTLER

To Carrington

Thursday, 8 February 1917 *Penn Studio, Hampstead*

My dear Carrington, Thanks very much for your kind letter—it was great comfort to get it. Your feelings of friendship are most valuable to me.

My father died last Monday at 6 o'clock—a few hours after I left him. He was buried yesterday in the Jewish Burial Ground at East Ham.

It is the custom among Jews for the family of deceased to sit "shiva" in the house where the person died. This means that the family sit on low stools for a week, say special prayers, and also the men are not allowed to shave for a month. I shall have to keep this up to some extent for the sake of my mother and also because I somehow want to. I shall not shave probably for a week and shall be going down to my people every day for that time to mourn with them. After sunset I am free, so I shall go to Monty's most evenings and also tonight where I hope to see you.

Thanking you again for your letter. Yours sincerely MARK GERTLER

To S. S. Koteliansky

Friday, February 1917

My dear Kot, Last Wednesday, the day my father was buried, was the worst day I've had in my life. I never wish to live to see another day like it. My people are making me sit "shiva" with them, so I spend my days with them. Also I am not allowed to shave. But apparently one does not "sit" on Saturdays, so tonight when I leave them I shall shave. . . . After sunset I am free, so will meet as usual at the Campbells.

I have had a letter from Mary Cannan to say she has finally decided *not* to live with Gilbert as he wants to live with her and at the same time have his young girl—to this she objects.

Well, till Sunday, 7 o'clock, Etoile. MARK GERTLER

To Carrington

Saturday, February 1917 *Penn Studio, Hampstead*

My dear Friend, Your letter this morning gave me new life; it was almost essential for me to get a letter from you this morning. Thank you so much. How sorry I was to be so wretched with you on Friday, but I have suffered so much, not so much because of the loss of my father, but for pity of my people and especially my mother. Oh, you can have no idea what I have gone through this week. To see my mother, whom I love so much, in such misery, crying and wailing aloud over the coffin that contained my father and her companion for over forty years, was a sight that nearly broke my spirits for ever. However, I am glad to say that I comforted her quite a lot, as hard as she clung to the coffin, so hard did I cling to her, declaring my passionate love to her and kissing her with all my might; but, dear Carrington, it was terrible. Never shall I forget this moment and certain other moments of this black week. The thought of my mother upsets me to the core—I can't bear it—and my brothers—they suffered silently, but awfully. I tell you these terrible things so that you may know why I am so unhappy. But how good it was to see your dear self again on Thursday. You bring with you such sunshine for me—my greatest troubles melt away as soon as I see your beautiful person. Thank you so much for saying that you will see a lot of me next week. How good that is to look forward to, how happy that will make me. But will you forgive me, dear, if when I am with you I seem sad and cold and unable to express myself. It will only be because I am sad and also because *I am always nervous and awkward in your presence and tongue-tied.* I have underlined this sentence because I want you *always* to bear it in mind. Then you always will understand why I am so curious in your presence and you will not get irritated with me and censure me. . .[1]

Yours with love MARK GERTLER

[1] The following letter from Carrington throws some light on the awkwardness that was developing between them:

25 March 1917 *Hurstbourne Tarrant, Nr Andover, Hants.*

Dear Mark, . . . But I think if we had a much broader relationship like old friends which nothing would move, I should not fear to hurt you, and you would not feel so nervous. I want you to meet my friends and share my interests more, not be cynical about them and make me keep them inside myself. This is rather my sin as I seldom take you with me, or tell you what I think and do. But I will in the future, only you must be very honest and not pretend to care and then go and say to Monty: "They are no good, they don't really feel things. How I dislike these people who only want life to be amusing." Because I know

To Carrington

Friday, April 1917 *The Mill House, Cholesbury*

My dear Friend, The trouble with Monty was momentary—it has passed, and our friendship is as before. He is really a most interesting companion. He always astounds me with his learning and knowledge and I learn ever so much from him.

He knows every bird, every flower, and all history. As I know mighty little about these things, I feel thankful for his information. He has also been translating some Latin poems to me, by Catullus, who seems to have influenced Donne quite a lot. They sound very good. I have been reading quite a lot, but only rather second-rate stuff but which teaches me quite a lot, just like second-rate pictures do sometimes.

I find Gissing and Gorky, however, quite good. Gissing is really almost great at moments, but never quite. Anyhow, he was quite a worthy fellow. Why should I be sarcastic because you like Plato?

As for trousers, forgive me for having grumbled—I don't really mind. *I* may even take to wearing a skirt!

I met Roger Fry the other day and he told me he was having a show soon of copies or translations by artists of past pictures. He asked me to do one, as I very much liked the idea and always wanted to do something of the sort. I have started a small copy of a Cézanne—whether I shall finish it in time for the show I don't know, as I cannot hurry. I hope when I return to London, if the army doesn't claim me, to set to work again. Lately I have been unable to work much as I have *been* far too preoccupied with life itself and the problems of life. These troublesome thoughts have put my work for the time being in the shade. As long as they go on I don't suppose I shall be able to do any continuous work. I am passing through terrible changes. I don't know what awaits me the other side, but I am not frightened. But in the meantime I am suffering much—more than you can imagine. Veil after veil I keep tearing off my eyes and the disclosures are more and more terrible. What I see is ghastly, almost too much to bear. MARK GERTLER

To Carrington

Monday, April 1917 *The Mill House, Cholesbury*

Dear Carrington, I am staying on here after all. I am longing to get back to my picture, but it is so very beautiful today. I have enjoyed my week-end immensely. I am very happy.

---

many people you would never guess would love in their way just as passionately as you do—only sometimes a different way. Jack's cynicism is quite all right but one rather believes it in time—it does dent into the brain—and Saxon [Turner] and James S[trachey] do become rather ridiculous people and not real, which they are just as much as Kot and Monty. Heavens, it is almost a sermon! . . .

CARRINGTON

Perhaps I shall be able to do a few sketches for future pictures, but more likely I shall just lounge in the sun and read. We have been reading Shelley's life. What a remarkably beautiful life it was. I am in love with him.

The woods are most beautiful here now. The flowers are really coming out now. Yesterday we startled an owl out of her nest in one of the Tring woods! Up she flew—very silently—a beautiful orange brown. There were two eggs at the foot of a tree. We waited for her to return but she didn't. In the same wood also there was a beautiful shaped tree—a twin tree—like lovers embracing. They clung to each other with such passion, their muscular thighs entwined. Nothing but death could part them. Happy lovers. Only we poor humans are torn roughly apart, our souls, heedlessly, left bleeding. But life is good since there are such enchanted woods to wander in and the sun. Yesterday at tea our happiness was spoiled for an hour or two, by second-rate company. Nigel Playfair[1] and Co.

Oh! But I am happy now, and I hope you are too. I hope your friendship with Lytton is a happy one. I shouldn't like to feel that you are unhappy there. The woods remind me of you MARK GERTLER

To Carrington

18 April 1917 *Penn Studio, Hampstead*

Dear Carrington, Thanks for your letter. I in no way blame you for anything that's happened. We have done well to part at last, and this time it does seem the end of that long and terrible struggle.

I shall commence right away to build up my future life, brick by brick, and I have hopes. My work will be the basis. From now onwards my life will be a more decent and spiritual thing than it's ever had a chance to be before.

I hope you too will find yourself soon on your feet and with a better knowledge of your mind and feelings.

Last night I told *everything* to Kot and Monty. I had to. They are my only friends and they are to help me with my future.

I shall not of course tell anybody else.

With my best wishes to you, I end this MARK GERTLER

P.S. Please send me my Greco when you have done with it.[2]

[1] The actor and producer.

[2] The following letter from Carrington is probably her reply:

[*1917*]

I am so sorry I made you wretched last night. Only don't you see you never go without a thing you want when it would make me less miserable.

You knew well enough how I felt. You could have avoided all that dreadfulness by just letting me go away quietly. And then you make yourself terribly injured. It is not that I do not love you, it is that I was sad and could not make love to you.

To Carrington

24 April 1917 *Penn Studio, Hampstead*

My dear Carrington, I cannot help writing to thank you for bringing me back to life, by giving me again your friendship. Seeing how it would shatter your spirit if I killed myself in the body, I decided, if only for your sake, to go on, but in spirit I was dead—nothing mattered to me. Now I can go on again. Today the warm sunshine is beautiful again.

You will in no way find me a hindrance. In fact, I hope to be of help to you. Trust me fully. Treat me like a brother. That's what I am to you now—a loving brother. I have taken my right place in relation to you.

In the meantime I am changing, I am being reborn, I am really beginning to feel my way now. I am beginning to feel now the reality of the abstract—the spiritual—one must be sooner or later *absolutely* self-contained. This is what I am struggling for. Dependence on people—on love—brings disaster. As yet I am dependent on you, therefore incomplete. Gradually, I shall grow more and more into myself, till at last I shall be *free*!

You have been wonderful lately. Really there is no one I care more for as a *person* than you. I can't tell you how much you've moved me these last few days. I must confess, I never knew how splendid you were. And do forgive me for all the suffering I caused you. The shock was too great for me. Now I am thankful for what has happened, and if you will be able to go on giving me the tiniest bit of friendship for some time yet, I shall be quite happy. As yet I cannot do without that tiny bit. So be kind and let me have it a while longer. Perhaps quite soon I shall be able to release you altogether. I can't as yet, as I am not quite fully reborn or self-contained, so I must perhaps prey on your kindness.

Well, Eiffel Tower, *1.30 Wednesday.* MARK GERTLER

To Carrington

28 April 1917 *Penn Studio, Hampstead*

My dear friend, Thank you ever so much for your letter. It was particularly important to me because it shows that *you too* care about our new friendship! . . .

When one is in sorrow one feels isolated curiously, and to be forced into another's animal passion suddenly makes it almost a nightmare.

Your interest in me frankly ceases when I am sad not about you or our relationship. But dear friend I know you cannot help it because you love me too much, so do not think I blame you in this letter. I am wrong I suppose not to have more control over my feelings.

I will come in one evening, perhaps Friday, to Monty's. But I won't see you alone till Monday next when we'll go out together. Please don't be sad about me for I do love you, and you know it really, only my way is so far from yours.
Your affectionate CARRINGTON

When I want to know what is right and what wrong *for me* I have only to think of you and somehow I know. And more and more you will help me. I cannot express here what I really feel and what a mass of beauty is being just now created in my soul. Some day, when we are together, perhaps the spirit will move me, and I shall be able to express it all to you. Then you will be amazed at what sort of stuff there is being created inside me just now. And for all this I have you to thank. I hope some day also to be able to tell you how deeply you have moved me lately, with your goodness to me during this crisis. When we meet I joke and talk nonsense for fun, because after all I am young and high-spirited, but under all this there is immense stuff inside me, which I am quivering to tell you and hope I shall now in the future with this much freer relationship that we now have.

Yes, we must now set to and paint.

I am simply full of new ideas for painting and sculpture. Will you please, when you have finished your Giotto, give it to me as a remembrance of this wonderful present? I should love it.

I know, dear friend, only too well how you suffered last week-end, and how it hurt. It tore my heart to see you, but I was helpless. But now it is over, so be happy—please remember that I have never been so happy and full as now. And as time goes on I will make you happier and help you in every way.

I am afraid I have not fully expressed what I feel, but some day I will tell you more, far, far, more.

Please remember me to Alix.[1] I like her so much. Ever your friend

MARK GERTLER[2]

[1] Alix Sargant-Florence, who later married James Strachey.

[2] The following letter from Carrington relates to this period:

[*1917*]

I am miserable, Mark, to think my selfishness in being happy this last week has made you wretched now. But I am sure it is impossible for us to part always. I shall only try later, if you still wish it, to spend more of my life with you. But I think it would be unfair if I promised to live with you, because I do not think I ever could. Do not tell Brett please this time.

Yes, it is my work that comes between us, but I cannot put that out of my life because it is too much myself now. If I had not my love for painting I should be a different person.

I understand, but I think a few months spent together in a year is worth it—but you do not think so. Later perhaps we might spend longer together. I really am certain I could never live with you sexually day after day. Only instead of a week like we have just spent, I see no reason why another summer it should not be a few months—we could *not* work better together. Do not try and believe it! I at any rate could not work at all if I lived with you every day.

It is because you do want me sexually that you are miserable. Do not deceive yourself otherwise you would not be so miserable seeing that only my corporeal body has left you.

Oh why did we ever leave those woods that Friday night? You understood me then for the first and only time.

Well I leave it to you. I wish to God I was not made as I am. CARRINGTON

S. S. Koteliansky

Oil painting ($36 \times 25\frac{1}{2}$ in.) 1917

Reproduced by permission of Mrs St John Hutchinson

The Acrobats

Bronze ($23\frac{1}{2} \times 16\frac{1}{2} \times 12\frac{1}{2}$ *in.*) 1917

Reproduced by permission of the Tate Gallery

To Carrington

15 May 1917 *Penn Studio, Hampstead*

Dear Carrington, I do indeed deserve to be punished for not writing to you as I promised, I am afraid I have no definite excuse to offer either. I could not get into a letter-writing mood. Also I suffer lately spells of most profound gloom, and the heat oppressed me, and I found the beauty of the country under this hot sun too intense to bear. To me intense beauty is painful. I can't bear it—such is my nature. Therefore I always suffer in the spring. I love the spring to a point of hatred! People would hardly believe it, but it is quite true, that, sometimes, on a beautiful spring day, I inwardly curse its beauty and the sun and I maliciously pray for rain and greyness!! Therefore I did not write. I wanted to wait for a good mood, so that I could write something that would show you how much I love our friendship, and how inexpressibly important it is to me—my development—my art—my everything. Thank you so much for your letter, for all your kindness, in fact. I enjoyed our last evening so much. How nice of you to read *King Lear* to me. You have no idea how much I enjoyed it and our talk and everything. You must read more to me and I to you.

I like your wood block very much and I shall look forward to seeing the painting of it.

I hope you will come and stay at Cholesbury this week-end. I shall be quite disappointed if you don't, because I think it is a pity not to spend more time together in the country. If you liked, we could even stay on a couple of days after Monty has gone. Later, I hope, you will come and stay a week with me at Wittering. I always think our relationship has one fault and that is we do not contrive to be in the country enough together in the summer—just when the beautiful weather comes, we are, as if on purpose, torn apart. Perhaps this year we might try, if you cared enough, to spend a few weeks together somewhere. But we can discuss that when we meet. I liked very much staying with Alix, she is so nice and so interesting to talk to. But I am afraid I was a little too critical in my talks with her. I should like to see more of her. Sunday we, Monty and I, motored over to see her. He also liked her very much.

I went to the Omega[1] today and liked the copies rather and had an interesting conversation with Roger Fry.

I am working hard on my "Bathing". If I succeed in getting a "certain something" into it that I want, it will be a great picture—I think, too, I shall get it. . . .

Please remember me to Lytton and tell him that I quite understand the mistake and I shall be pleased to have tea with him any time if he lets me know.

I am full of work—in this new picture I intend to make a definite step forward. But it is terrible hard work. I want to step right forward now on

[1] The Omega workshops.

all that I have discovered these last two years. My "Fruit Stall" commenced one period and this "Bathing" commences another. I wish I could describe in words what it is I am after, but it is impossible, so I won't even try. When you see it you will know. But how appallingly few people understand the worth of my work! I was so encouraged today by Roger Fry's appreciation and understanding of my work and especially my statue, which so few people can make anything of. *But I assure you that all that I have done so far is mere "child's play" to that which is coming!*

And *you* are going to help me. You have no idea how stimulating our relationship is to me and my work.

Your friend with love MARK GERTLER

To Carrington

7.30, Tuesday, June 1917 *The Eiffel Tower*

Carrington Dear, . . . Don't bother about my health, I shall soon be all right again. But you must know that it is impossible for me ever to be really well because my nervous output is so great. My body, although a fairly strong one, cannot bear the strain, but I feel that for me it is worth while always to be rather run down and get the best out of myself than to be well and robust at the cost of my work and spiritual life. Of course if I could manage to keep quite fit and to live my nervous spiritual life at the same time it would be ideal, but I am afraid that is impossible, in fact they don't go together somehow. Finally, I am happier at work though worried and ill in London than when I am feeling lazy and well and unproductive in the country—I soon get bored. No, I must live this nervous strained life always, always, and always. I must feel worried and ill—that is my fate. Therefore never feel worried when I look pale and haggard, it is part of me.

Dear person, don't talk about "worrying me for my help", because I am proud and happy to be able to be of use to you. Dear, dear girl, I would do *anything* to help you. *Never, never,* hesitate to ask me for help of any sort. If ever you want me, I shall always come to you, at a moment's notice.

I know you are going through troublesome times now and I feel your troubles as I would my own, believe me.

Last night, we both got into a mood. That is inevitable, as inevitable as rain, and we must be wise enough to treat it as such and never let such moods delude us into thinking that there is not good in our friendship.

Well, dearest friend, we must fight on and on and not despair. There are better times coming. Ever yours MARK GERTLER

To Carrington

June 1917 *Eleanor House, West Wittering, Nr Chichester*

Dear Carrington, It is indeed beautiful here. I am sitting now in the shed writing to you. We arrived last evening. We went for a stroll by the sea after supper and talked interestingly till quite late. This morning we went to the bathing place, but only Monty bathed as I was not feeling up to it. However, we both lay for hours on the sand enjoying the hot sun on our naked bodies. I am feeling much better in health now and hope to be able to bathe this afternoon, as we are going again. I keep thinking how you would like this place, it is so hot just now.

Yesterday, Friday morning I went by arrangement to Nevinson's to get some lessons on lithography. Schwabe[1] was also there for the same reason. Afterwards I called them back to my studio where we had an interesting discussion on art, which I enjoyed. I am feeling more and more the call to paint. My only ambition just now is to get into a sort of state where I can concentrate my whole energy on work. I have a great deal to do and I definitely feel the call to do it. . . .

Yours ever

MARK GERTLER

To Carrington

15 June 1917 *Eleanor House, West Wittering*

Dearest Carrington, Why so unhappy? But I think I understand. I wish I could help you more. I think I could, if you would let me, if you confided in me, and trusted me more. You seem to me too dear a creature to be unhappy, ever; *you* must be shielded, *you* must not suffer. . . .

If Monty had his car here, I should have made him take me to you at once and we should have made you gay. Yes, if only you were here, or I with you! But the Demon of life seems to take especial pleasure in tearing you from me. It has always been so.

Please do not burden yourself with the thought that you have made a mess of my life. It is not true; besides, my life is only just beginning. For proof that you have not messed my life, you have only to look at my work, at the progress I've made these last few years—that I've suffered is true, but don't you think that I am the sort of person that would always suffer? Carrington or no Carrington, I should always find something or somebody to suffer about. Besides, where is there a sensible or sensitive person who does not suffer? No, please don't blame yourself. I do not blame you. We are all in the same rocky boat—being constantly tossed, and shaken, by that Demoniacal power we call Life. Only now and then is there calm—a lull in the sea. At such moments we have to take breath, and gather strength for the next storms, and for these moments I suppose we ought even to be, or try to be, thankful.

[1] Randolph Schwabe, later head of the Slade.

Now for lighter things.

Wednesday evening Monty and I went to *Figaro*—in the stalls. I enjoyed the music, but it was a nervous business, because everybody was there, and I felt nervous especially in the intervals, when one walked about and talked to people. I was in fact almost too nervous to enjoy the opera. Afterwards the Jowitts, the Hutchinsons, and Monty and myself went back to the room. . . .

Thursday I had to go down to Battersea to see about my statue. It will not be completed before a fortnight, but I am so excited. Oh! you have no idea what wonderful things could be done in sculpture. They can gild bronze, silver it—gold and silver, mix metals, different sort of patinas. Wonderful, wonderful. Oh! what ambitious things I would like to create, and I think I shall! On my way back I went to the India Museum to see the bronzes there. How they inspired me. I think my statue will look beautiful in bronze![1]

Ever your friend MARK GERTLER

To Richard Carline

12 July 1917 *Penn Studio, Hampstead*

My dear Carline, My picture, the "Bathing", is giving me more trouble than anything I've ever worked on before. This I think is not only because the subject is a more difficult one but because I feel that I simply *must* get something new and better into this picture than I have got before into my work. Even as it stands, I believe it to be the best thing I've done, but God knows when I shall actually finish it—if ever. In the mean-time I feel very tired, and wretched generally. You have no idea how much I suffer. Some day, perhaps, I shall be able to tell you more.

Apart from my big picture, I have painted a still-life of tulips, which I think is rather beautiful. Also I am excited about my blue statue, as it is being cast into bronze! But the expense—my God! £22! This will ruin me, but I *must* have it in bronze.

The subject of women is such an immense one that I won't even attempt to discuss it with you by letter—we shall talk about it when we meet. Yours ever MARK GERTLER

To S. S. Koteliansky

29 August 1917 *Garsington Manor, Oxford*

My dear Kot, This morning I am very depressed. Yesterday a still-life that I had been working on for some time came to nothing. This of course is inevitable at my present stage. God knows if ever I shall actually finish

[1] Probably the "Acrobats", now in the Tate Gallery (Plate 12, facing page 145).

a picture again. Everything I do comes to nothing. This is simply because my mind has leapt into a higher consciousness, and I am not yet able to paint up to it. I might repeat the old song "My heart is good, but my hands won't let me". Only hands instead of feet, and it expresses absolutely my present state. But all this, as you will no doubt understand, is healthy and shows signs of progress. But it is very much a struggle and sometimes very depressing. I assure you however that my present failures are far more interesting than my past finished pictures. But all this doesn't in the least express really what I am going through just now, I mean mentally.

MARK GERTLER

To Carrington

August 1917 — *Garsington Manor, Oxford*

My dear Carrington, . . . Externally, I find everything very much as usual. It is peaceful, soothing. The weather has been awful ever since I arrived, yet I have found it pleasant and shall be almost sorry when my stay has come to an end. Besides the usual household, there is only Aldous Huxley and a younger brother of Murry's, rather a nice boy of fourteen who is learning farming on Philip's farm. Clive comes in occasionally and I have met Freddie Gonne.[1] She has asked me to tea one day. Today I experimented in water colours with Brett and discussed excitedly various problems of painting. Apart from this I have as yet done no work. It is a pity the sun is not here, because there is so much to paint around the pond. Oh! yes, the "Pro" is here too. . . .

I will not attempt to tell you what has been going on inside me, but my mind has been busy at work. I do not want to write about it, firstly because I would be unable to describe my thoughts in words, and secondly because the very attempt would cheapen what is dear to me. But externally, as I have already said, all is calm and uneventful here, yet pleasant. . . .

I am yours ever — MARK GERTLER[2]

[1] Fredegond Maitland, poetess.

[2] This letter provoked the following from Carrington:

19 August 1917 — *60 Frith Street, Soho, W.*

Dearest Mark, I just wanted to write at once and reassure you that I did not feel for a moment that you were being unfriendly when I read your letter in bed this morning. I suddenly looked back at a complete picture and saw the whole thing—saw that we were both friends who loved each other. Because right away I only felt how good that he is getting detached and happy and in the country, and I was so glad of that that I did not mind about not seeing you—only now later I am disappointed rather. But the main issue is so much better, and I am more than glad that you are happy in the country. Dearest Mark, if you saw the inside of me and knew how much I care, you would not have to write as you did and ask me not to be angry. Why should I be, dear one? Do you think I want to keep you unhappy and in love with me? I will be proud of you. I love you and your future work so much, and you will be a tremendous artist. Lately I have felt unhappy at not helping you more. When we are older, and all this is less painful, I shall tell you every single thing, and how hard it has been.

To Richard Carline

2 September 1917 *Garsington Manor, Oxford*

My dear Carline, I must read Goethe after what you say, but there is so little time for reading. I long to read more, but I simply can't find the time. The more I go on, the more does my painting absorb me. Really in order to paint at all, one must give oneself altogether and sacrifice everything. So it seems to me. Yet it is hard to give up some other things—reading especially. You see, I work all day, and in the evening one must see a human being.

I am struggling furiously with a still-life. But I can bring nothing to a finish nowadays. I am too particular—nothing satisfies me. I have started many little things but they have all come to nothing and caused me much anguish. Excellent form of exercise—"still-life"—I shall have to do many just now. It is through them that I hope to get that "something" that I am looking for. My head is full of new things about painting now and sculpture—so wonderful, oh, but so difficult. I paint marvellous pictures in my head and erect wonderful statues, huge and world-moving—but when it comes to doing it with the hand, it's another matter! Then I am also so much distracted by "things" in my life, so disturbing, so depressing, I suffer agonies of repression. And sometimes I look with longing into the pond here! Oh! it's a struggle—but one must go on, one *must* do something in spite of all the Devilish perversity and interference of the Demon of Life!

Yours ever MARK GERTLER

To Carrington

12 September 1917 *Garsington Manor, Oxford*

Dear Carrington, . . . I am still here, as you see. Would you believe it but this place suits me admirably! Really I am as happy here as I, with my peculiar temperament, can be. I like it so much that I have—for the first time in my life—a horor of returning to London! If I had a good place to work in here I assure you I would stay on. Philip talks of turning a beautiful barn he has into a studio for me. This is certainly tempting, but I have asked him to wait a bit before I decide.

I shall go back to London in October and see how London feels before

---

I am glad you like Oxford so much and the "feel" of it. It is so ancient, and also that feeling of a city where men sought to achieve great things. I always feel a body of human beings, wonderful tragic men, whom no one ever heard of, more wonderful perhaps than men like Shelley and Keats or Dr Johnson, who died, or passed away their time, in a foreign country, or in little towns and never achieved anything. It occurred to me first in a book called *Urn Burial* by Sir Thomas Browne, where musing over some ancient urns he discourses on the fragments of the dead, and says how many more amazing people may have lived than those we know of, and passed into oblivion—and Oxford has that for me—and the Byzantian book. What a discovery! . . . CARRINGTON

I decide. But I love working all day here and then the pleasant meal in the evening, with either the pianola or reading afterwards, and if one's work goes wrong one can seize upon someone to walk with at any moment. And Brett! She is invaluable, she is so good. She understands me and my work or what I want to do better than anyone—I do love her for this. You can't think how much she helps me, even to domestic details—such as washing my hair. Once she even came on her own account to scrub my back in the bath! This place has spoilt me! How shall I live without all this now! Brett has real talent too.

About my work there is so much to tell that I shall say nothing. Marvellous new and wonderful things have passed through my brain, but actually I have managed only to spoil a number of canvases. Of all the debris there are just two little canvases that are perhaps worth looking at—two still-lifes, but not much. Now I have taken up the pond once again. Oh! Carrington, real painting is so wonderful, but so hard—so devastating. I suffer headaches—I have worked terribly hard—my eyes ache—and nothing to show! My friends will be bored with me in the future, because I have got into the habit of painting the same thing over and over again. Yes it's all exercise—study, experimenting—wonderful internally, but no external results—and this will go on for how long? I don't know, I don't care. I am furiously interested in still-life again—wonderful exercise, I shall do thousands! How dull everybody will say, but I don't care. I may even do everything I've ever done again!

Aldous has gone now—there are no visitors. Brett for the moment is in London to see Zena. She returns today. Last week-end there was Sheppard,[1] a nice man, but curious—sometimes quite suddenly surprisingly critical. Before that there was Murry—"A String in the Wind"—shifty, backboneless, fearful, ill, but rather nice and pathetic. Of course Asquith alights and his family. I don't like them—they distress me. Elizabeth is awful. Lord Harcourt also asked me at once to come over to see his "pictures"! I declined—hateful man. . . . Fredegond and Gerald[2]—dear me, I like them. What attacks on the Bloomsburians. If you only know how sick I am of the talk, talk, talk—as for the "Bloomsburians", the very sound of that word makes me sick. They don't let *you* off in their criticism either. As for James,[3] he is always annihilated with one straight blow from the shoulder. I have learnt that Alix is desperately in love with James—alas poor Alix! What a sickly thing love is!

I have been reading Rousseau's *Confessions* and Sir Thomas Browne and now I am reading Green's English History. In the evening we are having readings aloud of Shakespeare, Henry James, the Old Testament. But I don't like being read to really. I can't take it in. There is a wonderful book on Cézanne here, lent by Clive—we are well off for reproductions. Also I study French three quarters of an hour a day with Mademoiselle. We are doing Voltaire now. We have most amusing evenings sometimes.

[1] Later Sir John Sheppard, Provost of King's College, Cambridge.
[2] Gerald Shove, who married Fredegond Maitland.
[3] James Strachey.

Fancy dress and dancing. Fredegond is wonderful. Oxford is still a great pleasure to us. The other day we saw quite the best Charlie Chaplin—*Easy Street*. . . .

I am afraid that your passion for L.S. estranges me more and more from you—I can't stomach it at all. It makes it almost impossible to see you. I am sorry, but I can't help it. I am afraid that I don't look forward to seeing you at all. It's poisoning my feelings and belief in you. I don't feel the same about you as I used to. Also I think now that you have been so unnecessarily cruel to me in the past. It's difficult for me to forgive you. However, never mind. MARK GERTLER [1]

To Carrington

4 October 1917 *Penn Studio, Hampstead*

Dear Carrington, It has been difficult for me to write because honestly, I do not feel the prospect of returning to you as at all enticing. I get on so much better without you. I don't see why the future should be any better than the past, and the past visualised in perspective is pretty ghastly. You have treated me abominably, Carrington—always until the last moment—and it is hard not to hate you for it. Your attitude to me has been most unhuman, and brutal, your selfishness appals me—it is terrifying. And you will be just the same in the future—you can't help it. You are made like that, and I don't like you for it. By your treatment of me you have done me ever so much harm. You have sown seeds of bitterness inside me, by your brutality. I have to spend all my time now undoing what you have done to me. And even if I could forgive and believed that you would

[1] Carrington was finding it difficult to accept a break in their friendship.

21 September 1917 *c/o Mrs Elford, Beery Farm, Boscastle, N. Cornwall*

Dear Mark, I am writing to you immediately—your letter has only just come this instant. Oh Mark, dearest friend, I was so glad to get it that I almost cried with joy, although it hurt me also. Today when I was gathering wood in the valley I knew that you would write this morning, yet I was surprised—I knew I must not complain. But if you only knew the number of times I longed to write and implore you to forgive me and write again. You need not dread meeting me in October because, will you believe it, we shall at last be friends I think. I have learnt so much now. I am humbled like the man in the Psalms "even unto the dust"—and do not hate me for my cruelty, it was impossible I should know what you felt. If I could tell you everything you would be sorry for me. It was not easy. There, now I'll tell you! When Monty washed your hair I was jealous, and when I read in your letter that Brett cares for you so well, again I felt miserable. Because I longed so often to look after you tenderly, to make you feel how good it was to be cared for, and like a nightmare I never could move hand or foot. The effort when I did get near to it was like strangulation. But I won't go on about this. Only be merciful, do not hate me.

I am so glad in reading your letter to know how happy you are, and about your painting—so splendid. What does it matter if nothing but exercises are produced for years if at fifty you produce work like Cézanne or Goya? . . .

CARRINGTON

be more human in the future, I still would hesitate in returning, since you had the bad taste to fall in love with that half-dead man. That alone finishes me—that proves how antipathetic to me you must be *au fond*. It proves also that there is something in you which I must always hate.

So what's the good? You are incapable of understanding a person like me. If your excuse to all this is that you did not love me, my answer is that it is not enough excuse for the torture you put me through. You treated me not merely as a person who does not love one, but like an enemy, as if you hated me, and in fact I absolutely refuse to believe that you ever cared for me a straw!

I will not write more because it is very painful to be so disillusioned about you, whom I loved so much and so beautifully—I could write volumes about how you spoilt my life. However in spite of all this I *will* try not to hate you and to forgive you. I will even see you sometimes, if you wish it. Yes, you can come and see my work whenever you like.

Yours sincerely MARK GERTLER

To Carrington

1 November 1917 *Garsington Manor, Oxford*

My dear Carrington, I am sorry to be away as I should have liked to have seen you. I came here last week because I was very anxious to work out some small charcoal studies, one a sort of clarification of my "Bathing"—upon which I am still working, and another of my Shop Window idea, I have finished the first ("Bathing") and am now working on the second.

I return to London on Monday next with Brett. But I am afraid that I shall have nothing to show you, as I have sent all my summer work away to exhibitions—the Omega and the London Group. But you will see them there. Do come and see me though, one teatime—any day after next Monday. But let me know soon when you will come. Perhaps you will have time to write me a longish letter about yourself before I return. I should very much like to hear your news.

I have already sold three of my Garsington studies for £25 each!! They are selling like hot cakes. But I shall tell you more when we meet next week.

Forgive my last letter—I don't blame you for anything really, and I feel quite friendly to you. I always shall whatever happens. You may trust me quite fully. Thank you very much for the kind letter you wrote me during the summer. I assure you, in spite of my detachment, they gave me great pleasure. I only hope that in the future I shan't worry you and interfere with your relations and affairs—but I am sure I shan't now as I feel differently about it all. So write me *at once* and tell me you too are friendly and not angry and that you understand that my detachment was necessary to me, and my bitterness quite natural to me with my temperament under the circumstances. Ever your friend MARK GERTLER

To Carrington

15 November 1917 *Penn Studio, Hampstead*

Dear Carrington, This morning I had a letter from Ottoline, a good letter; it rather moved me. It made me feel sorry, in fact, that I was slightly anti the other night. I really like her very much and value her friendship, and the idea of Garsington means quite a lot to me now. I miss it, even Brett's sisterly and "artistic" companionship. She says she loves you, and hopes that you will become friends again, but she feels that you do not trust her enough.

I was unnecessarily angry the other night. I ought to have waited to hear about it all myself. However, as you say, it is better left alone. I am only writing to tell you, as it were, that I feel I was rather unfair that night to them at Garsington and that I am sorry, because I am anxious in spite of your differences with the place to have a "good attitude" towards them, and *au fond* my attitude is a good one! . . .

Yours with love MARK GERTLER

To S. S. Koteliansky

26 December 1917 *Garsington Manor, Oxford*

My dear Kot, . . . I can't settle down to anything. If I do it is more likely to be writing. . . . I have written to Carrington asking her to forgive my last letter, but she has not yet answered. This alone makes me nervous and anxious. I sometimes think my real life will not commence before my passion for Carrington ends. But God knows when it will end. This passion of mine may yet ruin me. It makes life so hateful to me—so ugly, so crooked. . . . MARK GERTLER

To Carrington

29 December 1917 *Garsington Manor, Oxford*

Dear Carrington, I am glad that you were able to forgive me—I'd hate an atmosphere of Gilbert and Mary sort of anger between us, so much.

I am returning to London on Monday next, when I hope to be able to continue my work. Lately I have been prevented from work by certain mental problems other than painting and to my mind equally important that I was anxious to think out. Now I think I am clear enough in my head to recommence my work—but I don't know.

Murry, whom I got to like here, has left now. Berty Russell was also here. Now there is only Aldous, besides the usual household.

I am busy reading a big book on Keats, which interests me immensely; also I am reading Chekhov and Euripides. . . .

Yours sincerely MARK GERTLER

To Carrington

Sunday evening, 10 February 1918 — *Penn Studio, Hampstead*

Dear Carrington, I feel in the mood to write to you. It is just before dinner time. I am about to go out and dine with—who?—Marie Beerbohm![1] Yes, Marie of all people! at the Eiffel Tower.

Last night I had a good evening. I have a new friend, Suggia. Do you know her? She is beautiful and she plays Bach on the cello!! The cello is my favourite instrument and Bach my favourite composer. So you can imagine! She played to me last night. We also go to dances together; she dances excellently. It would take volumes to tell you what happens to us at these occasions.

But last night as she played I thought of you! and a good attitude came over me for you. I won't tell you what I thought, because you would become conceited! Some day perhaps I shall tell you! But I think I know now what it is I love in you. I thought it all out as I walked home in a pleasant mood from Chelsea (no taxis). I knew this meant a letter. But you have forgotten me now, have you?

I am working hard, but I will not go into painting now because that also would need volumes. Besides we have parted now, and this letter is superfluous and will no doubt bore you, so I shall stop, although I am in a mood to chatter on for hours.

Well, dear little person, my love to you. I never forget you and shall never stop loving you! MARK GERTLER

To Carrington

20 February 1918 — *Penn Studio, Hampstead*

Dear Carrington, I am afraid you have an exaggerated notion of my dissipations and evenings. I have been about twice to the Café Royal this month. Otherwise I have been out, one or two evenings, with some quite nice young men, whose company and gaiety and youth I have enjoyed, and felt the better for. It was such a relief after always being with people so much older than myself. Really you must not take all this seriously. You surely know me well enough to realise that my internal life will always go on, and develop, and struggle, and strive for decent things. What does it matter what I do in the evenings? Of course if there were better things or people to see, I should certainly prefer it.

It was a great blow to me, your moving to the country. If you were here it would be different. But as it is I never see you, and one must see somebody in the evenings. However I promise you not to drink or do anything of the sort, if it worries you, but please, always remember that that sort of thing is a superficial part of my nature, and that my real self never stops striving. If other people do not know this, *you* at any rate *must*. You must not be like —— who judges one by little parts, and turns her

[1] Max Beerbohm's sister.

back on one, because one "does not always carry one's soul on one's nose!" I am a complex being; there are many bad sides to my nature; but my real flame always burns brightly, and no wind or hurricane ever can extinguish it. Therefore, when you hear of, or see, a bad side, always try and remember *the side. My real being.*

I had not the vaguest notion that you were to be at Mary's party, otherwise I should not have turned up slightly drunk. Please forgive me.[1]

I am tired this morning so will you excuse me from writing you more about myself or my work? Only before I finish I should like to tell you how very anxious I am to build up a really strong friendship between us.

[1] After this party there was a fracas when Gertler attacked Lytton Strachey in the street, and Carrington had written to Gertler:

Sunday, February 1918 *The Mill House, Tidmarsh, Pangbourne*

Dear Mark, I was glad to hear from you this morning. I confess I was upset by that incident. Not so much about it but because I felt so responsible—that it resulted through a neglect of my duties to you, and lack of foresight on my part. I am rather worried about you altogether. What's to be done? Frankly I wish you had some better friends to keep you from getting dissipated, and wasting your time in the evenings. Monty is really not much good is he? I hate to hear of you at the cafés. It is just because I know you are worth more, and that more intelligent people like you would be friends with you. I am sure it is all too short, this life, to waste time in a boring way—and confess now you must be bored with those café people night after night? Perhaps I am wrong, but I hear from so many people of your careless evening life. Will you try, Mark, to get on with the other sort of people and not drink any more? I am not preaching, it did however upset me to see you drunk at Mary's party, and I felt it was so much my fault for leaving you for so long and making you unhappy. . . .

Tell me also when you next write more about your friend Suggia, the cellist. Remember I care always very much for you. Just as much as I used to. It is in no way changed and if you knew how much I felt your pains and grief it would lessen them for you. I shall look forward to seeing your work again next time I come to London. . . . CARRINGTON

Strachey's own account of the incident is as follows:

18 February 1918

. . . You've probably heard of the unfortunate occurrence in the purlieus of Ravenscourt Park, after M's party. Anything more cinematographic could hardly be imagined, and looking back it wears all the appearance of a bad dream. All the same it was at the time exceedingly painful, especially as a little more presence of mind on my part might have prevented the situation: but it all came about with a speed. Poor Mark! The provocation was certainly great and I am sorry for him. However, as he was obviously drunk, perhaps he was rather less conscious than one supposed. Characteristically, Maynard[1] came to the rescue, and eventually led him off, and pacified him, with amazing aplomb. Monty had already tried and completely failed; Carrington had fled, under the protection of Sheppard, who kept on repeating, during the height of the crisis, "Who is it? Who is it?" in a most pained voice; and Harry[2] supported my trembling form from the field. It was really an intervention of providence that they should all come up at the psychological moment, as otherwise Heaven knows what might have happened. . . .

The day after the incident Gertler went up to Strachey, who was lunching at the Eiffel Tower restaurant, and apologised. Strachey told him to think no more about it.

[1] John Maynard Keynes.

[2] H. T. J. Norton, to whom *Eminent Victorians* was dedicated.

You *must* help me, and understand me. You will never regret the trouble, because not only can *you* stimulate *me*, but I feel that *I* can help and stimulate *you* too! Only please do not allow too long periods to elapse between our meetings.

My love to you, dear friend. MARK GERTLER

To S. S. Koteliansky

18 February 1918 *Garsington Manor, Oxford*

My dear Kot, I feel better today. Yesterday I was terribly upset by a letter from Carrington. There was nothing much in it, but I did not like the tone, so I hastily wrote one of my abrupt letters back. Really until that relationship has in some way worked itself out I am a lost wretched creature. . . . My ambition now is somehow to have a place somewhere, perhaps in the country, where I can work without interruption for any length of time, because it is only when I am working and absorbed in my work that life is at all tolerable for me. . . . There is a limit to how much one can suffer. *Work is my only salvation*. . . . I think we shall drift apart very, very soon. It is like a dying candle which is nearly finished, but which shoots up every now and then, a brilliant flicker, more for the moment than it ever was when it was long and fresh, but still it is dying. So it is with my relations with Carrington. But the difference from the candle is that once it burnt steadily. Carrington and myself never, never had a *steady* flame. It was always "flickers" with long black agonising periods between. . . . MARK GERTLER[1]

[1] Clearly Gertler's friends found his doctrine of salvation through work was becoming too much of an obsession, to judge by the following from D. H. Lawrence:

21 February 1918 *Chapel Farm Cottage, Hermitage, Nr Newbury, Berks.*

Dear Gertler, . . . Then, as to work, I *don't* think that to work is to live. Work is all right in proportion: but one wants to have a certain richness and satisfaction in oneself, which is more than anything *produced*. One wants to *be*. I think we need, not to paint or write, but to have a liberation from ourselves, to become quite careless and free. And we need to go away, as soon as we can, right to a new scene, and at least for a bit, live a new life—you and Campbell and Kot and Shearman and Frieda and me—and whomsoever else you want—and in some queer way, by *forgetting* everything, to start afresh. We live now in such a state of tension against everything—*you* are also wound up in a dreadful state of resistant tension. Now I think, that between a few of us, this tension ought to go, we ought to be able to relax altogether, to be perfectly confident with each other, and free. As it is, if you meet me, at once there is a sort of tension between us, you holding out hard against me, I holding hard against you. I believe it wants only just a little change, and this tension of resistance could disappear, and we could be at peace with one another, at peace, and free, and spontaneous, no need to hold our own each against the other in a tension of self-conscious self-insistence. I believe this could be so between Shearman and Kot and Campbell and you and Frieda and me—a kind of fulfilment, as if we were all complete beings, and therefore all free by being together, as in a new world.

So I always want to have a plan of going away after the war—anywhere that is not England—perhaps Italy—going away and living in one place, all of us, at least for a while. But it is no good, if work, or love either, seems to you the

To Carrington

24 February 1918 *Garsington Manor, Oxford*

Dear Carrington, I am afraid that my last two letters were rather gushing and hasty. There is no reason why we should not meet when you come to town or even correspond. But there can be nothing much between us. You need not tell me things because *I know that you live with Lytton.* You are supposed to do so with other people too, but that I can hardly believe. But your living with Lytton Strachey, I confess quite frankly, does make it impossible for me.

I have to catch the post so cannot write more this time—I only felt that it was out of place of me to have written, now, so late in the day about being friends with you and so on.

Well I hope you will come and see me when you are in London, but write also when you feel like it. With love MARK GERTLER

To Carrington

2 March 1918 *Penn Studio, Hampstead*

Dearest Carrington, Thanks for your letter. I got the calling paper last Wednesday. I rushed to London at once and straight to the Recruiting Office, with the hopes that they would say it was a mistake again. But this time it was not a mistake. So I took out an appeal form the next morning (Thursday) and lunched with Monty and Jack for the purpose of filling it in. We are objecting on the grounds of my Austrian parentage, and anyhow, I have a conscientious objection to *fighting*, but I agreed to doing work of national importance, as it is quite hopeless to try and get off altogether. We also mentioned that I have been going to a farm lately, and that they are ready to take me there to work. You see the best of all would be if they let me go and work on Philip's farm.[1] That is what I am trying for first, as that would give me time to do some work of my own, but in any case the appeal gives us time to think and see what can be done. Anyhow I need not present myself on Monday now to join the Colours. I have put in my appeal yesterday (Friday) and I have to call in a few days to see if they consider that there are sufficient grounds for an appeal. After that I shall have to wait for the tribunal, which may drag on for some weeks, if I am lucky. In the meantime I have a breathing space, which is so important.

---

be-all and the end-all. Work and love are subsidiary. What one wants is a free, spontaneous, harmonious relation amongst ourselves, each of us being in some way a complete fulfilled being—whatever you think of this plan, we might try it for a holiday.

I should beware of Garsington. I believe there is something exhaustive in the air there, not so very restful. . . . D. H. LAWRENCE

[1] At Garsington.

Desmond MacCarthy is trying to get me something and also Lady Tredegar. People generally are being very nice and helpful about it and most sympathetic, which livens one up somewhat.

I will not depress you with how I feel about it all, but you can imagine. Painting was always my main support, and helped me to live through all my troubles. Now *that* is being taken from me also. Then just now, I was at a most thrilling stage of my development. It could not have come at a worse moment! You can't imagine what important discoveries I have been making for myself lately. People that have been with me this last month or so also felt it, and I have had many letters from them telling me so. Brett knows about my work, and now I have to leave it all in the middle and go and do God knows what! and come before tribunals, and talk to asses of men.

However, I am trying to bear up—and you must also; don't worry about it. Some day it will all be over. Then one can look forward to a period of painting, painting, painting. Already it gives me joy, the mere thought of it. In the meantime I am not wasting time—I am painting! It is a painful process, under my present state of mind, but I want at least to finish one of my studies before I have to go. I will keep you well informed of every detail that happens, and if suddenly something horrible happens, I will wire for you to come up.

Love MARK GERTLER

To Richard Carline

2 April 1918 *Garsington Manor, Oxford*

Dear Carline, I have finished at home in London the "Still-Life", and also Shearman's portrait, and started a plan of a large self-portrait, seen in my big mirror, with many reflections behind, and my revolving book-case, supporting a cerulean vase in front of the mirror. It is an interesting though complex subject, and in spite of it being so pleasant here, I am longing to get back to get on with it. Yours ever MARK GERTLER

To S. S. Koteliansky

[June 1918] *Garsington Manor, Oxford*

My dear Kot, I have heard also from Ottoline about Kerensky. She was at the Labour Conference and saw him. She was much impressed by him. For myself I confess to knowing nothing at all about the whole business, but it sounds interesting. Also I feel far too detached to understand that feeling *for a people* as a whole, as you feel about the Russians. It seems as uninteresting to me as many other sentiments.

I have had a letter from Lawrence.[1] He is wanting to know how it might suit him to be friends again with Ottoline, and in fact he suggests coming here and asks me to tell him what I feel about it. It puts me in a very difficult position. Ottoline particularly objects to Frieda. . . .

MARK GERTLER

To S. S. Koteliansky

[*15 July 1918*] *Garsington Manor, Oxford*

My dear Kot, This week-end has been crammed full. Mr and Mrs Snowden,[2] a Mr Whitehouse, M.P.,[3] Massingham,[4] Lady Margaret Sackville.[5] I am not really in a mood to give you a lively description of them. I have fallen into an apathetic mood from which I am unable to extricate myself. I can only say that Mr Whitehouse was the worst simply because he is a pure buffoon, though, I suppose, well-meaning. The conversations and discussions are still raging round Lytton Strachey's book. Everyone agrees that it is most wonderful, except the Bishop of Oxford, who asked the household if they had read that "mangy book *Eminent Victorians*". But even he thought it clever, nay brilliant. By the way I somehow very much like the Bishop of Oxford.[6] He is a nice man. We have all been reading Katherine's book *Prelude.* I thought it rubbishy, but the others say that, somehow, after reading it through, "it sticks in one's mind and then one suddenly realises that it *is* rather exquisite". Perhaps it is. Personally I've lost all sense of judgement. I am dazed into apathy by all the wonderful and "exquisite" books and other kinds of masterpieces that seem to come out every day like mushrooms in season. . . .

Murry wrote a scathing criticism of Sassoon's poems—Ottoline furious.

Best wishes MARK GERTLER

[1] The letter is as follows:

[*26 June 1918*] *Mountain Cottage, Middleton by Wirksworth, Derby*

Dear Gertler, I suppose you are at Garsington now. Is it nice? Perhaps we should like to come to London for a while, next month, to see you all again. We will come if I get that money from that beastly fund.

How is Ottoline now? Do you think she would like to see us again? Do you think we might be happy if we saw her again—if we went to Garsington? I feel, somehow, that perhaps we might. But tell me how it is—what you think.

We are alone again today for the first time for weeks—it is queer. I am very restless and at the end of *everything.* I don't work—don't try to—only just endure the days. There will either have to come a break outside or inside—in the world or in one's self.

Tell me about Garsington and Ottoline. Remember us both to her. If you feel like it, you can come up here from Garsington. You come from Oxford to Birmingham—Birmingham to Derby—and then you are soon here. If it attracts you at all, do come.

Frieda sends her love D. H. LAWRENCE

[2] Philip Snowden, Labour M.P., later Chancellor of the Exchequer, and his wife.

[3] John Howard Whitehouse, author of many books on education.

[4] H. W. Massingham, editor of the *Nation.*

[5] The poetess.

[6] Bishop Gore.

To S. S. Koteliansky

17 July 1918 *Garsington Manor, Oxford*

My dear Kot, . . . I have been working mostly in water colour, which is new and exciting. I am getting much out of that medium. I hope by the time I return to London to have a few saleable things done and so straighten myself financially. Lack of money gives the finishing touch to life in making it absolutely fifth-rate, tedious and altogether a bad tasteless joke. If I had the money, I could go on at any rate experimenting in different ways, but as it is, I must be covering canvas with paint because in that way alone I can get enough money to live. After all it is not pleasant to sponge on people. MARK GERTLER

To S. S. Koteliansky

19 July 1918 *Garsington Manor, Oxford*

My dear Kot, I think you are right in what you say about *Prelude,* but some people here still think that it leaves an "exquisite trace". It is a pity. I had a letter from Murry yesterday morning, just to say that he and Katherine are moving into a big house in Hampstead. He would like a drawing of mine. He says I promised him one—once. That's all! That same morning Ottoline got an angry letter from him in answer to one from her in which she expressed her unhappiness about his review of Sassoon.

You wonder how I can "harness" myself down to rules. Well, I find it good for my temperament to harness and regulate myself. Strange as it may seem, I wish I could do so more.

I have not heard from Lawrence. I think he must have been annoyed at the tone of my last letter. But it is something good for him to have got £50 from the Literary Fund. If you were willing I should quite like to go and stop with them for a short while. What do you think?[1]

[1] Two letters from Koteliansky about the Lawrences may be inserted here:
[*Tuesday*]

My dear Gertler, I do not scoff at the idea of our reunion according to your plan, but I want to tell you, if I haven't told you before, that it is simply impossible for me to meet the Murrys until a time comes in me when I could completely forget the wrong attitude that they had towards me. You see, I don't mind their false attitude to others, I could even excuse it, but I cannot, notwithstanding all my self-persuading, excuse their attitude to me. How could one? I gave them friendship, and they simply accepted it as something due to them. They took me as anyone other of their hundreds of friends—to receive.

But perhaps this is not the chief point. If you only knew what sometimes means the desire to be, to talk, to commune with one who understands, and how painful sometimes is loneliness (and still it is impossible to turn just to anyone, well, like Shearman or Hutchinson), you would realise that it is not so easy to meet again those who have been something to you, and ceased, of their own individual faults, to be.

I do not think Lawrence is cross with you. I am looking forward to next week.

Yes, I got a letter from Shearman. I am even going to stay with him and his people on August 15th for a week. He seems very troubled and disturbed about Dallas, who apparently has developed a complex character, quite a temperament—he drinks, weeps, mopes, curses his fate, loses his temper, abuses Shearman, pines with love for Nina Hamnett[1] and in fact is going speedily "down-hill', or (as he put it in heart-rending letters to me) "I am going to pieces". His last letter distressed me. In fact as he is going to Oxford this week-end, I have asked him over for a few days. . . .

MARK GERTLER

To S. S. Koteliansky

25 July 1918 *Garsington Manor, Oxford*

My dear Kot, I would have answered your letter before, but I have been busy with Dallas, who appeared on my horizon like a whirlwind. He came to Oxford on Saturday last to get his medical board settled, so as to take up a job in London which is waiting for him. When I met him at the station, I found him nervous, trembling from head to foot, and no idea where to stay or anything. So I took him straight back here. Everything went off fairly all right except on Sunday morning when his nose quite suddenly began to bleed. He oppresses one with his complete lack of independence and will or direction of his own. He must always lean on someone. But really after meeting so many "settled and great men", men who know "what's what", Dallas was a great relief with his recklessness and lack of ambition of any sort. Monday Philip took him to Oxford and plumped him down there. Wednesday morning I got a telephone message: "Come at once Dallas very ill." I rushed to Oxford, found him perfectly well and gay. However we had a good lunch and drink, which I enjoyed very much, I must admit. . . . MARK GERTLER

I had no letter from L. so I do not know whether he will come here on Friday or Monday week. If I hear from him again I'll write you.

Yours S.K.

26 August

My dear Gertler, The Lawrences left on Friday. They will be paying visits in a couple more of places. Then they may be back here. The idea of Frieda coming here again irritates me and gives me a kind of stubborn muddle-headed anger. If she disappeared L. would be saved, because she is devouring him bit by bit, gradually, permanently. We had a few more quarrels and she shed profuse tears, but, I think, she weeps only to benefit her digestion. Tears to her seem to be a kind of purgative, after which she eats with an increased appetite and gusto. I am bored, as a matter of fact, to talk that sort of thing about her but I can't really rid myself of that nauseous obstinately bad feeling.

I'll most probably stay on in the Cave. I have no desire to move or undertake anything.

How I wish Frieda disappeared. Lawrence is most interesting and of the real few who matter. I have no other news to tell you. Yours S.K.

Remember me to the Hutchinsons.

[1] Painter and author of *Laughing Torso*.

PART SIX

Success

The two years following the First World War were exciting years in Gertler's development. For one thing he was able to go abroad, and in 1920 he paid his first visit to Paris, where he could see the originals of so many paintings which hitherto he had known only in reproduction. It was, too, a period of excitement for the younger generation, when, after four grinding years of war (and philistinism), hope of a better world was renewed.

In summer Gertler continued to pass much of his time at Garsington, where the Morrells treated him as one of the family[1] and the society was nothing if not varied. Gertler repaid Lady Ottoline's kindness by a loyalty which seems to have been rather rare amongst her many brilliant intellectual guests. In London he plunged into a life of painting by day and entertainment by night, perhaps too much so for his health, to judge

[1] The following letter from Lady Ottoline shows how she valued Gertler's friendship.

[*I June*] *Garsington Manor, Oxford*

My dear Gertler, I very nearly wrote to you after you left to say very much the same as you said in your letter—for you don't know *how* much *I* value your friendship. It means so much to me to be able to get in *contact* with anyone that I like—and I feel I really *do* get into communion with you—and that we have an "understanding" together—you know what I mean—and really can understand each other without explanations. I have such awful health and feel so ill so often that it makes it very difficult for me to talk as much as I would. Today and yesterday I feel so well and I realise what a nightmare I have to fight through most days, for this last three months my head has nearly driven me crazy. I don't want to worry you with all this, only I feel I am often very dull. Really life and friendship and the world and nature and buttercups and poetry and spiritual and concrete images, their impact is so tremendous and great and vivid. Even when sometimes one sees it all too clearly and one is almost frightened by the truth. . . .

Yes, I saw Bertie [Russell]. His mind is rather wearing him out, beating itself against its bars—his hunger for companionship—and his mind works like a steel reaping machine—and shakes him too much without diversion. He was very interesting. I am now to write to him once a fortnight and have just written him four pages in tiny handwriting and my hand aches so from having done it and my *mind* aches too. . . .

With love, yours most affly O.M.

by several letters from Carrington reproaching him for a dissipation which, she felt, must impair his ability to work. It is certain that his health was in fact suffering. His success as a painter seemed confirmed when Marchant of the Goupil took him up as one of their "regulars", paying him a small monthly cheque against future exhibitions, an arrangement he later renewed with the Leicester Galleries.

Gertler's relations with Carrington had by this time passed from the stormy phase of passion, quarrels and reconciliation to a calm sea of friendship and a sharing of common interest in their art. She had made her home with the Stracheys at the Mill House, Tidmarsh, and Gertler had more or less accepted the situation. Amongst his other friendships the most important, perhaps, was that with Koteliansky, the Russian translator. Kot was a rather mysterious figure to whom all his friends have paid tributes. In the letters he assumes something of the role of a father confessor, and his stern integrity was certainly a powerful influence on Gertler for the rest of his life.

To Carrington

5 December 1918 *Penn Studio, Hampstead*

Dearest Carrington, I missed you this time, perhaps more than usual. I think that is because we got on so much more harmoniously than ever before and without the trouble and pains we used to suffer. I found your company stimulating and I loved talking to you and hearing you talk, also showing you my work and getting your opinions, which I value most highly. I do hope we shall meet fairly often, as I am always wanting to tell you things, to get your ideas about them—you are such a help.

I shall certainly give you that pen drawing. I shall get it mounted and framed, but you will have to come up and fetch it! Now I am bribing you again!

The last few days I have been suffering from an attack of awful depression; as you know, I get these fits—like a disease—but I am better now. Yesterday morning it was at its height and it was terrible—it is a sort of nervous depression. When in such a state I lose all control and my harmony. It's a sort of madness. You have no idea what it's like and unfortunately I suffer much in this way, but I must not burden you with this side of me, though I feel, now that we are so intimate, that I want to tell you all about myself and every side of me.

I am working on my "Circus" almost exclusively. It is coming along slowly, but it has undergone much alteration since you saw it last, *I* think for the better. However you must have patience with me, for it will be many years yet before I shall be producing my real stuff and only then if circumstances are favourable to my development.

Roger Fry came here the other afternoon to see my work. We had much interesting and feverish discussion on painting. He said something about buying one of my small pen drawings, *not* the one, fortunately, that you like! but one of the ballet.

Sunday for tea I saw Katherine, who seemed much better and our talk was interesting—I even told her about you! MARK GERTLER

To Carrington

15 December 1918 *Penn Studio, Hampstead*

Dearest Carrington, Yes, it is good to be getting letters from you again. I don't know how on earth I got along without them for so long!

I don't dislike David Garnett at all. I have no particular feelings about him, only he speaks so softly now that I can't hear what he says. I like him however for helping you by sitting for you. Nudes are really about the most exciting things to draw, I agree. . . .

I am still working very hard at my "Circus". It has undergone many changes and at one moment it came to a standstill. Now, however, it is going on steadily, though slowly. I am still not certain of it, as a result. It will probably be a long time before I shall produce anything at all, as I seem quite suddenly to be absolutely lost and am starting from the beginning again. This is not new for me however, as I am really always experimenting and never satisfied and this will always be my state probably. All the same I feel I am making steady progress, which is apparent through the chaos. What is to me of great importance now, through all my struggles, is our friendship. It has never meant so much to me and has never been so satisfying and helpful as it is now. It is all so much more solid and real than it ever was before. It is so good to know a person also whom one can respect and believe in, as I do in you. Altogether, it is very wonderful and I feel so grateful to you. It was certainly worth all the struggles and pains to have worked through to this. How wonderful it is to know, as I know now, that one can develop in one's relationships as much as in one's work! Just think of the different stages from the beginning until now! Only the thought of you spurs me on almost too much. I keep wanting to do extraordinary and outstanding things both in myself as a person and in my work in order to gain your esteem, but I shan't disappoint you. . . .

I should like very much to see more of your brother when he returns. Perhaps we might—he, you, Brett and myself—spend a little holiday together, in the spring or summer, a walking tour or something. Don't you think it might be nice?

I hope, anyhow, that you and I will have little outings together in the country later. I am ambitious to spend a few days in the country with you, occasionally. It would be so much better than London and you would find me quite a peaceful companion now—no troubles. We could do water colours or sit for each other. However there is as yet much time before the spring or summer.

I hope your work will go well and please let me hear from you soon.
Yours with love MARK GERTLER[1]

To Carrington

22 December 1918 *Penn Studio, Hampstead*

Dearest Carrington, I am sending you these which I hope will reach you safely.

I have been particularly distraught lately about my work. I have brought my "Circus" up to a certain point and shall now call it finished—it has a sort of completion: it is not without interest, but I am far from satisfied. I am anxious now to discover some form of logical and coherent expression, so that I can go ahead more steadily and fluently. I am in fact out of mood with all that I have done so far. For the purpose of this discovery, I have started a small study, which began in pencil, which soon became ink, then water colour and is now in oils (all on the same piece of paper), just three figures (nudes). Whether this will come to anything or whether I shall discover anything of that which I want through it, I don't know, but I am hopeful. Anyhow I am starting from the A.B.C. again. Right from the beginning as though I had never painted before—but we shall see.

The whole business meanwhile is a very painful struggle and terribly exhausting. I am ill and worn out with it all. Why should it be so painful and difficult? I don't know—sometimes I feel that perhaps one ought to paint more lightly, gaily, but if this is possible to some people it is *not* to me. *I* can't work without desperate seriousness.

Yesterday I went with Beatrice[2] to the National Gallery. Most things I found dull, peaceful, and too much like brown, grey or black oil-cloth. The new Ingres portrait, however, is magnificent, and must remain always a great problem to painters.

The other day I went to a "Thursday"—you know, that Lessore[3] woman and her husband and they have "Thursdays". It was pleasant. Lessore is a very nice woman and her pictures are certainly interesting. There was also a Miss Stock, very nice also and feverish about her painting. Sickert was there too....

[1] Carrington replied:

[*17 December 1918*] *The Mill House, Tidmarsh, Pangbourne*

Dearest Mark, . . . I do take such a pride in you as it is. When I hear what good things Roger and Borenius say about your work I swell out with pride! But also you know you are so progressed as a character, and that is very nearly as difficult as to have improved in painting. I found it altogether delightful being with you this last time. And that is more than we ever managed before—at least for four days on end. Yes, next year we'll stay in the country together—it will be enjoyable. CARRINGTON

[2] Beatrice Campbell, later Lady Glenavy.

[3] Thérèse Lessore, the painter.

Hutchinson came here today—he seemed to like what I showed him of my work. He is thinking of buying the "Boxers". As I did it, in spite of its size, in a comparatively short time, I am only asking £35 for it. Monty also is contemplating buying my "Ballet" for £50. This would be good as I still owe my brothers over £100 and I really get very distressed sometimes about money, especially when I am in such an experimental mood as now and not likely to produce much for some time. Everything is so expensive now—colours alone are ruinous. . . .

As you will notice from this letter I am very distracted, but I forced myself to write to you, as I did not want you to think that I am "off" you or anything like that.

With best wishes and love, Yours ever MARK GERTLER

To Carrington

31 December 1918 *Penn Studio, Hampstead*

Dearest Carrington, Thanks for your last letter and for answering mine so soon. Your letter was a very interesting one and excited and pleased me much. I am glad you are so engrossed in painting—that alone creates a bond between us. I am glad also that you liked the pen drawing so much. It gave me great pleasure to give it you. It is not true, though, that you do not deserve anything from me; your friendship means a great deal to me and it would take a good bit to repay you enough for that. You also make too great a division between our achievements or shall I say, rather, between our lack of achievements! I like your drawing of the two boys—it would certainly make a good subject! I hope you will be able to carry it out—that is the test. You will find it pretty difficult, but I wish you luck with it. Yes, what a nuisance it is when one's picture begins to grow, but you know very often one can manage by squashing one's subject into the canvas. Enlarging becomes a habit, a bad one too. If you have not already enlarged it, try "squashing". It may work. But I am sorry you are having that kind of trouble with it; I know from experience how tedious and depressing it is.

Why should you waste time with sawing wood and pumping and all that? Can't you get someone in the village to do that sort of thing for you? I should have thought a few pence could save you all that labour.

Garsington was quite pleasant. There were the MacCarthys, and children, and Aldous Huxley, and of course Clive Bell came over a good deal. Julian was home too. There was much interesting conversation and controversy and a village ball. I enjoyed also playing with the children. The MacCarthy children are remarkable—one, a girl of nine,[1] has as much sense and composure as a very sensible and dignified young woman of twenty-five!

Desmond MacCarthy came back the same time as myself (last Friday

[1] Rachel MacCarthy, who married Lord David Cecil.

morning). We lunched and went off to a certain Prince Bibesco,[1] who has two Cézannes!! Imagine my excitement when I heard of these at Garsington from Desmond! I could think of nothing else. At lunch, in London, I was so nervous and excited that Desmond (a most peaceful and quiet personage) caught my mood and became quite agitated! At last we arrived. Whether it was because I was too excited beforehand, or what, I don't know, but the Cézannes somewhat disappointed me! Yet they were typical. Do you know I fear that I may miss something in the originals that I get from the reproductions! In reproduction Cézanne stands quite alone. He doesn't somehow quite so much in the originals, at any rate those that I have seen. However, they *were* good and I have really not seen enough originals to judge. When I arrived back here, a slow sort of depression set in, even a sort of boredom, an apathy—I could not get going, and, although this mood still persists rather, I have now got started again.

I am working on a tiny composition in oils of three nudes, as a study for a big picture. So far it is not going with any fire or excitement and I don't know if anything will come of it, but I am still trying to almost "forge" out a sort of lucid and logical means of expressing myself, so that I can go ahead in the future more fluently. How soon I shall make the discovery, if ever, I don't know. It may come quite soon.

For the moment, the manner seems to be a sort of mixture of my big "Bathing" and "Fruit Stall" period—but I don't know. In my "Circus" I have already exhausted that manner which came to birth in the "Ballet" and pen drawings.

With my best wishes in the coming year, to *you, your work and our friendship*. Yours ever MARK GERTLER

To Carrington

5 January 1919 *Penn Studio, Hampstead*

Dearest Carrington, I am so sorry about your father—[2]I know what it feels like, because it's only two years ago since the same thing happened to me. It must have been awful for you, with your sensitive nature, to have to go through with it all. I mean especially being forced into contact with the rest of your family, under such circumstances. They are, I expect —your mother and sister—so insensitive and different from you. Anyhow, coming into contact with one's family is always *most* distressing, even if one loves them as I do. I think it is simply because one has become *so very* different and yet, somehow, one can't help feeling that there is after all some ghastly link. A link which one cannot shake off altogether, and so one feels it would have been better either not to have changed from them at all, or having changed, the link should automatically have broken itself. But no, a sort of link *does* persist in remaining.

[1] Prince Antoine Bibesco who married Elizabeth Asquith.
[2] Carrington's father died early in 1919.

I agree with you really about the little El Greco. I loved it too, perhaps more than anything else. About the Cézannes, I liked the Maynard[1] one more than the Bibesco's and, so far, more than any original Cézannes I have yet seen. In that tiny one there *is* that plasticity and construction one likes so much in him in reproductions. But I must see the Bibesco's again. Next time you come to London, we must go together. I should also like to go with you to the National Gallery.

What a pity you are always so far away! How much we could learn from each other and by studying together. There are always things I want to discuss with you, but there you are, always miles away, and people to whom you do not matter half as much have you always! . . .

With love, MARK GERTLER

To Carrington

12 January 1919 *Penn Studio, Hampstead*

Dearest Carrington, I hope by now you are more composed and happier about your family trouble. Of course it is absurd of your mother to expect you to live with her, in order to cheer her up—you could not do it. Yet I can't help feeling sorry for these elderly women who suddenly lose their partners with whom they have lived intimately for twenty, thirty or forty years, never parting and no other interests. Suddenly one of them departs—the other left, quite alone and nothing else to take its place, too old or perhaps too stupid to create a new interest for themselves. They always turn to their children, but it hardly ever works.

I am sure I should have liked your father. He must have been a fine simple character. I am sorry I never met him. No doubt all your good qualities are inherited from him.

I am sorry you are for the moment "stuck" in your work. I know the feeling very well—that "blankness" you speak of is indeed terrible. Yet it is quite a healthy state. It usually means that one is growing, that one is too dissatisfied to go on working in the same old way, that something new and more interesting must be found. In the meantime there is the Blank. I do understand that desire to have something solid in front of one to work from and as a matter of fact one *should*, when one feels like that, plant some thing or person in front of one, because it is about the best way of replenishing one's imagination. But looking at good pictures is a good tonic too. In your letter you say that ideas come but too vaguely to be of use—that's about the truest thing you've ever said.

No, I do not see Bertie much now; he is living at Garsington at present, but I don't think his book would interest me. As for those of his books which are supposed to be really important, they are no use to me since no doubt I could not understand them. Although Miss Wrinch[2] always tells me that I have a talent for mathematical philosophy!

[1] John Maynard Keynes.

[2] Dorothy Wrinch, distinguished mathematician and physicist.

People have not yet seen my "Circus". I am at this moment working on a still-life.

In your last letter you advised me to read Tolstoy's *Ivan Ilyitch.* Well, I read it last summer at Wittering and thought it about the most remarkable thing I've ever read! But what's strange is, that a day before I got your letter, I suddenly thought of that story at the Campbells' and made Gordon read it aloud!!! Tolstoy is an immense writer.

My love and best wishes dear girl. Yours ever MARK GERTLER

To S. S. Koteliansky

March 1919 *Garsington Manor, Oxford*

My dear Kot, I understand all you say and quite agree that it is the only way for a temperament like mine to look at things.[1] But it remains hard all the same. I did not talk to you of my troubles for several reasons. Firstly

[1] Koteliansky had written as follows:

[*Probably March 1919*]

My Dear Gertler, Lately it so happened somehow that you were avoiding talking to me of what troubled you. I was shy to question. But talk or not talk, I felt you're worried, and want to offer you that kind of "consolation" which one of Gorky's personages has when he is in great trouble. He remembers then that even Kings, throned heads, supposed to be happiest on earth, have sometimes awful troubles. The other "consolation" is that not being one of the many obliges. As on instance, take the attitude of the many and of the individual towards the war. Many (artists among them) went to the war and for years had been doing other than used to, desiring to get out of the state of war back to their work. Now, like in everything concerning the many, their state of war is finished and they are returning to their work, to the place allotted to them in the community.

But individuals who have to endure their own state of war—with themselves, with things important and unimportant, even with shadows and ghosts—*must* not desire the things and state of mind that the many possess. This is the price of *being*.

You know quite well that all personal troubles (I don't want to use the word tragedies) are, on the whole, reducible to whether one, notwithstanding all the great toll, wants to remain *being* himself, or one prefers quiet, peace of mind, the love of his "friends" and neighbours and the other blessings of the earth to negation, rejection of one's own being. In other words, if you want to be happy, prosperous etc., take your allotted place in life, a painter among many painters, do your work as others do, don't seek for anything, and since you possess talent, you will become one of their best. But once you chose a different path (what that different is is too long a discussion to enter into), then you must realise that also a different attitude to nearly everything is required in you—for yourself.

You aren't satisfied with your work at the present moment, you're obsessed with numerous troubles—well, face them: there are thousands of things, hard and bitter, outside and inside one, but you must always keep in mind that you are in a state of war—great battles, skirmishes, fluctuations.

This is not moralising. It is only my way of writing. What really does it matter to you if temporarily, at the present moment, you feel a bit at a loss? It *must* be so. I say must because I know that out of troubles and suffering for that which matters and which is incredibly difficult to attain, is built the way of real being and creating.

because it becomes more and more difficult to do so, and then they don't seem worth discussing. I am tired of them, they bore me as much as they make me suffer. There was a time when I felt a slight turn of martyrdom mixed with my sufferings that made it feel sufficiently heroic for me to want to talk about them. Now, since that is all gone, the causes of my troubles just bore me and so I don't like to talk about them. But if I do feel a desire to unburden myself, I should quite naturally come to you before anybody else.

I am calmer now. Chekhov's *Seagull* which I read yesterday helped a great deal to soothe me and when the spirit of work returns all will be well. For over and over again I rediscover that for me there is only *work*. . . .

We have talked and talked here till I sometimes felt quite giddy in the head and sick. It is bad to talk too much—especially about the very fundamentals of life, as it makes them even more rocky than they already seem to one's disturbed soul, or they leave one empty and depressed like the after-effects of copulation. MARK GERTLER

To S. S. Koteliansky

[*Monday, June 1919*] *Garsington Manor, Oxford*

My dear Kot, Well, here I am for the week-end.[1] There were Lowes Dickinson,[2] Virginia Woolf, Aldous Huxley. While sitting on the lawn, Saturday after tea Lord Durham was announced and instead of a venerable grey-headed elderly gentleman, as I imagine lords generally to be, a boy of eighteen appeared, just like any other English college boy. Though

---

I also had a letter from Lawrence saying that he is better and about Palestine. The difficulty is that he won't be allowed a passport before the peace has been signed.

Gordon Campbell was here. I dined with him on Saturday. He's absorbed in his work. B. and the children are well. After dinner with Gordon I went to see Katherine, and to compensate ourselves for your talk in Garsington, we also talked a great deal. Yours S.K.

[1] An extract from a letter from Lady Ottoline Morrell of about this time may be inserted here:

[*11 June 1919*]
My dearest Gertler, . . . Your description of Lawrence is terribly sad. It is what I felt—but oh how sad and how monotonous and boring really. I had a most wonderful letter from Bertie and the proofs of his new book—which is very interesting—on Socialism and Anarchy and Syndicalism.[3]

We have Rupert Brooke's Memoir by E.M. and it is *sickening*—so sentimental and one-sided, only giving his own "soppy" view of him—only as he was to that silly fashionable set—and never even a hint of the very interesting, complicated side of him.

It is a cruel thing to be put on the screen for the world to see—E.M. as the photographer. I am so thankful that you kicked off from him. It was a good thing. . . .

[2] Fellow of King's College Cambridge and well-known author.

[3] *The Practice and Theory of Bolshevism*, published 1920.

they say he is not at all ordinary, but broad-minded, the right sort of political views and all sorts of original accomplishments, to me he seemed just a nice boy.

Virginia received me rather coldly. Later I learned that [——] has been at work again—mischief about Mary, the usual boring stuff, not worth talking about. It is a pity though, because Virginia is really so interesting a person. Mostly we discussed a little book just out, supposed to be written by a girl of nine.[1] Perhaps you've heard of it. It is really wonderful stuff. But there were doubts as to whether it was really written by a child, especially as Barbellion, the author of *Diary of a Disappointed Man*, has come to life again.

Of course Lytton Strachey—his greatness or smallness—was also discussed. On Sunday there came over a brother of Carrington, and a friend of his, and a Miss Sands, a rich, ugly and elderly spinster, cultured and friendly. I have already started work, a landscape of course. I hear by the way that when Derain was taken round the London Group he picked out, without knowing the name, pictures by Roger Fry as being the best. Also at a party he saw a picture by Carrington and thought it excellent. So that Roger Fry and Carrington are the two best English artists, according to Derain. Clive Bell will have to change his mind. As for Picasso, he thinks all English art just pretty and sentimental. . . . MARK GERTLER

To Carrington

Sunday, June 1919 *Garsington Manor, Oxford*

Dear Carrington, I came here on Saturday before last. In town I finished off the large portrait of Mrs Dobrée[2] and a "still-life". Both were important to me, as, by their completion, they proved the reality of certain ideas that I have recently discovered. I think I certainly have in some points made a definite step forward. You must come and see the portrait some time in the autumn. I should like your opinion on it.

Here I have already started work. I work from about 10 o'clock until seven! I am working on three studies of the same thing. Two of them are tiny. Landscape, or at any rate the landscape here, is not altogether sympathetic to me. All the same it is good to do and I hope to get something out of it. The smallest one of the three is nearly finished. About my private life, as one might call it, it is awfully difficult to write as you must know. Also I am so bad at expressing myself in letters. I haven't even told you here a hundredth part of what I feel about painting. So you must excuse me if I don't tell you everything that happens to me. There are some things that are too intimate, even impossible, or that one fears to spoil by talking about to others, even one's greatest friends. . . .

Last week-end we were all busy reading that book by the young girl

[1] Daisy Ashford's *The Young Visiters* had been published on 22 May 1919.
[2] Valentine, wife of Bonamy Dobrée, critic.

of nine years. It *is* remarkable, but doubtful if it's really written by a child. I, personally, suggested Max Beerbohm!

Yours ever MARK GERTLER

To Carrington

[*22 July 1919*] *Garsington Manor, Oxford*

My dear Carrington, I have heard before that there are some Cézannes at Bath and I remember wanting to go there for the purpose of seeing them. Now you mention them again I feel I *must* go some time soon. I wish you had given me more details about them, the subjects, the sizes and a description, as far as you can remember, of the colour. Will you do this in your next letter? Also the Renoir—try and particularly remember the *sizes*. I am very interested in that point just now. Had you never read Vollard's *Cezanne* before? I read it some time ago.

I envy you, there, in your little cottage.[1] Here there are really too many people and sometimes I long for real solitude and also real country. I don't feel that it is real here at all. I keep remembering my stay at Swanage last year, and all the wonderful stuff I saw there. Next year, I feel, I must make an effort to move further afield and more alone—one is made to waste so much time here, one way or another. The older I get the more necessary does painting become to me, necessary to my very constitution. If I don't paint I become restless, bored and even ill. This is a charming place and on the whole I've been as happy here as I can be, but I find now that, from a serious working point of view, it has its drawbacks. Until now I have been painting on the edge of the pond and really it was like trying to paint in some market place, or rather pleasure ground. I suffered very much. Now, thank goodness, having finished with that place, I shall try and move to another, where there is less chance of disturbance, even if the subject is duller. There are many more disadvantages here, but I cannot speak of them now.

I have finished my three studies of the "Pigeon House", but I am really disappointed with them and am anxious to start afresh and do better.

Do you know, I was nearly drowned! Nelson[2] rescued me and none too soon either! It was a curious experience—I thought I was done for. I had got into deep water by accident and simply could not come up. Nelson didn't come sooner because he thought I was fooling, so that by the time he *did* come I was nearly done for!

Brett is here—yes—but above all is Mrs Baker here! You have no idea what consternation that little woman caused. The moment she came Philip and Ottoline took the most violent dislike to her and I must say, for my own part, I found nothing much to like in her either. Later, however, they became somewhat reconciled, but in the place of hatred,

[1] Carrington was having a holiday at Welcombe in Cornwall.

[2] Geoffrey Nelson, an artist.

boredom set in. Me she bored terribly too, especially as she shared her meals with Nelson and myself. Now after endless discussion and trouble we have managed to make her feel that she *must* go—so she goes tomorrow, thank God! Last week-end there were Birrell[1] and Eliot[2]—this week-end Lady G. Churchill, Mr and Mrs McKenna,[3] a Mrs Herbert.[4]

Saturday there was, of course, the Peace celebration, which was boring and disturbing enough.

I have had the last few days, what I call my "Garsington Headaches". I always get them here and they make me feel very wretched. Altogether I have been feeling depressed and wretched lately. Now I am glad I've come to the end of the sheet as I am sure I should become sorry for myself and tell all my woes!

So "Au Revoir" MARK GERTLER

To S. S. Koteliansky

13 August 1919 *Garsington Manor, Oxford*

My dear Kot, When I read your news, you could have knocked me down with a feather. That you should have actually gone off a motoring tour and . . . with Gilbert, Pluck[5] and Mond! Yes, I am glad somehow that you went. . . .

I have done quite a number of pictures, not so much because I have worked harder than usual but because they have just come off a little more quickly than they used to. But again a change is coming. From that small portrait of Mrs Dobrée until quite recently things went with a sort of flow and consistency quite unusual for me, but now things are working inside me. But I refuse to start them till I come to London. I cannot do them here on this "pleasure ground". I have only just one drawing which will be the beginning of the new and that is of a "Horse in an Orchard". I will start the painting when I return. I don't suppose I shall do much here till I return; this hot sun paralyses me. I just mooch about in a sordid morbid sulking manner, secretly hoping for rain.

Yet this August sun is most beautiful. To me as a painter it is ravishing and too wonderful, that's why I am unhappy. I have a special walk where I go to escape from everything here. In one particular spot I read. It is a beautiful spot, high up with endless fields of different colours and a few haystacks looking like half lemons in the sun against the intense blue of the sky. I won't say I feel happy at such moments, but it *does* feel good.

MARK GERTLER

[1] Probably Augustine Birrell.

[2] T. S. Eliot.

[3] Reginald McKenna, Liberal politician, and his wife.

[4] Probably Mrs A. P. Herbert.

[5] Gwen Wilson, nicknamed "Plucky Little Gwen", married the second Lord Melchett, then Henry Mond.

To S. S. Koteliansky

August 1919 *Garsington Manor, Oxford*

My dear Kot, You will be surprised to hear that I was in London the other day, Wednesday, for one night. We suddenly got a wire from Ottoline, who was in London, asking us all to come up at once to go to the ballet and see a show of French pictures which were being hung at Heals. So we rushed up and, as I was completely in the hands of the others, I couldn't snatch time to see you. . . . I did not like Picasso's ballet or even his scenery. Neither did I like running into all the old people again. It was very unpleasant and nerve-racking. I was tempted to come up merely for the French pictures. And they were interesting. You see it was a very representative show of all the interesting young painters now working in Paris. I am sorry Lawrence is in such a depressed state. But as you say, one can do nothing, especially when one is in the same boat oneself.

When I was in London I saw Carrington. We spent one stolen hour alone in a small café on Thursday morning at 10 o'clock. It was rather pleasant seeing her this time. She seemed, after all and in spite of whatever faults she may have, to be more interesting than the people I am with just now. But one is alone, always alone, and alone one must remain I suppose. The benefits of this place are wearing out for me now, I am afraid, and perhaps it is the last summer I shall spend here.

During dinner, before the ballet, I drank too much. I felt an uncontrollable desire to drink and I suppose I got drunk. Ottoline was angry with me and has not yet altogether forgiven me. I can't say I'm sorry, in fact I feel a secret joy at her indignation. Yet I hope I shan't drink again, because I merely become silly, and deprived the next morning.

At present I am not working, because a change is going on in my mind again, perhaps caused by the French pictures. They are all very nice and fine and clever, but *Exquise!* and *oh c'est formidable!* They all make me feel as if I were on the stage.

We walked round the pond by moonlight reciting Verlaine in the melodramatic manner. Sometimes I dislike poetry as much as I dislike French.

But worst of all Sunday for tea-time came, ssh, YEATS! The great Irish poet. I was sent for to come and hear the *interesting* conversation. (I had hidden because there were so many people.) When I entered the room, there was the Great Man. He seemed to be sitting on a chair much higher than anyone else's and holding forth. Everyone sat with rapt faces listening. The funniest part was Bussy[1] who, ill luck would have it, sat next to Yeats. The higher up Yeats sat, the lower little Bussy seemed to sink. The contrast was well worth seeing.

I have never met a more pompous and theatrical humbug of an Irishman than Yeats. I escaped from the room as quick as I could. . . .

I am painting Julian and reading Knut Hamsun, *Growth of the Soil.*

[1] The French painter Simon Bussy, married to Dorothy Strachey, and a friend of André Gide and Matisse.

I don't quite know what I think of it yet—a little on the heroic grand style!

MARK GERTLER

To S. S. Koteliansky

31 August 1919 *Garsington Manor, Oxford*

My dear Kot, It is rather interesting that Shearman should have wanted to see you just now because, when I last saw him at the Hutchinsons, I chaffed him so much about his "love affairs" and all that that he became quite angry and wrote a very critical letter about me afterwards. Some parts were so bad that Mary H. refused to read them to me even. Yes, he is more dignified now, fat and serious.

Last week there came again that French little painter Bussy, a nice comic little chap with an enormous stage laugh, but it affects one so much every time he does it that one cannot help joining in, and he laughs all the time. His wife is a Strachey. One fails to see where the relationship lies in between them, but it's there all right. Then there was also André Gide, a French writer, and a *supposed* nephew with him, a boy of eighteen and well....

Of course there was a great deal of French spoken and I hate the sound of French more and more. Why will they say everything is *Magnifique! Horrible! Terrible!* I am *not* a Frenchman. Anyhow, what I mean is that they made me want to paint as differently from them as possible, and not, as one would think, like them.

I am worried about money again. Goodness knows how much I now owe my brother. MARK GERTLER

P.S. Do you know what a Jew says to a "shatchan" when the proposed bride is unsuitable? He says, "Very nice, very fine, but not for me." That's what I feel about the French pictures.

To Carrington

December 1919 *Penn Studio, Hampstead*

Dear Carrington, Yes, it was characteristic of you not to turn up! And it was this same characteristicness which saved the situation! You see I have learnt by now to only expect you to keep one engagement with me out of four, so I was not surprised when you did not come. All the same I was disappointed, because I have been wanting you so much to see my latest two pictures, so much so in fact that, in spite of several letters from its owner demanding one of them, I have kept it still, hoping you would turn up soon. You see the first one of the two was bought by Siegfried Sassoon—the second by Moffat,[1] Iris's husband! But why I should expect

[1] Curtis Moffat, the decorator.

Gertler at the pianola.
Village fete at Garsington
(*c.* 1918)

Photographs by
permission of Mrs Igor
Vinogradoff.

Charades at Garsington.
Mark Gertler, Aldous
Huxley, Dorothy Brett

Self-Portrait

Oil painting ($16\frac{3}{4} \times 11\frac{3}{4}$ in.) *1920*

Collection and photograph: Arts Council of Great Britain

you to be as interested to see my work as I am to show it you I don't know. But you know what it is—when one paints, one has a few people in mind—one's audience as it were—and to me you are one of the principal of them.

So every time I heard you had been in town, it was a fresh disappointment to me that you did not come here. The only conclusion I could come to was that you did not care—and after all why should you?! You see, that little "horse" that you saw at Garsington was the first step to a new "ladder", which seems to me an important one and likely to last, perhaps even the beginning to my final path. And these two, (1) "Bathers", (2) "Petrushka", seem to me important evidence of the fact and important also in enabling you to understand the work to come. The important thing really is that I have at last evolved a sort of charcoal drawing which is so explanatory to me that I can paint almost the whole picture afterwards from it. You will remember having seen the charcoal drawing of the "Bathers" at Garsington. Well, I intend, for your sake, to keep back the "Bathers" until the end of next week, though I've heard again from Sassoon today—so if you *can* possibly come here by then, *do*. Try and let me know first as I rather dislike sudden visits!

It was good to see you again, dear Carrington, and to touch your hand! How wonderful! How I should love to keep up a more regular relationship with you, but you are so difficult—so elusive and capricious! You suddenly don't turn up at a critical moment and all is severed in one fell swoop!

Well, let me know if you can come and when. With love

MARK GERTLER

To Carrington

14 December 1919 *Penn Studio, Hampstead*

Dearest Carrington, Do you know I was almost pleased you did not turn up on Friday evening! That hour or so we spent together in the afternoon was so good, so satisfying, that I feared any more the same day might only spoil my mood! Thank you ever so much for that friendship which makes you feel so happy for me. No doubt you will meet her soon, but at present it is difficult and my instincts are still against it, but we shall see. You must be patient. What made me most happy in your very beautiful and stimulating letter was that you too see that now, if anything, we can be greater friends even than before! Also showing you my work was so wonderful. It is always a great day for me when *you* come to see my work, and especially when you approve as much as you did, this last time!

I too am proud to be *your* friend, because there are very few people in the world for whom I have a respect as great as I have for you! To be in your beautiful presence is to feel uplifted and stimulated the whole time. Whenever I am with you I feel the same as I do in front of a real work of art, or as one feels at a moment of some emotional or religious conception....

My best love to you, dear friend, and I hope we shall meet soon again.

MARK GERTLER

To Carrington

2 January 1920 *Penn Studio, Hampstead*

Dearest Carrington, My New Year didn't start well at all! I came back, eagerly, from Garsington last Monday in order to go on with my "Footballers". It only just needed finishing off but, alas, yesterday it all went wrong, and now it's done for—five weeks' solid work gone. I may take it up again, but at present I am very depressed and unhinged and I don't know what I shall do. Today I feel like swinging a knapsack across my shoulders travelling off into the world—anywhere.

Julian came only on the Saturday after Christmas. She *is* a fine big girl, for her age, and to my senses, very beautiful. I love her solidity and bigness, and just watching her is to me more thrilling than the most intellectual conversation! . . .

Sunday after Xmas came Prince and Princess Bibesco, Violet Asquith, Maynard Keynes—a short hectic visit and nothing more. There was also a village dance. I danced mostly with Mademoiselle—you know, the new one—a pale fair pretty chic thing with a very lively manner, half intriguing and half boring—and Monday I came back here. . . .

But we have *very* nice evenings here. I love my studio now at night—with a fire—you *must* come one evening. The supper consists of scrambled eggs and ham, fruit, coffee, later tea and buns. Doesn't that fascinate you? . . .

I could also show you the large portrait of Mrs Dobrée. It has come back now.

With much love and good wishes for New Year. Yours ever

MARK GERTLER

To Carrington

Hotel des Grands Hommes, 9 Place du Panthéon, Paris

9 April 1920

Dear Carrington, Although I've only been here about three weeks[1]—it seems like years—there's so much to tell, that I don't know where to begin, so I'll only write you a short letter and tell you more of my adventures when we meet. I have of course seen masses of pictures, but the most important was the Pellerin Collection, which contains the greater bulk of the Cézannes we know so well and for so long from reproduction. It was, I assure you, a most extraordinary sensation, seeing them at last, in the flesh!

[1] This was Gertler's first visit to Paris.

There are many Cézannes which I find disappointing, not so good and suggestive as their photographs. Others quite fulfil one's expectations and are superb. But Renoir has made an enormous impression on me. In fact I am not sure that I do not like him best! I have seen a magnificent one, done only two years ago, when he was seventy-eight! One of the finest things I've ever seen.

About the more modern stuff I am really not at all sure; there is nothing that takes one's breath away like those giants.

There is a café called the Rotonde—the equivalent of Café Royal—all the younger artists go there. It is really remarkable. They all go in for "bohemian" make-ups, and are rather dirty. Also there are hardly any Frenchmen among them; they are mostly foreigners and about half of them are Jews! I have been to some of their parties and it is all very much the same sort of thing we know so well and are so tired of.

Hutchinson, Iris, her husband are here, and I saw them yesterday, also Epstein, Nina Hamnett, Roger Fry, Duncan Grant, Vanessa Bell. I've seen Derain—he is a nice man. There is one young artist called Ortiz. I think he has talent—he's also nice. But I am longing to get back to London and work, and as soon as I've seen a few more collections I shall return. So probably I shall not be here by the time you pass through.

You see it is impossible for me to work here. Even if I wanted to I couldn't, because my bedroom is too small and dark and there isn't a room to be got in Paris suitable for painting. . . . MARK GERTLER

To Carrington

17 May 1920 *Penn Studio, Hampstead*

Dearest Carrington, Well I am working hard and with much trouble, chiefly on account of my sitters. Little did I know what I was letting myself in for, when I decided to return and paint again *only from Nature.* All went well as long as I was on "still-life", but I got panting to paint people, so with difficulty I procured a model for a nude and also started a portrait of Mrs Dobrée. After a few sittings of the nude (and it was going thrillingly), she became anaemic and run down and had to go to the country to recuperate for a fortnight! Then I thought, well there's Mrs Dobrée left, *she* won't fail me, but alas her heart has gone wrong and for the time being the sittings had to be abandoned! You have no idea what all this means to me, especially *now*, when I am full of a new motive and feverish to express it. Yesterday another model came—an old hag of forty-five. You should see her! But still I started a nude of her! I *must* be painting someone! But by leaving out the wrinkles and the crumpled skin I shall, I hope, turn her into a rather fascinating plump woman of thirty. Younger I *cannot* make her—but you know even *she* is full up and can't come again until next Sunday! So you see what I suffer!

Painting in the way I am doing now one is simply almost completely in the hands of one's sitters and this is an awful thought. Yet I can't paint any other way *just now*, as it is just *that* which is my *Idea*.

But I told you what I feel now when you came here the other day, at least as well as I could, because the suddenness of your visit took my breath away rather. Some day if we could meet in a more quiet and appointed way and for more than five minutes and perhaps more frequently than just three times a year, I could express more of myself to you.

Yesterday I saw Murry. We talked of my Paris trip and of Cézanne and Renoir. I told him *my* way of understanding these great men and how terribly misled one has been all along by the "wizards' and intellectuals'" interpretations of them. I mean Roger Fry & Co. And he (Murry) was very impressed and said that it cleared up much for him. So far so good; but he said he is going to "crib" it all and write about it! So look out for an "enlightening" article on "art" by Murry. This sort of thing makes me furious! I shall *never* again talk to writers! Murry has done that sort of thing before in his articles. Things one has said to him appear wholesale—I mean things I've said to him on painting—but *please* don't tell anyone I said so.

He asked me to write it, but I refused. Firstly because I *can't* write; secondly I don't want to write as my job is painting; thirdly I neither want nor believe in "enlightening the world" on the subject of art. There are quite enough articles being written already. Besides, these are my own *private* feelings and probably *only good for me*. . . .

To pass away time, when there is no one to sit for me, I have been and am still painting a small portrait of myself. Perhaps I shall finish it today. Then I shall start on my "Mantelpiece".

Thursday before last Augustus John suddenly turned up here for one of my tea parties! His presence rather bewildered and staggered us all. I am surprised to hear that Alix is going to marry James—especially as they have lived for so long already as husband and wife. But perhaps it is for the "sake of the children".

I would not be a bit surprised to hear any moment that you're going to marry L.S., or would it be Partridge?[1] Personally I rather hope not. Somehow it is easier to remain friends with unmarried people. As it is, it's rather difficult with you, because I hardly know anyone more married and domesticated than you are already!

Mrs D. is rather unwell; her heart is not strong. She goes away for Whitsun for a while—so I shall be rather lonely for a bit. When she came here on the day after you left, I was moved to tell her the *whole* of my past love story!

To Carrington

[*22 May 1920*] *Penn Studio, Hampstead*

Dearest Carrington, . . . I have been working on a little self-portrait, which

[1] Ralph Partridge, who married Carrington in 1921.

I've now finished, and also on my "Mantelpiece". But today my models start again and I hope regularly for some time now.

I have been offered a one-man show in Paris, but I am refusing. I don't somehow want to show in Paris yet. Also they want quite a lot of money from me to cover expenses and this I can't afford.

The last time I saw Mrs Dobrée she looked much better. For the moment she is away. I liked very much your skit on Rupert Brooke. I too will make so bold as to enclose something I've written in the same manner, only it doesn't rhyme—

THE SPRING

How lonely and unhappy one can feel in the spring!
The spring the freshest and most living of the seasons
Everything buds into life.
Women's breasts shake and frolic more vivaciously in their
  blouses as they walk,
They nod and point at one with derisive voluptuousness.
Young girls take off their stockings and their legs shine
  in the sun.
As they run across the lawn
  —suggesting desires and infinite possibilities.
How unhappy and lonely one can be,
Wanting these things!—
And in the spring one wants them more than before.

Let me hear from you again, dear one, and much love to you

MARK GERTLER

To Carrington

1 July 1920 *Penn Studio, Hampstead*

Dearest Carrington, Thanks for your letter and post-card. I am answering you at once, though I feel almost too bored and listless to do so. Yes, I've had rather a bad time, but it's turned out not so bad as it might have done. My chest is weak, they tell me, and generally my constitution is far from satisfactory. However, there is nothing actively wrong at present and I am to take great care of myself and all that. But it's all boring and I don't care either way—just now at any rate. Also I've had other troubles of a more romantic nature but none the less painful.

Altogether I feel about a hundred years old and as if I shall never again experience a pleasant or thrilling mood. But no doubt nature will some time again begin to play one or two of her pleasant tricks upon me as well as nasty ones. The only decent piece of news I have is that I have come to a sort of arrangement with Marchant of the Goupil Gallery to have a show of my work about next March, and meanwhile he is to advance me a certain amount of money. As I am not allowed to sell anything before the show, which to me is a great relief, and if the show turns out at all successful from a financial point of view, I shall no doubt be able to arrange something with him about a regular income, which would be wonderful.

I have been working hard all through my troubles and since you were here last I have done:

1. Flower Piece.
2. Portrait of myself.
3. Portrait of Mrs Dobrée.
4. Still-Life of my Mantelpiece.
5. Nude on Sofa.

Two more in hand: one of myself with interior and another of a pretty young girl that lives next door to 28.

I am glad that Duncan and Vanessa were encouraging about your work. I should very much like to see some of it.

Please do not trouble to send me flowers, but thanks for the thought. Would you like to spend a week or two by the sea in Ireland? Because the Campbells have asked me and suggested you as well. Some time in August would suit them best, from what they say. It must be wonderful country and we could do at least a picture each. If you feel like it let me know. *I* should love it—I've never been to Ireland, have you? (The fare would be found.) And the Campbells are really very nice....

Last night *everybody* went to a boxing school to see "Chile" box. For days before the excitement was intense, because he told us that he was a wonderful boxer—that soon he would be the heavyweight champion of the world and that he was called the "Eel". Though I doubted most of this, I didn't think he was quite as futile as he proved himself to be by this exhibition. It was awful! Shivers of shame ran down my spine. So much for Chile's boxing....

With love MARK GERTLER

To Carrington

22 July 1920 *Garsington Manor, Oxford*

Dearest Carrington, ... I must have given you a wrong impression in my last letter—I am *not* hopelessly depressed or unhappy. I was merely depressed by contact with doctors and disease. I never before realised what an evil disease was. The thought that I *might* be *really* ill took all the life out of me and made me reflect, more than before, on the horror of it. It has, in fact, left a permanent trace—and if *I* am not ill, others are, and I think now that disease is the greatest evil on earth. Now, however, I'm composed again.

I have had many invitations to various places this year, but with the exception of the Hutchinsons I am refusing them all, because it is much better for my work to stay in one place. To the Hutchinsons I go on Monday, 9th August, for a week. Then back here until the end of August, after that to London. . . .

I take it Partridge is in love with you. How much of it do you return, I wonder. I think, if I were a woman, he is the sort of man I'd love—he is so good-looking and *such* a figure! But I'm not a woman.

With love MARK GERTLER

To Carrington

26 August 1920 *Garsington Manor, Oxford*

Dearest Carrington, . . . I stayed with the Hutchinsons[1] for ten days. I meant to stay a week only, but I painted a portrait of Jack and it took longer than I expected. I also painted a small study of a china ornament there. They have such a good collection—I love them. I'm going to try and collect them myself.

My stay with the Hutchinsons was most pleasant. I could have stayed on forever. It all went so well. Then they drove me here—all the way, 112 miles—which gave me an opportunity of seeing the changing country. In certain parts it was magnificent. We lunched at Winchester and stayed for two hours looking over it. Then on to Newbury, where we had tea, and from Newbury to Oxford—the same road that Jude was supposed to have traversed and seen Oxford (Christminster) from a distance. We tried to imagine the spot from where he could have seen it.[2] Unfortunately, the car was a small one meant for two only and we were three—so I got crushed and cramped and my behind suffered cruelly. The Hutchinsons stayed the night here.

I am painting a portrait of Julian.

I cannot write to you about my work. You must see for yourself.

I now have fifteen pictures towards the show, which is exactly half of what I should like to get done for it—in next March.

Well, dear one, I send you my love. Write again. Ever yours

MARK GERTLER

To Carrington

12 September 1920 *Garsington Manor, Oxford*

Dearest Carrington, . . . Ottoline has nothing against you, only the day you proposed coming was to be filled with numbers of different and

[1] At Wittering in Sussex.

[2] From the Berkshire downs one can see Boar's Hill above Oxford, but not the towers.

difficult people already and Ottoline was dreading it. So were we all. When she asked me, I wasn't very encouraging either. What would have been the good, your sudden appearance in the midst of such nerve-racking turmoil?

I have now finished Julian's portrait.[1] It was a struggle and she was so bored sitting. I didn't succeed in getting a likeness, but as a picture it's not bad. She's almost too good-looking to paint.

I am dragging on here—too lazy to pack up and leave. Also I am at last working on two landscapes—one sunny one from the further side of the pond looking back at the house, and me from my bedroom window, over at the cottage ("gris clair one") of the pigeon house, with miles of distant country behind. I shan't leave until I finish these. And they will take at least another ten days to finish. I live very quietly here, really, just Ottoline, Julian and myself. We go out drives and play games when I'm not working. Once a very pleasant picnic on the Clumps[2] that one can see from the house here. They are very high up and the view all round is very remarkable.

Of course, it would make a great difference if you came to London more and saw me frequently. Aren't I always trying to meet you? Brett? What does she do? She plays tennis with Murry and likes him very much.

Yes, that little book of Gorky's on Tolstoy[3] is wonderful. It meant more to me than anything I've read for ever so long. It's a classic. But I was also overwhelmed and much struck by Wells' *History of the World*! I read the first few volumes furiously, greedily and really learnt things from it! So you mean to know *everything* about me do you? Well, you can't, so there! As for sins, there aren't many to confess really. Who am I to sin with here, eh?

Yes, I think the portrait of Jack[4] was a success.

Well, I am tired of writing, so good-bye, my dear. With much love

MARK GERTLER

[1] Now in the collection of Mrs Igor Vinogradoff.

[2] Wittenham Clumps, near Wallingford.

[3] *Reminiscences of L. N. Tolstoi*. Translated by S. S. Koteliansky and Leonard Woolf, 1920.

[4] St John Hutchinson.

PART SEVEN

Sanatoria and Régimes

If the years following the first war are marked by Gertler's maturity as an artist, they also saw his first collapse in health. At that time tuberculosis was the most dreaded of all diseases and took its toll particularly amongst the young. His friends Katherine Mansfield and D. H. Lawrence were already stricken. Gertler saw enough of the disease's ravages at the sanatorium to determine him to remodel his life. Henceforward he organised his day, his week, and his year to a carefully planned régime which he practically never varied. Ordinarily he would work for a couple of hours in the morning and then walk for an hour on Hampstead Heath. In the afternoon he would paint till half past four. After which friends might come to tea. In the evenings he liked to meet a group of intimate friends for conversation.

There are frequent references in letters to "Thursdays" or "Saturdays" and "Sundays", some at the Campbells, some at the Hutchinsons and some at Gertler's own lodgings. These evenings became almost sacred. Generally they were exclusively masculine. In the early twenties the regulars were, besides Gertler, Koteliansky, Murry, D. H. Lawrence (when in London), J. W. N. Sullivan (scientist and biographer of Beethoven), Ralph Hodgson, W. J. Turner, the poet and critic, and James Stephens. Sometimes the rendezvous was a restaurant. At one time Brett was allowed to preside at her Pond Street house, because, as she said, she was too deaf to intervene.

Part of the summer was usually passed at Garsington, where he had his own studio, near Chichester with the Hutchinsons, or with a few other friends such as Montague Shearman. Visits to Paris continued to influence him, as may be deduced from his paintings, but he remained always on his guard against succumbing to any movement or fashion.

To Carrington

19 November 1920 *Sanatorium, Nordrach-on-Dee, Banchory, N.B.*

Dearest Carrington, I arrived here last Saturday at nine o'clock in the morning, after a fairly pleasant journey. There was something romantic about the "sleeper", only very stuffy, and I couldn't find out how to open the window before morning, when it was no longer any use.

This place—what shall I say about it? It's obviously a very good sanatorium, very comfortable and efficient. At first I was put to bed, that being the rule, and kept there for a day or two. At present my out-of-bed hours are still rationed. Today I was allowed half an hour walk in the morning and the same again in the afternoon—4.30 to bed again.

Your letter has just come. Thank you ever so much for it, also for G.B.'s[1] letter. I will read it later and send it back in my next letter. I am glad you like Valentine.[2] She is the most genuine and satisfactory young woman I have as yet come across. Yes, it was an interesting little period just before I came here. Like old times, yet how different!

I am sorry you continue to have "love difficulties". But I am afraid that's inevitable and eternal—the everlasting "problem of the bedroom", as Tolstoy puts it—and that's what it amounts to, doesn't it? *I* am free from it *here* at any rate! Alas poor me!

Now it is my "rest hour" so I must go down and lie on an easy chair, among a lot of bank clerks in sporting get-ups and smartly dressed young women (yes, it's mixed).

To S. S. Koteliansky

19 November 1920 *Banchory*

Dear Kot, . . . All the same I don't feel well. I keep feeling so exhausted. Yesterday for the first time I was allowed downstairs with the others on the verandah from 11 to 3 o'clock. All the patients who are up look quite healthy; some of them even look robust. Then there are so many fat ones. I never knew there were fat consumptives in the world. There were also some old ones. One grey-headed and grey-bearded fellow looks like a Kilburn Jew. He keeps muttering, "Golf needs concentration and concentration is not good for people like us. We ought to dream, to dream. . . ."

MARK GERTLER

To S. S. Koteliansky

22 November 1920 *Banchory*

Dear Kot, . . . Today it was sunny, so I rested outside, then 1 o'clock lunch in my room. After lunch I misbehaved and took a much longer walk than I was ordered and was caught by the doctor! He was very stern with me and I actually blushed like a naughty schoolboy. I apologised and

[1] Gerald Brenan, a friend of Ralph Partridge and Carrington, had settled in Spain.

[2] Mrs Dobrée.

promised not to disobey again. I only did it because a longer walk simply passes more time. . . .

During tea I chatted with a man about our health. I suggested it was a bit boring here. "Well," he said in a strong Lancashire accent, "one must make the best of it. I've had some bad moments when I first came here, and so do they all. They *look* happy but they're *not*. They all want to get away." Somehow I found my chat with this fellow comforting. I came back to my room and went to bed. . . . MARK GERTLER

To Carrington

26 November 1920 *Banchory*

Dearest Carrington, It was so nice of you to write so soon again. I was most excited to get your letter and it was long too—I am getting more used to this place now, and almost resigned. Things are a little better now. To begin with, I feel better in health—very much as I used to feel before my collapse—and also my exercise hours are longer. This morning I walked for one and a half hours and in the afternoon I played golf—or a sort of golf. It is called putting. This game intrigues me rather, but I've only played three times, so I'm not very brilliant, and therefore rather shy of asking people to play with me. They play so well, but they are very nice about it, I must say. In fact I am getting to like some of them now! Once a week we are weighed and the surprising thing is that in spite of my depression I am gaining weight! I have gained several pounds since I've been here! It is a queer sensation—that of "filling out". Those few pounds have already made such a difference to my appearance that when I catch a sudden glimpse of myself in the mirror it seems to me that my face is swollen! It doesn't suit me: it makes me look coarse—my neck gets so fat. It rather depresses me, also, to think that human beings, even sensitive ones like me, can be fattened like pigs! What one gets fat on here is milk and the boredom. I have to drink three pints of milk a day! But I never knew what a fattening thing boredom was. . . .

No, no works of Matisse, Picasso or Lhote or Derain have ever given me that hard blow of satisfaction that one gets from a real picture—you know the sensation I mean. I don't get that from anybody after Renoir in France, and as you say "We know better!"

You must send me more of Brenan's letters and work. I enclose here the last one you sent me. It *was* nice of you to send me it. I was so interested, but of course I don't altogether approve. Some of the things he says are rather silly. The part I like best is his appreciation of Gorky's *Tolstoy* and the quotation he chooses is a good one. He seems to me detached and philosophic and disinterested all right, but in a sort of picturesque and "flowing bow" kind of fashion. He seems to lack also in human experiences, but I don't quite express myself. I think you'll understand what I mean. Of course I am judging only from one solitary letter, but what do you think, am I wrong? There is even a something—just a suggestion of something superior in the tone of his letter. He is talking just a little down to you, just a little humouringly and that I don't like, and what about that "flattering" that you "lay on so thickly". I *do* hope you don't do that! It's a tiny little bit the great man's letter and in fact could go straight into a book. He writes so glibly and easily, and that again I don't like, but I envy him the clarity of his handwriting.

But please send me more. I'm so interested and don't be hurt at my criticisms. But to do so gives my mind a little rest from the continual boredom of this place. I enjoyed thinking about him, and trying to work out a character just from a letter. Probably I'm all wrong!

Yes, do send me some prints of your wood block work.

I do hope your portrait of Lady Strachey[1] will go well, and don't worry too much over "situations", my dear. Time settles and ends everything all the same.

Well, thank you again for your nice long letters and don't forget your poor forlorn little friend and write. Ever yours MARK GERTLER

To S. S. Koteliansky

28 November 1920 *Banchory*

My dear Kot, . . . No, they do not forbid me work. Then they do not realise two things. (1) How much painting agitates me. They call it a "hobby". You don't know how narrow and stupid these doctors are on any subject outside their work. God knows, perhaps they are stupid in that too. (2) That the days are so short. By the time our exercise is over there is no more daylight. The light, as far as painting is concerned, is gone by three-thirty this time of year and will continue so for the next few months.

All the same, as it rained yesterday and we couldn't play our game, I started painting—a landscape seen from my bedroom window. Somehow it did not go well. I got agitated and hot, so I chucked it in disgust and despair. Afterwards I got terribly depressed and last night was the worst I've had since I came here. Today I feel better, especially as I took up my painting again and this time it went better and now I hope to do about an hour's work a day. . . . It'll make all the difference to my spirits. . . . There is a servant girl whom I long to paint. She's about seventeen, extremely plump, with a face like a doll. Only her eyes black instead of blue and the red parts of her cheeks are absolutely scarlet. She has all the beauty of an apple with the additional charm of being human—a living apple. What could be more desirable!

Painting today seriously for the first time since three months had an extraordinary effect on me. I don't know how to describe it. My old paint box, my brushes so well known to me, the very same with which I struggled at Penn Studio and Garsington, it was so extraordinary and for some

[1] Mother of Lytton and James Strachey.

reason so sad. I really don't know why it affected me so much, but I wanted to cry. My poor old paint box in a sanatorium. . . . The only sensation I can liken it to is—supposing you loved a person very much, but whom you saw only occasionally and then only among other people—always in a bustle—and suddenly one day you and your beloved are shipwrecked on a deserted island. Just you two. . . . MARK GERTLER

To S. S. Koteliansky

3 December 1920 *Banchory*

Dear Kot, . . . Is Brett going to have "Saturday evenings" then? I have just had a long letter from Murry in which he sends his sympathies, admiration and advice, mixed with romantic reminiscences and offers of friendship and help! One of the many troubles of this life is that some people *will* not make up their minds what attitude they intend to take up towards one but cry with the times. Do you remember what Blake says somewhere to a "friend".

> Oh *do* be my enemy
> For friendship's sake!

It was a nice letter Murry wrote. I wish you could see it. I was quite touched. You know I am really very soft-hearted. He writes, by the way, that he doesn't consider this place or any sanatorium good for me—that I ought instead to go abroad and live my ordinary life. I don't agree with him and I think on the contrary that Katherine[1] ought to come here. I am sure it would do her good.

But all painting possibilities seem to be fading away again. To begin with, the doctor won't allow me to work after all—not for another fortnight—because I would have to stand. Dr Lucas, however, promises to get me a high stool, so that I can be raised to the right level for the particular subject I am doing. But the prospect of doing work here really isn't very promising. "You have come here primarily for your health, remember," one doctor told me. Yet whenever they come in they always ask, "Well, done any sketching yet?" The inconsistency of fools!

MARK GERTLER

To Carrington

7 December 1920 *Banchory*

Dearest Carrington, There is a middle-aged man, a patient here named Brahms, and his wife is staying in the village near him. I was out for my

[1] Katherine Mansfield was already suffering from tuberculosis.

walk one day, when I met this couple. They stopped me and asked if I wasn't Mr Gertler! Well, they knew me—met me at the Cannans—the Old Mill!—and said she, "Where is that charming young girl you had with you that time?" (meaning you). You could have knocked me down with a feather! That anyone here should know me and Gilly and Mary and Plucky little Gwen and the good old mill! I could have cried. In a place like this everything that's ever happened to one—every blessed memory—seems charming, wonderful, thrilling; and these people, the Brahms, dull, stupid and Jewish as they are, became for me here almost enchanted, just because they have crossed my path—if only for a moment—ah, some period of my past. . . .

The country round here is truly magnificent—the best I've seen. It is cruel to see it all and not have the freedom to get at it and paint. . . .

MARK GERTLER

To S. S. Koteliansky

12 December 1920 *Banchory*

My dear Kot, . . . The other night we had a cinema here. It was quite amusing. The nurses—some of them—sat rather close to the male patients. There was an unfortunate circumstance, during the early part of the first drama, which led up to a note which the hero finds on his table, and of course the note was flung large on the screen as usual for the benefit of the audience. It ran something like this: "It is no use our staying here. There is no hope for any of us, nothing to look forward to. We may as well give up." Everybody saw it and received it, however, with a roar of laughter. . . .

But the greatest boon here is that funny chap I told you about. He is really very funny. He also suffers from bad rheumatism and he gets no end of jokes out of it by the way he walks and groans. Even his cough he turns into fun. He coughs so loudly that it can be heard a mile off. I like him very much and not only for his jesting. . . . MARK GERTLER

To Carrington

17 December 1920 *Banchory*

Dear Carrington, Yes, you kept your promise and your letter came. Thank you for it, and also for the Brenan letter and the wood blocks. I would like to write to you even more often than I do, but my correspondence has grown rather large lately. I suppose people are feeling "compassionately" towards me just now; so they write me lots of letters. It is very nice of them, but I have to answer them all, which is *not* so nice. But that feeling of compassion will no doubt smoulder out soon—like most feelings—and then I shall write more often. I rather feel like writing to you these days. In fact, altogether, I feel more like writing letters here than I used to, simply because there is positively no one here you can open your mouth to—in any decent sort of way. There's no one to talk to and writing is the next best thing.

I liked this second letter of Brenan very much, especially in parts, but it seems such a waste to put it all into letters. He obviously, in spite of what he says, feels a craving to write, and it is a wonder to me that he doesn't write essays—or just descriptions—of the country and people around him. Somehow it all seems out of place and wasted in a letter. Your wood blocks I like very much too—they are so nice and definite.

As regards myself, I am really not in such a bad mood now as when I first came. I am almost completely resigned now. It's only just a question of patience, and after all it is worth while giving up a few months to be set up in health again. Already I feel far better than I've felt for years! And it is quite amusing to watch oneself growing plump every day! It's like magic. I get fascinated every time I bathe. I have gained half a stone since I came. I now weigh 9½ stone in my pyjamas. Not much I know. But for me—who has never weighed more than 9 stone, clothes and all—it makes quite a difference to the appearance. Then the country here is so fine that it makes up for a good deal. It's so interesting watching country in winter —a thing I've never done before. The colours of the mountains are so beautiful. They vary so. Sometimes they seem painted with those old master browns, golds and varying russets; at other times they suddenly become gay and assume Matisse blues and purples. Looking at them I sometimes suffer from a rather fascinating form of optical illusion. Suddenly they all turn into painting! I mean that instead of solid earth and stone, over which men can walk, it appears to me only as a picture, an oil painting done by some super genius! When this happens to me the illusion is so strong that I simply cannot—for some time—turn back again and see the scene in front of me as real space and solid earth—just as one suddenly imagines that the train one happens to be travelling in is going the wrong way.

How wonderful it was today; the weather was so glorious—frosty and sunny—and some of the mountains—the highest—wore snow caps, and how they glistened—a nice creamy chunk of flake white against a smoother layer of white, only slightly tinged with blue!

With Mr Brahms I play golf every afternoon—after my hour's work. But I dislike him. I hate his appearance and his manner, he's worse than any of them here really. Yet he thinks that between him and me there's a bond, and that *we* know more. The wretch has never heard of Renoir! And he has the damn cheek to talk about painting! "Those wonderful Italians," he says—and "My dear old Giotto," his wife exclaims suddenly, apropos of nothing.

The view I'm painting from my window has not turned out so dull after all. In fact, when I've finished the one I'm doing I shall start another, because in the present one I could not manage to get quite the right spacing. It began to grow over the top edge of the canvas, and I should have liked a band of sky[1]. . . .

Your suggestion that I should do some of my pen drawings is a good one, only, somehow, I seem to have lost all interest in work which is not done directly from Nature. I don't even see things in black and white. I have positively no desire to draw! I feel now that I only want to paint—and in oils—that which is in front of me. It doesn't matter how insignificant the object in front of me is. I'd rather paint it than compose a large and imaginative subject. Those are my present feelings. I may change, of course. It is a pity, in a way, because if only I was still in my charcoal period I could have worked away quite a lot here by artificial light, but it's all passed away.

Yes, I have had several letters from Ottoline. She doesn't seem especially happy—only so-so. She has run into Mary Cannan![2] And being almost as lonely there as I am here, Mary is I suppose almost an excitement!

Ever yours MARK GERTLER

To Carrington

December 1920 *Banchory*

Dear Carrington, . . . During my rest I talked to a pleasant young man—he's a medical student and does pen and ink "sketches" of the people here. He's heard of Nevinson and I found myself boasting that "Nevinson is a great friend of mine"! So you see I acted like a sort of St Peter—the other way about.

But, how queer it is to be among people—a little world in fact—where nothing is known about one or anything one cares for. Not a soul here has heard of Cézanne or Chekhov! Everything we care for—think about—is nothing to them. The things we really live for, in fact, are unknown to them. Sometimes I can take this extraordinary fact calmly.

I had quite an exciting day last Friday. Exciting in contrast to my present mode of living. I spent the day in Aberdeen, which is eighteen miles from here, with my young friend the medical student. We went first of all to the Art Gallery there, which is putrid (my friend liking all the worst pictures there, especially a horrid still life by Brangwyn). Then we lunched with his brother and another young man in the sort of Café Royal of Aberdeen, where we had a very good lunch with much wine *and* port *and* liqueurs *and* a fat cigar!!!!!

Oh! How good these things tasted after so long a period of abstinence and sobriety! Of course I got pleasantly tipsy. Then we went to my friend's house for tea, where I found his mother reading Rupert Brooke, of all people! She asked me if I knew the one on Painters. I said no, but I knew Rupert Brooke, lui-même! This caused great excitement in his

[1] Probably the painting reproduced opposite.

[2] Gilbert Cannan had left his wife Mary.

Trees at Sanatorium, Scotland

Oil painting (43 × 19 in.) 1921
Reproduced by permission of Mr Luke Gertler

Garsington Manor

Oil painting (22 × 30 in.) 1921

Reproduced by permission of Mrs Igor Vinogradoff

The Queen of Sheba

Oil painting (37 × 42 in.) 1922

Reproduced by permission of the Tate G

mother's breast and I went up heaps in her estimation. I find that in the world I live in now there is only one chance of distinction for me and that is to shelter under the wing of such great men as John, Epstein, Nevinson and Meninsky![1] (Meninsky has a drawing in the Aberdeen Art Gallery.) My own poor self counts as nothing here!

I also got my friend to get himself a whole set of oil painting materials and have started him off on a self-portrait!—over which he is now in a flutter of excitement, and doing not at all badly. He is a nice young man—good-looking in a sort of athletic way, sensitive and intelligent. I am going to paint his portrait. Today, a little tailor man from some obscure little town in Lanarkshire, a patient here, who, though unassuming and negative to look at, I got to like very much, left. I am sorry. He was one of the most lovable little people I've ever met! To look at him you would never have thought it—very small, bald, pince-nez'd, with a little moustache—yet so sensitive, kindly, intelligent and altogether lovable.

Much love

MARK GERTLER

To Carrington

1 January 1921 *Banchory*

Dear Carrington, Thank goodness we've pushed the old year by—that time should pass and pass is my chief wish just now. In a place like this, it sometimes seems to stop dead, and one thinks that tomorrow will never some. Here an hour is a year, a day a hundred, and a month five hundred years! Now they tell me that I ought to stop till May! and that it would be foolish of me to take risks and leave before this, in spite of the fact that I am "progressing excellently"—so they say—and according to them six or seven months is supposed to be a very short time for a cure and that I ought to consider myself lucky that I *am* curable etc. etc. But to me from now till May is an eternity of time, a life time—no, more—five thousand years!

However, time *does* pass—even here—and some time in the misty future May *will* come, and then I shall be free and well! It is better to suffer once and for all and get it over. I haven't been really well for years, and it will be worth while to feel so at last. Already I feel better than I've done for ever so long. . . .

I have finished one landscape. I am pleased with it, but I have got another going of the same subject, with a different and rather better spacing. Also a still-life of apples, which is nearly finished, and a self-portrait. The strange thing is that I am having a bigger struggle with the apples than I had with the landscape! And I've painted apples on and off all my life! However, it was worth the struggle as I have now managed to extract some good colour out of them and the paint has got into a peculiarly interesting condition. . . . The portrait of myself is not yet sufficiently advanced for me to say anything about it yet. Of course I am working under

[1] Bernard Meninsky, a member of the London Group.

great difficulty. My bedroom, in which I work, is dark in grey weather, and the moment there is a suggestion of sun the whole room from corner to corner gets flooded with it! How I long sometimes for Penn Studio where I could work for hours and hours with a "gris clair" light—I love painting in a good large convenient studio with a steady light, where things look the same for ever. To me comfort is more important than subject—I mean that I infinitely prefer painting a dull subject under comfortable conditions than something thrilling under conditions that are constantly changing. Then it's questionable if there is such a thing as a dull subject. . . .

Ah! those Goyas! How subtle—yet how vivid. Sometimes it seems to me that those old fellows were of a different species—else, how did they get that undesirable delicacy and mysteriously beautiful technique?! It seems almost as if they used different materials, so superior is their craft—and I *love* craft—beautiful paint—that kind of paint that makes you say "What lovely stuff." Since Goya there's only been Cézanne, sometimes Renoir—no one else has that *sense of paint*. I have never yet loved a picture whole-heartedly unless it has had that *sense of paint*. But I won't go on. *You* know what I mean.

They have been festive here for Xmas—champagne, fancy-dress dinner New Year's Eve—I was forced to go as a pierrot. Imagine me sitting about eighty strangers, dressed as a pierrot! drinking champagne. Really it wasn't altogether unamusing. The great comfort is that hardly any of the patients look in the least bit ill! I have never sat down to dinner with a healthier lot of *looking* people in my life. Some of the young ladies are pretty. There is one, especially, who is very good-looking. I send these two photographs as a token of my love and esteem for you, along with my very best wishes for a happy New Year. MARK GERTLER

To S. S. Koteliansky

5 January 1921 *Banchory*

My dear Kot, . . . Meanwhile that violent and active kind of boredom that I felt here at the beginning is passing. If I'm depressed ever now, it's no longer because I'm in a sanatorium, but the good old depression one always had, over no particular or tellable thing, simply the dissatisfaction with life in general. . . . When I think of what I am missing by not being in London I find there's mighty little. There's a lot of time for me yet to spend playing bezique with Brett or dining with Shearman. What else does one do there? It is not as if there were a bevy of beautiful young women whose love and caresses I miss by being here. No, the last few years the whole of life seems to have turned into one huge sanatorium without the health benefit of a real love. . . .

One never seems to lose the feeling that there are good and exciting things somewhere round the corner and that tomorrow, the day after or next year, perhaps, they will come to one, and everything will end with a wonderful climax, a sort of final and eternal embrace; But meanwhile. . . .

To me the most satisfactory thing is the process of work. As long as I work I feel somehow that I am really *functioning*, to use one of your words. . . .

You see, I've already done two pictures and two more are well advanced, which is not so very much less than the rate at which I've turned out pictures before my illness.

Yes, how good it was pushing that miserable year. In its disgusting way it was most eventful. It was only last March, nine months ago, that I went to Paris, saw pictures I longed to see for years, came back, and in the following few months did a sufficient number of pictures for a one-man show. In April I spat blood and went through that wretched unforgettable time waiting for results of tests. Then Garsington, and September brought my collapse and here I am. I leave out more soulful events. Events, let us say, of the heart, of which I have not told you and of which somehow I cannot speak. But there has been quite a lot.

MARK GERTLER

To Carrington

17 January 1921 *Banchory*

Dearest Carrington, . . . Being kept in bed for two days was more boring than I can tell you. I nearly lost heart completely! Cursed my fate and the day I was born and vowed that the moment I was allowed up I would run away or take poison!! However, they have allowed me to get up now, and to be at the ordinary routine again seems bliss after being confined to bed! That shows you how much everything goes by comparison. I mean, what was once tedious and almost unbearable has now become pleasant in comparison to an experience which was worse—and so on.

Yes, my work is now in full flow; but of course I *shall* be limited as regards to choice of subjects as long as I am here. There *are* certain subjects I have set my heart on, and which cannot be done here, such as large life-size portraits, nudes, nudes *with* still-lifes, compositions of several nudes *all done from nature* and so on.

But meanwhile I shall be able to keep the pot boiling here well enough. I am glad you agree with me about the paint of the old masters. We must see what we can do to rival it! Apart from the satisfaction of the result if we succeeded, we should be original enough for the *mere trying*, because, as far as I can see, no one else seems to care about it. Or do they try and fail *so* badly that one can't even trace the attempt?!

I am also very interested in your description and appreciation of the new Piero di Cosimo. I wonder if I should like it as much as a good Goya? If you can *possibly* get hold of a reproduction of it, *please* send it me. By the way, did that little Goya ever appear in the Burlington? or any of those Goyas? If it did, do for Christ's sake get hold of that particular number and send me it. I have come away foolishly enough with *no* reproductions! *Do* send me any you come across. I must ask Brett to send me my Goya and other reproduction books from my studio. But she is *so* lazy about that sort of thing!

The fame and peculiarities of Picasso reach even to here! People come and ask me to "explain" him, and cubism generally. Sometimes I almost seriously contemplate giving a lecture on "Art" here! Because, you know, I really *have* got a gift of clearing their minds up a bit! What I try and point out to them is really quite simple and primitive, and which is as yet so little realised by people of the pig-headed world. I start off by telling them, to their *utmost astonishment*, that, just as there is such a thing as an *ear for music*, so is there such a thing as a *sense for painting*. This sense does *not* consists of merely judging how *like* the painting is to the object represented, but that with this sense one *can* get pleasure from the mere juxtaposition and balance of coloured forms!!!!! And that in any picture, realistic or not, that part is *always* important if not *the most* important part. Granting that, then it is only logical and right for some painters, if they choose, to leave out almost, or quite completely, the representive part. They seem to grasp that and quite frankly admit that they never thought that anyone *could* get pleasure from the mere harmony of coloured forms, just as a musical person gets it from the harmony of sounds. What I tell them is of course crude, but you have no idea how necessary it is to drill this into them. Half the battle between the artist and the public is because the public is quite unaware of the existence of this, shall we call it *eye* for the juxtaposition of coloured forms as an equivalent to that in music of the ear for sound. Of course I talk it much more clearly than I write it, and honestly over and over again I have been thanked quite seriously by people who started off by being cynical and almost quarrelsome on the subject! The reason why people *don't* understand what I've been writing about here is of course really quite simple. The reason is that the sense for painting at its purest is the *rarest*, *rarest* sense in this world! Cézanne says somewhere that "In painting one addresses oneself only to the few". The fact is that painting at its best *does* only address itself to few, because there are damned few who have it in them to *be* "addressed" by it. Forgive this long lecture, but I am excited and angry, and allow me to finish up with one final expression of sadness on our art, namely that our poor art, Painting, is by far the most misunderstood and unappreciated art that ever was, and to my mind the most *truly aristocratic* one. . . .

My show is supposed to be coming off on the third of next month (February). My one desire is that I should sell well, as it is really very expensive here. Well, I shall stop now. I've written so much about "Art" in this letter that I feel there's no room for other subjects. For some reason I always write "shop" only in my letters to you!

But before ending I want to tell that your letters mean ever so much to me here, and I should be glad if you would continue to write regularly to me as long as I am here. Your labours will not be wasted, and after all it isn't for so very long now.

With ever so much love — MARK GERTLER

To S. S. Koteliansky

20 January 1921 — *Banchory*

My dear Kot, . . . Yes I used to like Desmond MacCarthy but, as you say, after a certain point, he falls asleep. The reason is that he is awfully fond of food and eats a great deal of it. He loves being asked out by "Society" and given a good dinner. At Garsington he used to "kindly" offer to carve the ham and relieve Philip of the trouble, in spite of the latter's assurances that he loved doing it and that it was no trouble at all. On such occasions none of us grumbled at not having enough to eat. MacCarthy used to help himself to a second helping. He used generally to become so absent-minded and conversational that half the ham changed its original place for MacCarthy's plate. At such moments Philip's counter-talk became rather disjointed. Toronto[1] is quite a nice young fellow. I could never make up my mind whether he is a fraud or genuine, but even if he is a fraud, he's a nice homely one. . . . Women seem rather taken with him, goodness knows why. . . . I used to like going into Oxford with him and having a fling—that is to say a drinking bout, on which occasion he made an amusing companion. He could drink ever so much without getting drunk. . . . — MARK GERTLER

To S. S. Koteliansky

6 February 1921 — *Banchory*

My dear Kot, . . . Apparently my pictures at the private view did not sell like hot cakes exactly. Only two sold and one of these was bought by our poor friends the Hannays. . . .[2]

My fame has at last penetrated to here. They keep finding notices in the papers. The other day the little plump girl came rushing to me, breathless with excitement, flapping a *Daily Mirror* in my face in which was a notice about me headed "*Mendel*" etc. This is really most unfortunate because they all want to know about this book of which I am the "hero". . . . They look at me now with a new eye. It is most embarrassing. . . . They are awfully nice here but surprisingly provincial. . . .

My work goes fairly well, though as often happens to me, I have for the moment come against a sort of hitch—a knot in the grain—but it

[1] Frank Prewett, a Canadian poet.

[2] Howard Hannay had married a Slade artist, Lynton.

will pass. I am working pretty hard now, in spite of which I am making progress in my health, which is a good sign. . . . MARK GERTLER

To Carrington

18 February 1921 *Banchory*

Dearest Carrington, You were unnecessarily alarmed over my "spree" in Aberdeen. I only drank two or three glasses, I assure you. I am careful enough over my cure. I am going through it with the patience of an ox, and I'm sure that in the future, far from their having to find fault with me for carelessness, I shall bore people with the excessive care I intend to take of myself in the future! I am so glad you thought the pictures at my show looked well. I have heard from many people who thought the same. I had a nice letter from Roger Fry, though I do not like his review in the *New Statesman* as it is too patronising and harping too much as to the future, instead of dealing with that already achieved. That is to say, he should have said what he liked and disliked about the pictures at the present moment at the Goupil and not gassed so much about my "handicaps" and how well I overcome them, and how much more I may yet overcome them in the dim distant future!

But please do not tell him this, if you happen to see him, as his letter was very nice and congratulatory. I can't help feeling that my work is really *not* for him, that he and I are too fundamentally different for my work ever to really appeal to him or his kind. Also, he is altogether too hopelessly French just now for my work to be really understood by him. Hence the mincing, grudging and ungenerous review of his in the *New Statesman*. In his letter he calls this review an "appreciation"! No, do not send me any newspaper notices of my show—I hate them all equally whether they happen to be "appreciations" or criticisms. Besides I get them all here; every day somebody else comes rushing at me with a new and ghastly notice. Ugh! . . .

I have written to tell Brett that for the first fortnight, at least, I shall have to keep very quiet—and only gradually break myself in to the old excitements of life. Like a man who comes out of a dark room into brilliant sunlight, he can open his eyes only by degrees. I am afraid there isn't a photograph of the medical student. At least it would look rather strange if I asked him for one in order to send home to a young lady friend of mine! . . .

Much love, dear MARK GERTLER

To S. S. Koteliansky

28 February 1921 *Banchory*

My dear Kot, . . . G's reason for not buying a picture is everybody's reason. Everybody seems particularly hard up just now when for the first time in my life I happen to have a one-man show! . . .

I shall have to live almost exactly under the régime of this place. But I shall be all right, I'm sure, at Hampstead with the help of Mrs Horne and my people, at least for the first few weeks. . . . It is a terribly capricious disease, this T.B. One can't be too careful. I know a great deal now and one thing I *have* made up my mind about is that it is worth sacrificing anything for one's health. What I have felt and seen here confirmed me in that. . . .

I have at last arranged for the apple-faced maid to sit for me. I am much excited. I am also doing my young medical student friend and two fairly large landscapes. . . . MARK GERTLER

To Carrington

14 March 1921 *Banchory*

Dearest Carrington, Thank you so much for your letter and the magazine on Renoir. I enjoyed seeing reproductions of Renoir again—immensely. How good they are! How massive and grand! I am struggling also with the text, but I find I can still understand very little French, which is really a great nuisance. Yes, you must be humble indeed if you are pleased with Roger Fry having said, "There is something to be said for your work" etc. I confess I am not so humble; also I prefer people to say they like or dislike one's work, rather than hold out hope for some distant time in the future. One doesn't live forever, you know.

Personally I have no views about your work, for the simple reason that I have not seen any!—or about three things I think within the last ten years—and the last one I saw was three years ago at Monty's. I was looking forward to a nice little tête-à-tête tea with you and seeing your work at Gordon Square that day after Taylor's[1] lunch, but you seemed to have forgotten, or pretended to, and went instead to see Julian! The reason being I think that you wanted to see the king of Spain—of all people—in the morning!! However, I may yet see a work by you one of these days. I shall look forward to it.

I am sorry, my dear, but the little painting you like so much has sold! I don't know who bought it. Probably I shall do another one like it this summer when I stay with the Hutchinsons, which no doubt I am sure to do—then perhaps I will give it you.

Out of the whole of my show I made only £139 11*s*. Hardly enough even to pay my fee here for three months. But better luck next time perhaps.

I wonder which is the most Renoir-like, your girl or mine, the one I am painting here? Did I tell you about her? She is wonderful to paint—vermilion cheeks—I could do a half a dozen pictures of her right off.

There is no doubt about my getting well, but I shall have to be so very

[1] Walter Taylor, friend and patron of Gertler's, and himself a painter.

careful in the future—and that's the bother. I don't even know how much I shall be allowed to live in London or even England—I may have to live abroad, especially in the winters. My future, in fact, is very vague and foggy at present. My actions and movements will have to be guided entirely by my health—and goodness knows where I shall be driven to in the end.

I don't even know quite where to go for my summer, I should like Garsington, because there I could see interesting people again, which would be a pleasant change after being cooped up here for so long. There are two reasons against Garsington: (1) I am not sure of the air there, and (2) if I could get the enormous quantities of food I shall need now. But no doubt it'll all work out somehow. . . .

My work continues to go well in spite of the adverse circumstances. Last Sunday I felt very bored—the weather was so awful—so I flung the rules of this place to the winds (and it *was* terribly windy) and painted all day from nine in the morning to six at night! The longest day's work I've done since my illness—and I completed a flowerpiece! The next day I fell ill with a bilious attack and frightful headaches and so the doctors had the excuse to put it all down to my long day's work. I am better now, though I lost a lot of weight this week. So I am now being made to stuff like a prize pig in order to regain it—and only one hour's work a day for the week! . . .

Much love MARK GERTLER

To Carrington

21 March 1921 *Banchory*

Dearest Carrington, . . . Thank you also for the thought of asking me down to Tidmarsh.[1] But, even if you did and it was healthy and all that, I would not think of plumping my troublesome and invalided self down upon you.

No doubt it will be Garsington for the summer as usual. I don't much care. All I want for the moment is to get out of this—this month has been, and is still, horrible. I don't know why, but it is being more of a trial to me than all the rest of the time put together! . . .

No thank you, I *don't* want a Mary Cannan—nor a good wife nor a good mistress!!! Get me rather a £1,000 a year, and all would be well. For a £1,000 a year I could get a nice house anywhere and hire a good cook. For the rest I like women to be my friends and equals, or superiors as the case may be, not half mistress and half slave. I hate that state of affairs. I also hate that dual sort of feeling between a man and a woman, sort of "Beatty and Babs". Ugh!

I really couldn't think of letting you *buy* one of my pictures. Your

[1] Tidmarsh Mill, near Pangbourne, home of Lytton Strachey and Carrington at this time.

money would choke me. But I will really quite soon now *give* you a picture. . . .

I assure you I *have* got your enthusiasm for travel, only there is just one thing I have even a greater enthusiasm for and that is painting—and I swear that moving about is bad for one's work. When I was young I felt that instinctively and now I know it consciously. Also travelling always exhausts me so much that the pleasure becomes doubtful. Though some day you are going to take me to Spain, aren't you? . . .

Much love MARK GERTLER

To S. S. Koteliansky

11 April 1921 *Banchory*

My dear Kot, . . . The doctor said I could leave any time—that is before May, if I wanted to. But the reason I am staying on till the beginning of next month is that I want to finish a certain rather large landscape. In fact I could not bear to leave it unfinished. . . .

I have to keep showing my work every day to the people here. They all want to see them, which is a bore. But I have to show them out of politeness. I have three people up at a time. Three different ones every day. Well, if a strike or any other mishap doesn't prevent me, I shall be in London on Tuesday a fortnight. . . . That same evening you must come round to see me—after supper will be the best time.

Today a boy of about eighteen died, rather unexpectedly. I liked him very much. He was such a nice quiet and modest boy, with something awfully nice about his eyes. He was expecting to leave here in May and looking forward so much to going home, which he missed dreadfully. It is very strange to think of him lying dead a few doors away.

MARK GERTLER

To Carrington

13 April 1921 *Banchory*

Dearest Carrington, Thank you ever so much for your charming letter and the book of reproductions. It was really most kind of you to send them, and I enjoy looking at them so much. I am also reading the letters and articles on Cézanne—the reproductions are excellent.

When I last wrote to Brett I was feeling very wretched and despairing, and very nervous and apprehensive as to what the new chief doctor would say about my condition—he seemed to be finding all sorts of additional diseases in most of the other patients. In my young medical friend for instance he discovered that his throat was tubercular—which is a ghastly disease—and as I was suffering from discomfort in the throat too, I imagined that he would find the same in me too! However, when at last my turn came, all was well. His report was even better than I expected. He said I could leave as soon as I wished!! But I am staying on till May in spite of it, because I want to finish my long landscape.

Now I know that I am well and that I *can* go if I want to, it is not so tedious being here, especially as the weather has been so fine lately.

The doctor gave me a long talking to as to how I shall have to live in the future and it appears that I shall have to take the greatest possible care for about two years—as it takes all that time for the cure to what he calls "*solidify*"! No cinemas, theatres, restaurants, woman, wine—or any place that's stuffy, etc, etc! So you see it doesn't leave me much room for "dissipation" exactly. He is also not certain as to my being able to live in London next winter—I have to consult Dr Latham about that in the autumn—so I may have to undergo another exile somewhere or other next winter.

However, I am well again now and free to leave this wretched place, and for the time being that's pleasing enough in itself. Yes, only you, Brett and me remain single. . . .

I confess that your recalling of memories saddened me rather. It might have been so much better—I loved you so. . . . I wonder if you ever realised how much I loved you! What agony and suffering I went through on your account! How terrible it was when you turned to L.S. . . . I used to start up in bed at night—all in a sweat—from sheer agonies of jealousy. Ugh!

However that moment you mention was good—for once you were amiable, and you actually *let* me kiss the rain off your face. You even went so far as to point out a particular drop and asked me to catch it quick, which I lost no time in doing—and how good it tasted!

Yes—it is spring. Beautiful? yes, but I am sitting at this moment in a sanatorium—my health uncertain—and I'm nearly thirty! Well, forgive this melancholy outpouring, but you brought it on yourself by those "memories".

You were quite right to send your picture of the maid to the International. I think it is good to exhibit—and among other pictures too—because very often one can see one's faults more clearly when contrasted with other people's pictures. But I should ever so much like to see it. Also I am *very* pleased that you got £25 for "Lady Strachey". . . .

Much love MARK GERTLER

To Carrington

26 April 1921 *Banchory*

Dearest C., . . . You are right. The "pleasures" I am forbidden are really very doubtful ones in comparison to work and talk and a quiet dinner with a friend, though I must say I *shall* miss the cinema—also I have a strong desire to go to dances! I wanted to go and dance with nice girls!

And I should like to dig up students, like we used to be, and go to their parties—surely there must be some somewhere. Taken in the right spirit one could, I feel, enjoy them now. When one is no longer so hot-blooded—and more detached—who knows, I might even impress them like a sort of John! Surely there must be some nice short-haired girls with heavy boots and young eager natures wishing to be "advanced" and seeking for "free love"!? I should like to meet such people now. They would not find me wanting in "free love" anyhow!

Yes, Kot has told me about the Russian doctor's visit to him, but he has already left the country for Paris where he is going to work at the Pasteur Institute, whatever that may be. But if I do get ill again perhaps we may with Kot's influence get hold of him and try his cure.

The strikes are awful indeed and I quite agree with you. I think people who undertake to do such unpleasant and dull labour should be well paid for it. Why on God's Earth people who do nothing but *own* mines should be so disgustingly rich, while people who do the nasty part of work in them should be so much less rich is beyond my apprehension and out of all sense of justice. But you seemed so very worried, dear—you must not worry yourself over it. . . .

You are not old my dear—that is a fable—and you are as beautiful—both internally and externally. I at any rate shall always think you so and love you. To me your presence is always beautiful and stimulating—like champagne—only the excitement is of a more spiritual and intellectual nature. I think of you when I paint.

When I come to London I shall have to pay a visit to the Garnett[1] shop and see these books of reproductions. . . .

There has arrived here a beautiful boy patient in kilts—twelve years old, slim, a pale face, long white legs and a charming and affectionate nature. I wish he had arrived before as he makes such a desirable addition to a place like this.

Much love and may we meet soon MARK GERTLER

To Carrington

17 May 1921 *Penn Studio, Hampstead*

My dearest Friend, Thank you so much for your two letters. How good it is to get letters from you, but how much better still to see you in the flesh!

It was really wonderful—that Wednesday evening—and how nice you were to me! That night we created another memory to add to the long list. I am glad also that you liked my work, but you must not despair about your own—a person of such outstanding and beautiful personality

[1] Francis Birrell and David Garnett had just started a bookshop in Taviton Street, Bloomsbury.

as you are is sure to do good work. I should like very much to see your signboard.[1]

My plans for the summer are not absolutely fixed yet, but to begin with at any rate I hope to go to Garsington—that is about the first week in June. After staying there a while it is possible that I may go abroad. If I don't, I should be delighted to come and stay with you at Tidmarsh—later on. Thanks for asking me. Only, if I do, you will have to allow me to pay for my week-end food. I insist upon that now, wherever I go to stay in the country, since I need so much milk and cream and butter.

I have not been to many parties yet, firstly because there have not been many to go to and secondly because I don't want to go out much as yet. Taylor, however, gave a party especially to me! last Monday. It was nice of him to give it, but I must say I found it boring, and I was chiefly conscious of the stuffiness and heat of the atmosphere, which was making me feel nervous. Ever since I've come back I have been suffering from stuffiness. Sometimes people will not open their windows.

Yesterday I lunched with a Mrs Braham, a Princess Obolensky, a countess of the same name and three other ladies at the Ritz! I enjoyed it very much!

I am sorry you are a little harassed by "situations". I suppose that is inevitable with a person as beautiful as you are. I am afraid being forty won't help you—you'll probably be just as beautiful. To me at any rate you become more beautiful every time I see you. I don't mean by this just externally, but the "tout ensemble".

Whatever you do, don't tie yourself irrevocably to one man. A person like you should *never belong* to anyone—never be so and so's *wife* or even so and so's *mistress*. There ought to be no one person who should be able to say "*she is mine*". Live with men if you like, but don't pledge yourself in any way. You are too good for that—you belong to the *world*. God knows *I* love you enough and *I* should like to own you. But I have learnt to curb my desires, and not even to *expect* to possess all the parts of a person like you. I am satisfied with what little you can give me—at moments.

And others *must* learn the same, and *not* be greedy. As it is they get so much more than I do or ever did. How pleased *I* should have been to see you so often or to live with you in the country or to travel with you to Italy! None of these joys fell to my lot. Yet I dare say people who get all this and more from you are not satisfied. No, *don't* allow people to be greedy, and for goodness sake keep me my little share. Remember I love you as much as anybody else, and it is only out of respect to *you* that I curb it, and don't worry you with it.

A good thing has happened to me. Marchant has seen my work from Nordrach and liked it so much that he is going to advance me £25 per month! And Taylor has bought the "Scotch Maid" for £35.

Forever yours MARK GERTLER

[1] Probably the one she painted for the Spread Eagle at Thame, John Fothergill's inn.

To S. S. Koteliansky

25 June 1921 *Garsington Manor, Oxford*

My dear Kot, The chief fault about this place is that it feels so much like a pleasure ground, so that I am not able to work with such regularity and concentration. There are two things which cause this effect more than anything else and they are hot sunny weather and Julian. Julian would like to be gay and playful the whole time and this rather demoralises me. It is also very difficult to treat her as a child, because she is as full grown and has precisely the same effect as a very attractive young lady of twenty-five. I see no difference whatsoever. The business about age is absurd. I think she ought to wear a placard with "Please remember I'm only fifteen."

However, today the sun has gone. It is grey and dismal, and I feel my good old self again. I like grey weather: it suits me. It keeps my blood pressure down. I also prefer painting grey landscapes. The sun is terribly difficult to paint, and it moves and alters everything all the time. And it burns the back of one's neck till one feels giddy, and dazzles the canvas to such an extent that it is quite impossible to see what one is doing. A sketching umbrella on the other hand makes it too dark. Altogether painting out of doors is a terrible business. One of these days I shall give it up. I like painting landscape from indoors, where I can sit in comfort.

I have been having terrible dreams lately. They say it is my liver. I dreamt that I accidentally shot my elder brother and the first thing that struck me was that my chief source of maintenance was gone.

Then I dreamt that I had a haemorrhage and lost all my teeth—and that I had a frightful quarrel with my elder sister, because she happened to come in just as I was drawing a nude model and criticised the shape of the model's legs. "Ha!" she said, "look at those legs! Like sticks! Those are the sort of legs you like, I suppose." So I got furious and told her what I thought of her and her legs! . . .

I find I must see people. I hate being alone. That is why I like being here. One gets people without any trouble. You don't have to ask them to come or go to see them. In London I feel lonely because I hate bothering to make arrangements to see people and therefore I am very much alone. . . .

The only person I can get information from, so far, on the quality of Murry's lectures is "Toronto". He says that he only went to one: that they thought it was very learned, and that the general impression from others is that they were a great success, especially among the young ladies, and that he had a great ovation on the last one. . . .

Yesterday Julian forced me, in the middle of painting, to take a riding lesson. So I went out on horseback. It was not bad and I did not fall off, though I could not control the horse at all. He just did precisely what Julian's horse did. When she galloped, I galloped, and so on. My horse seemed to utterly despise me and completely ignored my demands from him. At moments, if I didn't sit quiet, he would turn his head and look round threateningly at me, as if to say, "Do that again and I'll bite you." So in the end I left it to him, after which we got on very well. . . .

MARK GERTLER

To Carrington

1 July 1921 *Garsington Manor, Oxford*

Dear Carrington, I hear from Ottoline that you have some intention of coming over here. Well, I am writing to beg of you not to do so, if you have any feeling left for me at all, as it would be most painful for me to see you just now.[1]

Please do not tell Ottoline that it was I that put you off. Make some excuse, as I do not like people to know my private feelings.

I am extremely sorry to be so tiresome, but I am fairly happy here, and if you came you would spoil it for me and I am not often happy.

MARK GERTLER

To The Hon. Dorothy Brett

13 July 1921 *Garsington Manor, Oxford*

Dear Brett, The place you are at certainly sounds remote.[2] The last time I heard from Valentine she had not yet definitely taken a house there. I wonder if she will.

I am quite happy here. I have had an awful struggle with the painting of sunlight. I never knew how difficult it was to do and how much it stood by itself as a problem for the painter. However, after a terrific struggle I have managed, at last, to get somewhat into it now, and I have finished one sunlit picture and another is well on the way.

The weather has been remarkable. I never remember such a summer. Broiling sun all the time and though everybody wants rain it still continues —sometimes it gets too hot even for work.

Toronto is staying in the village. He has become a cheese-maker and is settled here more or less permanently. Siegfried Sassoon is also staying here for some time. Those are the only permanences. Julian is just a little bigger all round and very nice. Taylor has been staying near by and came over several times, once for a week-end. He enjoyed his visits, enormously —I think Julian added vastly to his pleasures.

There came also for last week-end that man with the eyebrows, Gill.[3] Do you remember him? At the Slade he was—with a sister—rather nice, not unlike Carrington to look at.

[1] Probably because Carrington had married Ralph Partridge on 21 May of that year.

[2] Probably Callendar in Scotland, where Brett's family had a house.

[3] Colin Gill.

The week-end before that there were the Bussys, with a daughter of fifteen[1] who looks like a sort of Lytton Strachey in petticoats!

Ottoline, Julian and I have started last night to sleep on the roof, as it is so terribly hot in the bedrooms. I liked it in some ways but I am not yet quite used to sleeping out of doors as I have never really slept completely out of doors before.

We play croquet golf now. It is all the rage with us. My health remains good and the few times I have weighed myself all was well. Well perhaps you will come here soon for a week-end. Let me know. MARK GERTLER

To Carrington

14 July 1921 *Garsington Manor, Oxford*

Dear Carrington, I am afraid that it is quite impossible for me to change my mind—at any rate for the present. I also do not feel inclined to give you "logical" reasons as you desire. Firstly my reasons would take up too much time and space and would be far from pleasant reading for you, and secondly logic doesn't matter in this case as much as feelings—and my feelings are strongly opposed to you. Surely that is enough reason for not wanting to see you.

As for regretting in the winter that we have not met in the summer, or the "exile" from my company that you speak of, that is all nonsense. You know very well that you never put yourself out for a single moment ever to come and see me. As for "perfect hot summers", whichever summer *did* I see you even in the best of times!?

So it is rather hard for me to believe that you are going to miss so much my company, when you chose to have it only for about two half-hours a year for the last three years! In any case I would not consider your feelings in the matter, since you never in any one instance in all the long years I have known you considered mine, but always and invariably did precisely what suited your own convenience, completely regardless of the suffering it might cause me.

"You can't have your cake and eat it!"

I have told Ottoline my difficulty about seeing you so that she will not expect you and will understand your not coming. I thought it best to do so.

Yours sincerely MARK GERTLER

To The Hon. Dorothy Brett

[? *1921*] *Garsington Manor, Oxford*

Dear Brett, You are one of those distressing people that have a way of pointing a critical finger at one the whole time. You tell me now that I

[1] Jane Simone Bussy.

"clip life like a yew tree is clipped", that people cannot talk to me for any length of time, that I do not understand others etc, etc. If you won't mind me saying so, your criticisms seem to me vague, not at all to the point. No doubt I have faults—who hasn't? But one thing I refuse to do and that is to correct myself according to the suggestions of others. Think what a muddle I'd be in if I tried! MARK GERTLER

To S. S. Koteliansky

1921 *Garsington Manor, Oxford*

Dear Kot, It is a pity that things are always so imperfect. This place is in some ways so attractive to me—like a second home. They are so kind and yet it goes wrong somehow, and I have to fly.

I have a sort of horror of my future. I am afraid of it. It all seems utterly black—so desolate. There isn't a single point I can look forward to, and say that will be nice—worth waiting for.

I hear Toronto's voice, below, at his cheese—he is humming some tune—shaky and uncertain like himself. Toronto, you know, bores me infinitely now—he more than bores me, he gets on my nerves. He doesn't know what he wants, and is always trying to gain the ladies' sympathy by his grumblings—even to Julian he grumbles and whines, and looks at her with glossy eyes. Ugh! Every view he expresses is romantic, unreal and sickly. In fact, he has a sickly soul. . . .

I am going to London from here by car. My brother is coming to fetch me. I hate partings. There is a sort of dismal feeling about everything today. I dread the parting. I long to be away—yet I will come here over and over again. This place has a magnetic attraction for me.

There came here some people called the Turners[1]—friends of Sassoon's. I liked them. I have taken their address. I also liked the Eliots[2] when they were here, so I took their address too. MARK GERTLER

To Edward Marsh

7 November 1921 *Penn Studio, Hampstead*

Dear Marsh, Thanks very much. It was extremely nice of you to bother. I must say I was rather surprised they didn't have anything of mine at the Tate. Especially as they have a few of my pictures bought by the Contemporary Arts Society, and I believe that the pictures hung were a selection from the Society's purchases. It is a pity, in fact, that they did not select one of those for the Gallery, or one of my more recent works, instead of robbing you of yours.

[1] W. J. Turner, music critic and poet.

[2] T. S. Eliot and his wife.

The Servant Girl

Oil painting (24 × 15 in.) 1923

Reproduced by permission of the Tate Gallery

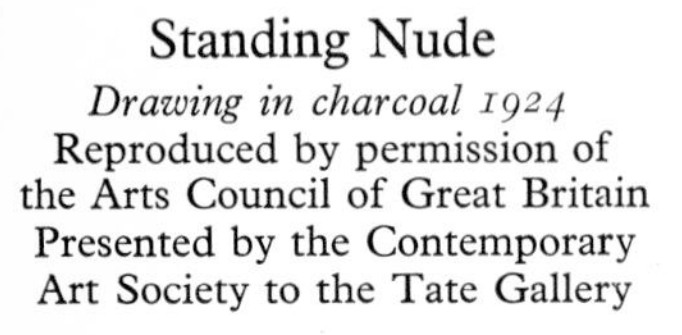

Standing Nude

Drawing in charcoal 1924
Reproduced by permission of
the Arts Council of Great Britain
Presented by the Contemporary
Art Society to the Tate Gallery

Young Girlhood II

Oil painting (53 × 25 in.) 1925
Reproduced by permission of
the Arts Council of Great Britain
From the collection of Mr Tom Balston

I am well again now, thanks, though no doubt you heard that I had a rather serious breakdown in health about a year ago—one of my lungs was touched and I had to go to a sanatorium in Scotland for some months. Now I am right again, but I have to take great care for a year or two yet.

Perhaps you would care to come to tea one Sunday? Do come if you would like to.

With all good wishes and again many thanks MARK GERTLER

To Carrington

[21 December 1921] *Penn Studio, Hampstead*

Dear C., I cannot but help writing to thank you for the two very good reproductions you sent me for Xmas and also for your kind wishes. I am afraid it is rather difficult for me to promise right away that I will see you again. The situation is too complicated for that, but I promise to try my best to get myself into a state of mind that may allow of our meeting again, since you seem to want to see me so much. This is only a few words to thank you, but very soon I will write again, more fully, to try and explain my state of feeling about you and give you more information about my life etc. If I can manage to explain what I feel, you will see that my wanting not to see you is not just a whim or a piece of narrow-mindedness or a form of cruel and unjust obstinacy.

Meanwhile please accept my best wishes for a Happy Xmas and New Year. MARK GERTLER

To W. J. Turner

4 January 1923 *Penn Studio, Hampstead*

Dear Turner, I have your cheque. I am glad you like the drawing.

I came back from Garsington on Tuesday, as usual, more dead than alive, with a fearful headache and sickness, which I still feel. The life somehow or other is very hectic there. My life in London is in comparison to Garsington like that of a monk! What with seeing people like the Asquiths, Miss Blake, the richest heiress in the world, or the "Shy Bride", Mrs Rose, a young woman who owns a husband with £50,000 a year, a dozen or two of young lords, a smart but elderly woman who cannot open her mouth without making an epigram, and whose name is Mrs Lindsay, then there is Toronto, who mooches about like a faded Hamlet, and so on—

Siegfried was there too, or the "Captain" as we call him. I can never look at him without wanting to slap my calves with an imaginary whip in "A hunting we will go" style! . . . MARK GERTLER

To S. S. Koteliansky

[*7 August 1923*] *Lyme Regis*

My dear Kot, I myself was going to write to Lawrence to take some steps about his health, as from what you write it sounds suspicious. I would strongly advise him to go to the doctor. He will then know exactly what is the matter. . . . For the last month I have not been able to get painting out of my head—night or day—I can think of nothing else. At moments I am worn out by it. I have read Vollard's *Renoir*. I was thrilled, but with Renoir, not with Vollard. He is such a liar, an artful cunning liar. He so cunningly makes people say and behave as he wants them to, and explain beliefs that he either believes, or disbelieves in, according to his like or dislike of them. He does it all in a sort of "naive" simple way. . . . He makes a libellous caricature of Rodin in the book. . . . MARK GERTLER

To W. J. Turner

28 September 1923 *Penn Studio, Hampstead*

Dear Walter, . . . I am glad you have got the picture. The fact that you like it is most encouraging to me. I should feel much happier if the people I see and like, my friends in fact, would take a greater interest in my work and appreciate it more. But so many of them happen to be writers and intellectual in another way, and really they take very little interest in not only my work but painting generally. The result is that I often feel, as an artist, very isolated. . . . MARK GERTLER

To Valentine Dobrée

6 April 1924

Dear Valentine, . . . The Picasso show did interest me, as his work always does. But frankly I don't know what I really think of it. He has *such* a lot of talent, yet sometimes it seems to me that, as results, his are too much *made up*. I wonder if he has anything moving to express—but I "don't know". I was somehow more moved this time by the happy gay decorative colours of Dufy! He is doing a beautiful screen, and now keeps a sort of workshop with young men assistants, like the old days, and full of work. Making money too! Also Matisse is nice, with his bright spontaneous colours. Yes, we at last got to Durand Ruel's, and I was disappointed! To begin with most of the ones I wanted to see were not there or were not shown to us and there were *so* many Monets and Pissarros. Also the house is so badly lit that it is almost impossible to see anything. Renoir is exquisite—delicious, but that is also his fault. I prefer him in reproductions. He is really too "tasty". It is too refined for us—too sweet. We must have something more brutal today. There were one or two Cézannes there and I felt the same about him—far too *precious*. No, I was really rather put off. . . . Of course I was panting to get back to work again. My ideas are somewhat changed—no big pictures, no romance, just chunks of Nature. It's design that matters, not subject. The less subject the better. The artist of today expresses himself no longer by religion, romance or literary illustrations, but *purely by design*. In my case *the realisation of Nature in terms of design*—and any bit of Nature. . . .

Yours ever MARK GERTLER

To S. S. Koteliansky

6 April 1924 *Hôtel Sube, Saint-Tropez*

My dear Kot, I arrived here yesterday. My journey was horrible, even worse than I expected. It was the Channel crossing which was so bad. . . . only an hour, but unfortunately it takes me two whole days to recover from that hour. . . . The day at Marseilles I enjoyed in spite of a sick headache. We went to Aix where Cézanne was born and spent the last twenty years of his life. We drove to his house and the coachman who took us happened by a curious chance to have been Cézanne's coachman, and a servant in the family before that. We went round the house and plucked a laurel leaf each from some bushes near the gateway as a memento.

The evening was spent differently. We went to a brothel and saw an indecent cinema. It was truly indecent not because of what they did, but because we knew that these people were doing that for a living, and in front of a camera . . . and my goodness how insipid and uninteresting they made vice seem.

This place is gay and vital, like so many little ports in this part of the world. There is a sort of lively stink about the place, except in the hotel, which has a more normal and intimate stink about it. There is quite a colony of artists here, social life, a cinema, dance hall, brothel, a few cafés and so on. Nelson, who dresses like Vie de Bohème, has been deserted by his wife for an American boy of eighteen. . . . MARK GERTLER

To S. S. Koteliansky

22 July 1924 *Garsington Manor, Oxford*

My dear Kot, . . . I wish we didn't talk and argue such a lot here, but unfortunately Turner, in spite of being a nice man, is inclined to arouse discussions of a rather superfluous nature, in the midst of which one finds oneself very excited but entirely at a loss to know what was the point. He has one other fault and that is bad taste with regard to people. He calls it "tolerance". I call it complete lack of discrimination. He likes what he calls "brilliance". I hate it. . . .

All the same it is nice to be here—at least for a while. For a change it is good to be among people, after living alone as I do. And when there are too many people here I just skip off—disappear. Ottoline knows it now and does not mind.

I see that in spite of those rascals, the Sitwells, coming up to me so friendly the other day, they have written a book with a malicious description of me in it![1] I am so glad I was cold to them. MARK GERTLER

To S. S. Koteliansky

6 August 1924 *Garsington Manor, Oxford*

My dear Kot, . . . I heard today that my little old lady from Hampstead died. I am sad about it. She was a lovable old thing and I shall miss seeing her creep about the studio, always anxious . . . and suspicious. She thought, I am sure, that she and I were the only decent people in the world, that the rest of the world was contriving its utmost to ruin and destroy us, that we must fight our hardest against them to survive. Even her brother-in-law, old May and his family, she was mistrustful of. She would refer to him merely by a sarcastic nod of her little head and say "Him". She used to look carefully at me every morning with a consoling look, as if to say, "Hm, the world *has* done it on you *this* morning, to be sure." She very often would know before I did if I was going to be ill. I therefore used to dread her careful scrutiny, and would often try to avoid it by looking away. Her smile was worth seeing—I loved it—but, if I sympathised with her over any little grievance, her eyes would immediately grow red and be on the point of tears. I am sure she loved me and I her. I am so unhappy that some flowers I sent her will have arrived too late, as I know they would have made a difference to her. I am also sorry that I was away and unable to see her before the end. . . . MARK GERTLER

To S. S. Koteliansky

30 December 1924 *Garsington Manor, Oxford*

My dear Kot, A day or two ago I heard from Phyllis[2] to say that she had got her father's consent to our marriage. So when I return I expect I shall become what's called "engaged". If you or Farbman are writing to Mrs Farbman you might tell her. . . . Of course I will bring Phyllis along to Acacia Road on the first available Monday. Here it came to them like a thunderbolt and my people are excited and pleased. I will tell you more when next we meet. MARK GERTLER

[1] I cannot trace the reference. It may be the same story about Epstein and Gertler which Edith Sitwell afterwards told in her memoirs.

[2] A young Jewish girl to whom Gertler was engaged. At the last moment he broke it off.

To S. S. Koteliansky

28 January 1925 *Hôtel Sube, Saint-Tropez*

My dear Kot, I had a comfortable journey, a smooth crossing and the Blue Train is certainly luxurious. . . . I have taken the little villa of which you must have heard me talking as a studio, just to paint in. There are beautiful views from every window. I have taken it for a month, 125 francs. Two rooms and a kitchen, neat and comfortable, and heart-breaking to think how cheaply one could live if only one was sufficiently self-contained. I look round and say to myself, "This is where I was to bring Phyllis," and I feel sad. Perhaps it was the sight of this beautiful little cottage in the middle of such ideal surroundings, when I first saw it last year, that helped me in the dream. I imagined myself here with a loving young wife, and so on. Well, such ideals may be beautiful, but they cannot be manufactured. They must *really* happen to one. So here I am, in the little villa all right, but alone as usual. Of course I sleep and feed at the hotel. I am glad to be here, as the peace and quiet will help me to think myself out again. . . . MARK GERTLER

To S. S. Koteliansky

[*1925*] *Hôtel Sube, Saint-Tropez*

My dear Kot, I am sorry your money affairs aren't more satisfactory. . . . For my own part I have ceased to worry about money now. I am even ashamed to think that I ever gave it serious thought. But I only did during that extraordinary period in which the theory of marriage played such a conspicuous part. . . . I had a letter from Waterlow.[1] He tells me that last Thursday you all met at my room and that it was pleasant. It is good to feel that the rooms are put to some use while I am away. . . . Waterlow is enthusiastic about Huxley's book, and yet in the same breath almost he says it wasn't worth doing. . . . But if anyone were to tell me one of my pictures was absolutely wonderful, only it wasn't worth doing, I should certainly take it as a very doubtful compliment. . . . But I entirely agree with you that people are so easily taken in by surface things. They are deceived in this way all the time. . . . I mean they actually prefer the superficial. In fact the real thing or even the serious effort frightens them. They hate it. I am speaking, of course, chiefly of painting, about which I know. . . .

So far I have not been able to get along with my sunny landscapes, but I feel fairly contented here, and the great thing is that I am really re-finding myself, and can now look forward into my future with more resignation and less horror than before. The main keynote being *absolute devotion to my work* and without compromise of any sort. MARK GERTLER

[1] Sydney Waterlow, later Ambassador to Athens and knighted.

To S. S. Koteliansky

[*1925*] *Saint-Tropez*

My dear Kot, I am glad your money worries are not acute but, if you would like, I could lend you some cash until your £50 arrives. . . . My own finances are somewhat brighter for the moment because I sold my mother's portrait for a very good price. I was so anxious to keep the picture for myself that I stipulated with Marchant that I would only let it go for £200, and a few days ago he wrote and told me he had sold it for that price, the largest sum I ever received for a picture. Then he tells me Lady Cunard is just moving into a new house and wants me to decorate some walls of her dining-room. Decorative work is not exactly in my line, but I think I shall undertake the job, because it might lead me into new and interesting paths and improve my work. . . .

Today everything looks marvellous. There is that sparkling sun again which I love so much and makes everything so very brilliant and intensely coloured, and even the girls of Saint-Tropez look really beautiful, as they go about shading their golden-coloured faces with their little brown hands. There is a little thing that I adore, from the cake shop we have our tea at. This morning I came across her sweeping the steps and you should have heard our conversation—in French! How awkward it is not to be able to speak the language. MARK GERTLER

To Edward Marsh

3 July 1925 *Penn Studio, Hampstead*

Dear Marsh, Thank you for the card inviting me to the "at home" next Wednesday. I should like very much to come, but I am in a bit of a dilemma. It occurs to me that a tail coat is necessary for such functions and I haven't got one—I only have a dinner jacket. What do you think? Would it be absolutely outrageous? Please tell me honestly, as I should feel most uncomfortable if I were the only person in a dinner jacket. Meanwhile I shall try and borrow a tail coat—or even hire one. I believe it is possible to hire such things. Do kindly drop me a card.

Yours sincerely MARK GERTLER

I was so interested to hear that you have translated La Fontaine into English. I shall now be able to read them. I am interested because Renoir loved them so. He used to say "tout est là".

To S. S. Koteliansky

22 July 1925 *The Spread Eagle, Thame*

My dear Kot, . . . I am enjoying the rest of this very much. Up till now I have spent most of my time lounging in the garden, basking in the sun, of which there has been a plentiful supply, meditating and reading Amy Lowell's *Keats*. This is a suitable book for a sunlit garden. I am enjoying it, chiefly because I have never got over my youthful love of literature about great men. They somehow stimulate me. . . . I don't think I shall be doing quite so much lounging now, however, because I have commenced several pictures of the gardens. Lots of people turn up and there are a few queer ones staying here. . . . Among the other lodgers is an enormously fat and romantic-looking woman, with two very large high and separated bosoms, and perpetually raised eyebrows as if in a continuous state of romantic surprise. She has also a maid. The other day, seeing I was reading Keats, she started, "How wonderful is the Ode to a Nightingale," and "How they *loved* and *lived* in those days." After which remarks she seemed literally to wave her bosoms at me *separately* and raise her eyebrows still higher. I did not encourage her "amorous propensities", as Dr Johnson called it. (I am rather enjoying that book too, by the way.) . . . The other day Taylor drove with me over to see Cholesbury. For old time's sake. Yes, I saw the Old Mill and everything. But it left me cold. I don't know why. . . .

MARK GERTLER

To S. S. Koteliansky

29 July 1925 — *The Spread Eagle, Thame*

My dear Kot, . . . My lady of the bosoms is still here. I find that she is quite a character and is nicknamed "The Duchess". I studiously avoid her. I quite agree with you about people's "living and loving" desires. It nauseates me, but unfortunately I find on self-examination that there is a great deal of that sort of greed inside me too, and I don't even know how good it is to eliminate it. However, time will perhaps solve many of one's little problems. . . .

My stay here has been far from peaceful. To begin with last Friday Turner phoned up and said he was coming down here for a few days. For the problem still rages. Many letters came from Ottoline to guide me in my advice to him. But for my part the picture of this Apollo being tug-of-warred by two desperate women had by that time become so distasteful and nauseous that I felt an equally strong dislike of all three—even for life itself. However, down he came, sighing and groaning, explaining that there is Delphine on one side suicidal and desperate, and the lady on the other side ill in bed with a temperature. . . . He went on Monday and, much as I like him, I was glad because the affair bores me to death.

Last Sunday we had a whole crowd. Ottoline came over with Asquith and a few others. . . . Asquith was chatty and friendly, rather nice, but he is beginning to look old. Julian was stopping at Garsington, so we motored over to see her. Letters from Ottoline still complain bitterly of

her cruelty. But really it is not my business. To me she seems very nice.
MARK GERTLER

To S. S. Koteliansky

11 September 1925 *Sanatorium, Mundesley, Norfolk*

My dear Kot, I write again at once because I have been examined and the report is so good, with regard to my lungs. It is only the old wound opened a little and that caused the bleeding. There is no active trouble at all. As for my throat it is perfect, only a little anaemic, caused or brought on when I am a little run down. . . . But the doctor says it is a very little affair altogether. . . . All the same I was pleased my brother came with me: it made my arrival more homely. . . . The doctor here knows my work and has been to the Goupil. See how famous I am! MARK GERTLER

To S. S. Koteliansky

24 September 1925 *Mundesley*

My dear Kot, . . . The death of Marchant, about which you have perhaps heard, is a very great blow to me. Certainly troubles don't come singly. . . . As all my things have sold only through the Goupil, Heaven only knows what will happen. . . . My future seems dreadful to me. What with this pernicious disease hanging over me, and a still great uncertainty about money. . . .

I continue to get well. Why? Because the life is regular and I am kept away from nervous exhaustion and strain. Strangely enough, boredom does not seem to do one harm physically. I am sure that when I get back to London, I could continue to improve myself as well as anywhere in my own rooms, provided I live quietly and regularly.

There is an artist here called Unwin. He says he met me years ago at Aniton's place. He is in a poor way. Like myself he has had it for a second time, but *his* second attack was a dreadful affair. He has been in bed since last February. Think of it. The germ has attacked his heart and stomach. He will have to be in bed for another three months at least. He says what knocked him out the second time was "mental trouble". Later he confided to me that his wife had left him, and that was the trouble. He is not exactly a happy spectacle. But I feel I must go and see him, as it must be indescribably horrible to be in bed so long with no friends near by. He is a nice man, forty years old—and very broken.

I am working from 2 to 4 and that makes a great difference.

MARK GERTLER

To S. S. Koteliansky

[*29 September 1925*] *Mundesley*

My dear Kot, . . . I was rather depressed by a letter from Taylor who, as a consolation, advises me to live abroad, where he says I could live so cheaply. He has no imagination; that is his fault. No, I should be bored to death living all alone abroad, apart from the fact that I couldn't work abroad for any length of time, as I feel my roots are in England. Perhaps if I were married, I might try, but by myself I couldn't. All I want is enough somehow to keep my rooms. They make all the difference to my life. I shall have to stay in a certain amount in the future for the sake of my health, and if I hadn't a fairly decent place to stay in, I don't know what I should do. . . .

My work is going pretty well. I have actually finished a picture, a landscape. I should like to finish up by quoting this appropriate piece from your Dostoevsky—letter to his brother.

"Brother, I have not become down-hearted or low-spirited. Life is everywhere life, life is ourselves, not in what is outside us. There will be people near me, and to be a *Man* among people and remain a man for ever, not to be down-hearted, not to fall into any misfortune that may befall me—this is life: this is the task of life, I have realised this. . . ."

MARK GERTLER

To Carrington

1 October 1925 *Mundesley*

Dear Carrington, Thank you very much for your letter. It was nice of you to write. I was so surprised and excited to hear from you after your long silence that I could hardly eat my breakfast and I continued to tremble slightly half the morning!

But why I wonder did you have a resentment? I have often wondered at your silence and half thought that you *might* have a resentment, but for the life of me I could not think in what it could consist of. Someone must have made mischief. . . . Believe me, I have never said anything malicious or bad about you. How could I when my affections for you and goodwill have never really ceased?

You do, and always will, mean something special to me, and I confess that I have felt hurt at your silence. For my part I have always thought of you, and asked whoever I could find who knew you how you are getting on and if you are happy. I used to ask your brother and Desmond (who gave me a more coherent account than anyone else), and lately I saw Ruth, who was able to tell me something about you.

At times, I have had a positive craving to see you. And, dear Carrington, I do hope you will no longer nurse any resentments against me. How can you? And if it is possible, write to me and tell me about yourself—every detail will interest me. In any case letters are desirable things in a place like this. However, don't bother if it's a nuisance—only *don't* bear me any ill-feelings.

Now with regards to my illness, I was keeping perfectly well ever since my exit from the last sanatorium, until a few weeks ago I suddenly coughed up blood—I was dining with the Morrells at the time. I was naturally terribly upset and disappointed as I foresaw in a flash that it meant my being banished immediately to a place like this. However, it turns out to be a very slight affair this time, and I have only to be here until about the middle of next month, which will make two months altogether. I believe I overdid it this spring. The Morrells were in town, and I went to too many parties. I am afraid that sort of life is no longer for me. I must keep remembering, I suppose, that I am a beastly invalid, and to add to my troubles, Marchant goes and dies just now. I had an arrangement with him—a contract—which entitled me to so much money every month whether I sold pictures or not. This was a great boon to me, but now that he is dead, I doubt if the firm will continue the arrangement or in fact continue to exist at all!

Well, I will not bore you with any more. Forgive me for writing so much, but believe me I appreciated your little note and it made me happy. So thanks again. Yours ever MARK GERTLER

To S. S. Koteliansky

8 October 1925 *Mundesley*

My dear Kot, I am surprised to hear that there is a probability of Lawrence coming to London: I wonder if with or without Brett. For my part I have no desire to see him and shall not be sorry if I miss him. At one time I used to blame myself for fearing to be disturbed by him. I put it down to a sort of cowardice. But now I have altered my mind because I think the kind of disturbance he creates is of the wrong sort, and does one only harm. . . .

With this disease it is not easy to make plans. Once you have come to a place like this with a "weak spot" you never know when you'll get away. The doctors themselves can only make vague guesses. MARK GERTLER

To S. S. Koteliansky

20 November 1925 *Mundesley*

My dear Kot, . . . Brett is going to Capri apparently and after, I believe, back to Mexico . . . but I do not believe that Lawrence is trying to get away from her. It is somehow not his way. I do not even credit him with that kind of decency. He seems always to prefer hurling himself back into relationships with people, even when they have long since become rotten. Take for instance his relationship with Murry. Of course he cannot do that with you, because you are different. But with Brett I should not be a bit surprised if he were *still* intrigued, though knowing in a way what she is. If he wanted to get rid of a person I think he could be pretty direct, and if he couldn't, Frieda could. No, I think he and Brett will drag on for ages yet, probably even conspiring against us. . . .

A few days ago I was examined and all my forebodings were dispelled by the report, which was as good as it could be. . . . So I shall probably be in Hampstead before the New Year, and although they advise me to stay in Hampstead a week or ten days, I shall stay till the end of January, as I *know* I shall be as safe there as anywhere. MARK GERTLER

To S. S. Koteliansky

30 November 1925 *Mundesley*

My dear Kot, . . . In spite of my approaching release, I had a fit of the glooms recently . . . there were moments when I felt I must pack up and run away. . . . This mood of super depression was brought on by several events. First Unwin died a few days ago, and the day before his death he sent for me to witness his will. He *would* not have anyone but me and one man (patient) I would choose to bring. Previous to this I hadn't seen him for ten days, and the change for the worse was so marked that I was profoundly shocked and depressed, and knew he was done for. Then the weather has been terrible—Siberia not in it—so we have been unable to do our walks and consequently our routine is disorganised. And we depend entirely for routine for the passing of time. . . . MARK GERTLER

To W. J. Turner

[? *November 1925*] *The Sanatorium, Mundesley, Norfolk*

Dear Walter, . . . On the whole I share your surprise that we should still persist in living on, after about the age of 35—though I should make it somewhere roundabout 25! When we have really experienced all, or at any rate experienced things with that freshness which makes an experience worthy of the name. Still more extraordinary is it, when you realise as you do here, how strong that persistence is even among invalids of the most wretched and hopeless kind, when to an onlooker death seems far more preferable than the state they exist in. But the will to live at all costs is very strong. However I do not agree with you that an artist need necessarily have exhausted himself at 35, nor even be repeating himself after that age. So many of the great artists, I refer particularly to painters as I know more about them, have gone on improving all the time, in some cases right to the end—although it is true that at quite an early age the germ or foundation of their final achievement is already laid. But as time goes on they build and embroider on this foundation to such an extent, simplifying and intensifying their statement so much that it becomes almost a different thing. Anyway it would be a great loss if some of the pictures painted by great artists after 40, were for some reason lost. . . .

MARK GERTLER

To S. S. Koteliansky

11 December 1925 *Mundesley*

My dear Kot, . . . The life of Benjamin Haydon, which I am reading now and with great interest, is a most extraordinary life. Here is a man who devoted a whole life to painting, with the utmost passion and self-sacrifice, without creating a single even moderately good picture. He had great conviction and definitely thought himself a great genius, on the scale of Michael Angelo. But he was all wrong. He adored all the great painters without ever understanding them. Never for a moment did he understand what painting was. All the time he tried to paint literature. To me it is all *most*, *most* interesting. I could go on for a long time about Haydon. In fact I could "write a book about it". But I shall leave it till we meet, when we can talk about it. MARK GERTLER

To S. S. Koteliansky

19 August 1926 *Salisbury Hotel, Brighton*

My dear Kot, I was motored here by Turner on Monday—a very long journey . . . me with a splitting headache. I have been passing through a bout of headaches . . . and, as usual after holidays I shall have to depend upon recuperating in Hampstead. Holidays never agree with me physically, I believe contrary to all the laws of humanity. Apparently most people feel benefited by them. Lyme Regis was a stuffy, steamy place—awful mists, heavy and liverish—I was glad to get away. Here it is nice and bright. I love Brighton but I am longing to get back to Hampstead and my work.

. . . The sea is filled with plump Jewesses of all ages, and the language of Brighton is Yiddish. So thank God I can make myself understood. . . .

Hardy[1] is very, very old. It was rather depressing, our visit. Old age terrifies me. He is charming and nice, though, and fairly active still. We talked about many things, including Murry, about whom they were *not* very enthusiastic. MARK GERTLER

[1] He had paid a visit to Thomas Hardy when in Dorset.

To Carrington

Tuesday [? *1926*] *Penn Studio, Hampstead*

Dear Carrington, I only got your letter this morning. I was glad to hear from you and should very much like to see you again, but much to my regret both the afternoons you mention aren't convenient. Today I shall have to leave the studio at 5 o'clock as I have to be at Hammersmith at 6.30. It takes a full hour to get there, and I must wash and change first. On Thursday there are some people coming to tea—Mrs Juliette Huxley, a Mrs Stoll, and probably Matthew Smith (the painter) and Valentine.

And I suppose Friday you go back.

I am full on Wednesday tea-time (Catharine[1] sits to me every afternoon but would go early) or if you are doing nothing on Thursday morning you might come and walk with me—I walk every morning from 11.30 to 12.45. Won't you do that? Will you stay and have lunch with me that day? Let me know.

If all these proposals are no good, do come next time you are in town. It is always better for you to write first, as you did this time. Your little picture has been much admired, especially by Mrs Turner.

Yours MARK GERTLER

P.S. If you don't mind the others do come on Thursday afternoon—I would tell Valentine and she could then turn up or not as she pleased.

To Marjorie Hodgkinson[2]

25 September 1926 *19 Worsley Road, Hampstead*

Dear Marjorie, Thank you for your letter. I am sure mine won't be half as amusing. It won't be amusing at all in fact, because for some reason or other, I feel peculiarly flat and bored tonight. It is Sunday night and I am alone. Nora Edwards[3] was to come to dine, but her mother suddenly had a fainting fit, and so she was unable to leave her. Also I am dissatisfied with my work, to a point of utter disgust—I really am unfit for the job. If only I had taken up a trade or remained a furrier like my brothers.

The landscape at Lyme Regis is good, but the climate awful—suddenly everything disappears in a mist, and then you feel as if your head was in an oven. Of course a bout of headaches came on and reduced me a good deal. Brighton was better. I was motored to Brighton—it took a whole day. I arrived with a splitting headache. In spite of which I noticed immediately a lot of nice girls with bare arms, so I thought I too must have a young female companion with bare arms, and I sent for Nora. She came and stayed a couple of days—bare arms and all. It was nice. I enjoyed her visit. But I always like Brighton. Some day I shall write a book about Brighton

[1] Catharine Carrington, sister-in-law of Carrington.

[2] An artist whom he later married.

[3] Later married Bernard Meninsky.

—a sort of eulogy—to show that we have a gay little Paris in our midst. Honestly it reminded me of Paris in some queer way. We must go there together one day. . . .

I have been pulled about by the nose a bit lately, because D. H. Lawrence and his wife are in London for the moment. They are a disturbing pair. . . .

Come back soon and see if you can liven things up a bit. Much love

MARK GERTLER

To Marjorie Hodgkinson

9 November 1926 *Penn Studio, Hampstead*

Dear Marjorie, I would have written or phoned before but I have been in a state of perturbation and depression owing to the long-dreaded and expected tragedy having really come about, that is my relations with the Goupil have come to an end! That corpse of a Gallery is really to be buried at last. It ceases to be at the end of this month and with it my monthly cheques. They even could not afford to give me the three months' notice according to the contract, but sent me away with my last cheque in my pocket a week ago. At the end of the month I shall be penniless and ready for the workhouse, where I hope you will come and visit me. Meanwhile let us not hearken to rumble of the distant . . . but have tea together here on Saturday at 4.30. And what about the party? As I staggered down from the office into the Gallery more dead than alive I ran into Dick[1] who told me there's to be a party on Sunday. Could we not collaborate for dinner before the party?

Yours MARK GERTLER

To S. S. Koteliansky

29 April 1927 *Arden Hotel, Stratford on Avon*

My dear Kot, At first I felt rather like a fish out of water here, and somewhat depressed. But today for the first time I feel comparatively happy. One can be too near a company of actors and actresses. This is my plight. They are all very nice and good natured and hearty, but somehow tiresome. They are superficial and third-rate. I don't mean as actors or actresses. I am no judge of that, but as people. . . .

I do not see so much of Lydia[2] as I should like, only in the afternoons—some days not even then, as there are two matinées a week. Every morning she rehearses. In the evenings I sit alone in the theatre and watch the play. It is a long time now since I first began to dread the idea of seeing Lydia act and so when, at last, I went to see *Hamlet*, which was my first evening, I felt very nervous, and when she first came on, as Ophelia,

[1] Richard Carline, whose studio at Downshire Hill was a frequent scene of parties.

[2] Lydia Sherwood.

looking tall and stately, I did not recognise her. But as soon as I realised it was she I felt most uncomfortable. The beginning of the mad scene she did so well and realistically that I was quite overcome. She received a great deal of applause for this piece of acting. And that was a strange experience—listening to so many people applauding her.

You seemed depressed of late. Are you so still? It is difficult to be happy, especially I think after thirty. One's youth is spent unhappily through over-ardent seeking for happiness. But at least one is hopeful. When youth has gone, there comes to take its place, gradually but surely, the ever-increasing horror of approaching old age and the realisation of that awful and inevitable final, death. So how can we be happy? No, there is no such thing as true happiness. There is only its make belief—forgetfulness—and to forget is a form of cowardice.

This place is enough to put you off Shakespeare for good. The whole place trades on Shakespeare. It is quite disgusting. Everything is either "Ye Olde Shoppe or Ye Olde Shakespeare" in one form or another, and a shilling to see Shakespeare this or that. Soon they will produce a Shakespeare piss-pot and one will have to pay a shilling to see it, and goodness knows what the Americans would give to be allowed to piss in it.

MARK GERTLER

To Thomas Balston[1]

[*5 July 1927*] *19 Worsley Road, Hampstead*

Dear Tom, I am very glad and encouraged by what you say of my work. The main thing one wants is to be steadily improving and, if one succeeds in this, one is sure to reach something worth while in the end. I agree with you. I too think that I am making headway, though one does not seem to do so continuously as much as by sudden spurts—every now and then one beats one's own record, as it were, and this is what I believe I've done with the nude. It is better than the best before it. . . .

MARK GERTLER

To S. S. Koteliansky

[*9 August 1927*] *Mullion, S. Cornwall*

My dear Kot, I had this letter.[2] I thought you would like to see it. I don't

[1] Tom Balston, publisher and collector, became one of Gertler's greatest friends.

[2] Lawrence had written:

[*31 July 1927*] *Villa Mirenda, Scandicci, Florence*

Dear Gertler, I am up and creeping round—feeling limp—but better. I had the best doctor in Florence—Prof. Giglioli—head of the Medical Profession for Tuscany. It's chronic bronchial congestion—and it brought me on a series of bronchial haemorrhages this time. I've had little ones before. It would be serious if they didn't stop, he says: but they do stop: so it's nothing to worry about—only one must lie in bed when they come on—and always be a bit careful—not

know what "bronchila congestion" means. I rather think it means nothing. He obviously has lung trouble and should take special care. I will write to him again later and tell him how he ought to live and what sort of precautions to take. However, he is better for the time being.

I was not really serious about "securing myself and getting married". Only, when I look on the life of a married couple, I sometimes feel peculiarly isolated and anchorless, and undoubtedly there are certain things which only a woman can supply.

Today we motored over to see Bertie Russell. We met him on the Wednesday. He and his family were coming from bathing. He was so astonished to see me that he forgot who I was. Besides his wife and his own two children there was a whole host of other children knocking around, and we all had tea in his place. He seemed much older and quieter. His wife wore knickers and bare legs. They are opening a school for children in Sussex, for children from two to seven. They are to employ special methods, the chief being apparently to teach the children to be happy.

I am working very hard. I have done a flower piece and now I am on a seascape. I cannot rest. My work is a great worry to me—for hours on end I cannot get my mind off it. Especially here where there are no other distractions. The worry is how to interpret. There are so many ways and nature is infinite, and doesn't help me *very* much.

To hold a philosophic discussion with Dobrée[1] is very soothing, like dessert after a good meal, especially when Valentine is quietly sewing a "gown", as you say. MARK GERTLER

To Marjorie Hodgkinson

[*20 September 1927*] *19 Worsley Road, Hampstead*

My dear Marjorie, I was glad to hear from you. I thought you had decided

---

take sea-baths, as I did at Forte. I think he's about right. He says now we're to go to the mountains so we're leaving for Austria—D.V.—on Thursday night. I can get into a sleeper in Florence, and stay in till Villach, so I should be all right. I'll send the addresses there, as I'm not sure. These haemorrhages are rather shattering—but perhaps they take some bad blood out of the system. The doctor says no good going in a sanatorium, if I will only lie down when I don't feel well—and not work. Which I shall really try to do.—I don't really feel bad.

So tell Kot to get a doctor himself, and not bother about me.

We saw Sullivan—he came with the Huxleys—and he was nice, but sad—I thought he would be rather bouncing—not a bit. He's coming back to England directly.

Ask Kot to tell Barbara I'll write from Villach.

I do hope you're well—cheerful. Frieda sends her love, with mine. D.H.L.

Did we ever thank you for your booklet of pictures—everybody looks at them. They nearly all like the Child best.

[The "booklet of pictures" would be the small book on Mark Gertler published by The Fleuron in 1925.]

[1] Bonamy Dobrée was at this time Professor of English at the Egyptian University, Cairo.

Coster Woman

Oil painting (23 × 16 in.) 1925

Reproduced by permission of Mr Peter Pears

Reclining Nude
Oil painting (30 × 40 in.) 1928
Reproduced by permission of Mr Thomas Balston

to cut yourself off and be a hermit again. I would have written you a letter before this, but I kept thinking that you'd be back any moment.

Yes, I wish I had been with you that romantic night. We really must try and spend a holiday together some time or other—I am sure we'd get on very well and enjoy it. We ought somehow or other to get round the "scandalous" part of it—I mean your relations and people "talking". From that point of view I suppose it would be better if we went in a group, but some day we really must do it. I would suggest Brighton as a start!

As for Surrealism, I don't know anything about it, but I am becoming more and more suspicious of "movements", with intricate and *startling* ways of painting and writing etc. I am more and more convinced that the best methods are after all the simplest and the traditional—and at the moment they are even the newest—because to *attempt* to be new and unusual for its own sake is so common now that the only possible newness and freshness left is in the simple and traditional. If a man is a bore he'll *be* a bore even under the most startling and "original" of methods. If on the other hand he really has got something personal to say, he will say it all right without having to attach himself to any of the innumerable new "isms" that have sprung and are apparently still springing up like mushrooms everywhere.

I am working hard and I think well, but am not in an absolute first-class condition of health. Nothing special, only peculiarly nervy, perhaps only that run-down feeling one experiences so often after holidays!

With love MARK

To Marjorie Hodgkinson

4 February 1928 *19 Worsley Road, Hampstead*

My dear Marjorie, How awful your journey sounds, and how well I know the horror of such an experience. I hope you have quite got over it by now. Of course I miss you too. First I feel conscious of a sort of blank, then I realise it's your absence. What you say is true. The moment one feels intensely about another person, there's trouble. And yet our relationship seems to me remarkably satisfactory. We actually "get on" so well and are, I think, a real support to each other. But the most remarkable part, I think, is that our feelings should be growing more intense, and not stopping still or dwindling. I certainly think you have reason to be happy rather than otherwise.

I have been struggling with my flower piece. I believe I've discovered how to do flowers without having to be in such a desperate hurry, which is simply by replacing the faded ones—I have for instance replaced the mimosa—and other tricks I've discovered too—such as, when a flower has grown to about twice as tall as it was, cut its stem. Then it is in its old place again, etc.!

I really believe I am acquiring something that my work needed. My experiments in working higher in key, brighter in colour and more fluid in the contour are I think repaying me. You will see.

With love MARK GERTLER

To Marjorie Hodgkinson

10 February 1928 *19 Worsley Road, Hampstead*

My dear Marjorie, I have finished my flowers and I really do believe they are *very* nice. In fact there are moments when I'm enthusiastic. They are so nice and bright, and just the effect I've been trying to get for ages. I believe all my future work will be beneficially affected by them. I really believe that I have at last added a something to my work which was wanting, but we shall see. . . .

There is a wonderful show of French pictures at Knoedlers'. I have been twice—Matisse, Bonnard, Derain, Picasso, Vuillard, Marchand, Segonzac etc. All good examples. But they have there the Bonnard you told me of—"The Girl in the Bath". It is a masterpiece. He is a *very* fine artist. There is also a show of his work at the Independent Gallery—all very exciting. . . .

Yours with love MARK GERTLER

To Marjorie Hodgkinson

29 February 1928 *19 Worsley Road, Hampstead*

Dear Marjorie, I went to a party at Nevinson's. It was crammed with fourth-rate celebrities, including all the critics and dealers.

I have finished the portrait of Miss Denny. I believe I like it very much. Mamma and Mr Jonas (fifteen years) came to see it. Mamma was bewildered but Jonas liked it. Now she has gone away; will be back in a few weeks when I hope to do another one of her. I have an idea that she is a nice girl, but too popular. There is a waiting list of six men, all of whom have proposed to her, but she cannot as yet make up her mind. Meanwhile they all buzz around her like so many amorous bees—what a life!

I have sold "The Girl with the Violin", £85—all mine! Saturday a week, the 10th, starts my show. I too am plodding through Napoleon—also Pepys's diary. They both bore me a little. . . .

With love MARK GERTLER

To Marjorie Hodgkinson

7 March 1928 *19 Worsley Road, Hampstead*

Dear Marjorie, . . . My show (private view) is on Saturday, 10th. I *am*

Basket of Fruit

Oil painting (32 × 40 in.) 1925
Reproduced by permission of
Mr Thomas Balston

Still Life with Staffordshire Pottery

Oil painting ($38\frac{1}{2}$ × $44\frac{1}{2}$ in.) 1926
Reproduced by permission of Mr M. G. Farquharson

Still Life with Violin and Flowers

a bit anxious, but of course from a financial point of view only. I find I owe as much as £480 to the Leicester Gallery, and in order to repay that I have to take about £800! because of their 33⅓ per cent commission. This means I must sell at least 50 per cent of the work, merely to repay them what I owe! and then at least they will continue to forward me £30 per month, which is what I want. My neighbour is Miss Laura Knight, who was introduced to me during the hanging. She said she had an admiration for my work. It was awkward, as I could hardly return the compliment. Her work is extremely clever and able, only somewhat vulgar in outlook.

With much love MARK

To Marjorie Hodgkinson

15 March 1928 *19 Worsley Road, Hampstead*

Dear Marjorie, My show has been quite a success. On the very first day pictures sold like hot cakes (probably due to the cutting which I enclose) and now on about the third day twelve paintings and five drawings have gone, about £700! My debt is already repaid and so enough of that.

The Beerbohms[1] sound awfully nice—I am glad they are there for your sake. I read that part of your letter out to Kot, who was interested in your account of them. . . .

Jas[2] rang me up about my show—a long rigmarole—congratulations—how he liked them—why he liked them—until I was very bored and he very involved—and it all ended rather with embarrassment, but it was nice of him to telephone.

It has become extremely cold and dark again lately—rather gloomy—and in spite of my "success" I feel depressed and empty. This afternoon I am going down to see the show for the first time. I dread it, as I sometimes loathe my own pictures beyond words!

Much love MARK

To Carrington

28 March 1928 *19 Worsley Road, Hampstead*

My dear Carrington, I am glad that you were impressed with the show. Fortunately I am doing well. I have sold a sufficient number of pictures to repay the debt to the dealers, in fact they owe me a little now, I think!

Roger Fry wrote a very good article on my pictures in the *Nation*—perhaps you've seen it. What a relief and comfort it was to read what he had to say, after all the usual "favourable" meaningless bosh of the average critic. Thank heavens we have at least *one* critic in the country.

I should like to stay a week-end with you. Please when the time comes

[1] Marjorie was staying near Rapallo, Max Beerbohm's home.

[2] James Wood, a painter and collector of pictures, friend of the Carlines.

try and give me a week or ten days' notice, as I generally become rather involved with engagements. Meanwhile if you are in town do come and see me. I enjoyed your last visit.

With love MARK

To S. S. Koteliansky

11 April 1929 *Paris*

My dear Kot, We had a pleasant journey and we are enjoying our stay. We are being a little social too. We ran into Nevinson and Fry. We are dining with Nevinson tonight and Fry tomorrow. We lunched with the Huxleys and are staying with them the week-end, though Aldous will be away. The news of Lawrence is very depressing. He seems to be ill in mind and body. The picture they gave us was gruesome and preyed on my mind all night. While Frieda was away they managed to get him to see a doctor, who pronounced his lungs to be in a bad state and his general condition serious, but he would not believe it and won't allow himself to be X-rayed. According to the Huxleys it is mostly Frieda's fault, and from what they say of her, it really seems almost as if it is she who is slowly killing him. Can she be so bad? They say it is sheer stupidity, and that her influence is so great that nothing can be done. I thought I'd tell you the truth—as I heard it—and what other details there are I shall be able to tell you better when we meet.

We will try and find out about that painter you mention. But I have never heard of him. However I will ask Nevinson and Fry, though I am sure that neither of them, like myself or any other sensible painter, would separate the idea of a good portrait painter from a good painter. Only a good painter would paint a good portrait and if he is a good painter I somehow feel I should have heard of him. . . . MARK GERTLER[1]

[1] The last letter from D. H. Lawrence to Gertler may be inserted at this point.

24 May 1928 *Villa Mirenda, Scandicci, Florence*

Dear Mark, Kot said you'd like to see these photographs of my pictures—they're only snaps a neighbour took—there was another snap—"Resurrection"—but I'm afraid I've not got it any more. There are seven big pictures—oils—a "Nymphs and Faun", all dark orange, not photographed. Also a "Fight with an Amazon". I think I shall send them to the Warren[2] for her gallery, because when we leave here—in about ten days—God knows when we'll come back, and it's no good just abandoning them. Would you take the big pictures off their stretchers and roll them?—paint is a bit thick in places, it might crack off. But they'd need a *big* packing case—I gave the seven water-colours and three smaller oils, on boards, to a friend to take to London for me: Kot's old acquaintance, Enid Hopkin! now Mrs Enid Hilton. She stayed in a little inn near here with her husband. . . . If you felt like it you could call at her house—flat, that is, top floor—40 Great James St, Bedford Row, WC1, and look at the pictures she took. Perhaps you'll dislike them. I myself prefer the big oils. The Hiltons won't be home, though, till 1st June—a week from now.

And would you tell me where you have your pictures photographed, and how much it costs? I'd like to have photographs of all these—but not if it's too expensive.

[2] Dorothy Warren, owner of the Warren Gallery.

To Carrington

26 June 1929 — *19 Worsley Road, Hampstead*

Dear Carrington, I only got your letter this morning, as I was not at the studio yesterday. There is something wrong with me again—I am hoping it is not the old trouble, but I am a bit suspicious. I am feeling awfully tired and my temperature is inclined to rise in the evenings. I shall be seeing my specialist soon, and I shall know. Meanwhile I am taking every precaution, not working etc.—it is very tiresome indeed.

I should have loved to come otherwise—and I'm sure Marjorie would too. You must ask us again later and, unless I am by that time tucked away in a sanatorium, it will be nice to spend a day or two with you. . . .

With love — MARK

To Carrington

6 July 1929 — *19 Worsley Road, Hampstead*

My dear Carrington, Thanks for your letter. For a wonder it is not my lungs this time, but I am very run down and nervously overstrained, due to overwork. In spite of the good condition of my lungs I have decided to go back to my sanatorium for a month, because there can I pick up thoroughly and quickly. My weight has been sadly reduced and at the sanatorium I shall soon regain it. My specialist agrees with me about the

---

What do you do with the shiny places on your pictures, when you want 'em *not* to shine? Mine *do* shine—some all over, because there's so much oil in them. But I don't mind all over.

You'll be sick of my questions—I am now doing the *last* proofs of my novel-so it won't be long. I expect some people will want to annihilate me for it: but I believe in it, it's got to be done. One's got to get back to the live, really lovely phallic self, and phallic consciousness. I think I get a certain phallic beauty in my pictures too. I know they're rolling with faults, Sladeily considered. But there's something *there*. Wonder how your work goes. I've seen nothing for two years—but that nude you were doing in Sept. 1926 seemed to me to have some phallic glow too—I hope we can send you your copy of the novel within a fortnight. Nice of you to order it.

I was so awfully sorry to hear of Ottoline so very ill. Poor Ottoline, when I feel she's down, my heart bleeds for her. After all, she's a queen, among the mass of women.

Of course I had to have a bit of flu; have been in bed some days. But am up again. I shall be really better at a higher altitude—when we get to Switzerland. Did you ever try the mountains—between 3 and 4000 ft? It's really rather marvellous, if you stay long enough. I think we shall go to Annecy, just in France, south of Geneva, and look round from there—I wish I really got well again—it's such a drag, not getting back to oneself. You know yourself how it feels. I do hope you're better, and feeling fairly chirpy.

We shall come to England, probably in August. Where will you be?—But we shall see you. We're not dead yet. We'll still show the world what's what.

Tell Kot I had his letter—and it's cold even here.

Frieda sends all sorts of messages. — D. H. LAWRENCE

sanatorium. I have been suffering from the most excruciating headaches but I am getting better now.

Yes, that Renoir was magnificent. How many painters are capable of painting a picture which one might almost describe as "pretty, pretty" and which is at the same time a masterpiece? A picture that could be appreciated from a servant girl to a Roger Fry!

Well, some day, we really must fix up a visit to Ham Spray.[1]

Meanwhile, my love, from MARK

To S. S. Koteliansky

15 July 1929 *Mundesley*

My dear Kot, I am not exactly happy. I arrived with an awful headache which set me back very much. The next morning I was nearly annihilated altogether by Dr Pearson telling me that he thinks the lung is *not* quite right . . . if it wasn't for Marjorie I should lose courage altogether. But she makes this place just tolerable. . . .

She is looking very well and is obviously benefiting from the very good air here, which is a great relief to me, as *I* haven't given her much pleasure. I'm afraid she's had a great deal to put up with. But seeing how unhappy she was enabled me to pull up if only for her sake. . . . MARK GERTLER

[1] Ham Spray, near Hungerford, home of Carrington, Ralph Partridge and Lytton Strachey.

PART EIGHT

Later Years

The last decade of Gertler's life was marred by the ever-increasing menace of ill health, not only recurring attacks of tuberculosis, which had first declared itself ten years before, but bouts of intense depression, headaches and melancholia which made work impossible. Yet, as he so frequently writes, only in work could he find real contentment and satisfaction. No diversion or holiday could satisfy him for long.

He found much happiness in marriage and in the birth of his son, but both his wife's health and his son's were also frequently the cause of added anxiety. His later exhibitions of paintings were not rewarding and he took to teaching at an art school in order to make ends meet. Those who learnt from him spoke highly of his teaching, but he grudged the time. His last show in 1938 suffered from the atmosphere of Munich which affected plants much less delicate than art. Nor were the critics, at least of the younger generation, any longer so favourable to an artist who had always gone his own way. All this was to add financial anxiety to his other cares. Indeed he was hardly ever free from worry about money for the last five years of his life. In a pocket diary for 1938 three entries repeat themselves with monotonous regularity. His weight, his headaches and his overdraft. Ill-health made work impossible. He could neither pay his way nor do the only thing which he felt worth while—paint.

In 1936, finding that he must return yet again to the sanatorium for treatment, he endeavoured to end his life. He was saved and restored to health, at least enough to make a further effort. Much of his finest work dates from these years.

The ranting of Hitler, the collapse of art patronage and increasing bouts of depression were too much for nerves already overstrained. He died by his own hand in June 1939.

To Marjorie Hodgkinson

3 March 1930 — *19 Worsley Road, Hampstead*

Dearest Marjorie, I am still going strong—feeling pretty well, and no moods of black despair. I have finished my flower piece. I'm glad it's finished as I wanted to have a goodish time to mooch about in, and do little things before going abroad. Now I shall "shut up shop" and shall probably do no more painting this side of the Channel. This enables me to feel, for the first time since my breakdown, that I am about to make a *new start* at last. The feeling is pleasant anyhow—even though it may be fictitious. Last Wednesday I went to a second Sickert lecture, but found it boring. I don't think I shall go to any more. Friday I had the Mavros[1] and the Turners to tea—it did not go off very pleasantly. Little Michael was rather distracting, during picture-gazing. Walter arrived late and in a very bad temper. I *think* they liked the pictures. Saturday evening the usual company foregathered here; a tremendous political argument took place with some awkwardness between Kot and Delphine.[2] It went on till 12.30. Yesterday (Sunday) I went for a drive with the Mavros to Elstree, but the enjoyment was somewhat marred by the prospect of Zena's engagement party in the evening. However, the party wasn't so bad after all. There was a charming little girl of seven, with whom I danced.

Lawrence really seems to be very ill. I believe it's serious. That is all the news, I believe. Keep well. Much love, MARK

To S. S. Koteliansky

26 March 1930 *Paris*

My dear Kot, . . . We are settling down to the Idea now, only at moments we feel hopelessly bored here. As you suggest I am giving people the reason of marrying here, "to avoid fares". And in a sense it's true. I am not going to tell my people until the day before the event. I don't want to be bothered with their objections until the event is over. . . .

I saw the Huxleys on Monday and talked to them about your taking part in the editing of Lawrence's letters, etc. He seemed genuinely agreeable. In fact he seems anxious that there should be someone in London to collect letters. The only trouble is Frieda. Apparently she keeps changing her mind about everything, publishers, etc.—keeps promising first one publisher and then another. She is in Paris at present. I have written to her to phone me or write, but so far she has taken no notice. But I may see her yet. She is going to London, so you will be able to see her yourself.

MARK GERTLER

To S. S. Koteliansky

3 April 1930 *Paris*

My dear Kot, Well, we've just been married. It was quite simple and took

[1] John Mavrogordato and his wife.

[2] Mrs W. J. Turner.

only a quarter of an hour. It was done by the British Consul himself, assisted by the proconsul. They were very nice to us. Thank heaven it is over. It has not been so quiet after all. Lots of letters and telegrams and we haven't altogether escaped the Press. We had a wire from the *Daily Mirror* asking for confirmation and permission to publish. We felt somehow obliged to answer.

But the most harassing of all was that my people object strongly; just what I expected. At first I got a wire from Jack and his wife, which was nice, but next day another from the other brother to say "Hold over wedding, writing." Then came a depressing letter. But of course it *is* unpleasant and probably my relations will continue cold for a long time.

Marjorie's relations are agreeable, except one religious aunt who wanted us to marry in church! . . .

I am glad you like Ottoline so much, but I don't know that I altogether agree with you about her having good friends, etc. I mean that it's a good deal her fault that she hasn't had many real ones. She does get rather bored with one—in a way—when one ceases to perform, as it were, though in another way I must say she does remain faithful too.

Just been disturbed again. From photographers. Marjorie and I had to pose arm in arm in the rain for American papers. I must stop now and escape from the hotel.

With love from us both — MARK GERTLER

P.S. My mother just phoned me!! She is pleased!

To S. S. Koteliansky

9 April 1930 — *Bandol*

My dear Kot, . . . Marjorie has a very religious aunt that is causing a certain amount of worry. She wants us to get married in a Roman Catholic church and is making herself quite ill over it. She writes that it can be done quite easily in spite of the fact that I am a Jew. . . . Only my people must *never* know of it or they would *never* forgive me. There is the beastly Press that might get hold of it. That's the bother. One can do nothing without their knowing it. Then there is the question whether the children have to be brought up as R.C.s. What do you think about this point? I couldn't hurt my mother to that extent. This aunt is absolutely devoted to Marjorie.

We had a perfectly beastly journey. . . . Here it is nice though, *really* beautiful. Only too picturesque and far too overdone by French artists, so I do not feel like painting it. However I am working just to keep going. . . . — MARK GERTLER

To Marjorie Gertler

15 May 1931 *22 Kemplay Road, Hampstead*

Dearest Marjorie, Tuesday afternoon I started Bliss's[1] portrait. It's rather an interesting composition, and they were excited with the start. I felt like saying "Wait till you see the finished article!" He has asked me to bring along the flower piece—in spite of his admiration of the Matthew Smith one—so perhaps he'll buy it.

In the evening I dined at Ross's, "the Jew's", but for some reason I'm not happy with the "Wednesdays" in a group and even my meal was ruined because of Sullivan's chin which was dripping with grease and beer! However I enjoyed the end of the evening—drinking tea with Kot at Acacia Road and resting on the sofa you sold them. Heavens! what a pity that was! It is a *most* comfortable sofa. Yesterday I started painting on the Heath at last! It was *very* pleasant. I hope to enjoy myself there, only the things *are* heavy to carry and I couldn't get as far as Ken Wood, but made a start from a point before you get there—quite good. Though the only unfortunate thing is that a few yards away General Booth's grandson is also vigorously working in a smock, and a Scotch policeman has made friends with me, and threatens to have a short "chat" with me *every* morning!

Well, I have several interesting "starts" now, but tomorrow I have to leave them all, and go off to Hastings! It is a pity you are not here tonight, because Mona has asked us to dinner to meet Sickert! I'm going of course—couldn't resist meeting the old man once more. MARK

To Carrington

20 February 1932 *22 Kemplay Road, Hampstead*

My dear Carrington, Now that I have seen Catharine[2] and she has paved the way a little, I feel more able to write and tell you how deeply I felt for you over Lytton's death. I was shocked that his end should have come at such an early age, but still more at the enormous blow I knew it would be to you.

There's very little one can say on such an occasion, but I do hope you will be able to muster up all the strength and courage that is necessary to make one go on and rebuild some sort of purpose in life.

I find that I have one or two letters and poems of Lytton's which you must see some time.

When you feel ready for it let us meet again. Meanwhile all my love and best wishes MARK

[1] Sir Arthur Bliss.

[2] Carrington's sister-in-law.

To Carrington

[*1 March 1932*] *22 Kemplay Road, Hampstead*

My dear Carrington, It was nice of you to send us a wedding present at such a time as this. It arrived quite safely and will make a good addition to my collections.

It is curious that you should have been reading some of my old letters lately, because I went through all yours a few months ago. I was alone in the flat with a bad cold one day when one of your letters fluttered out of the bundle in a drawer where I was looking for a book. So it struck me I might pass the time by reading the whole bundle through. It certainly made most moving reading. It must have been a most extraordinary and painful time for both of us. But we were both very young and probably unsuited. And it is over now and nobody's fault.

Do come and see me when you are next in Town. With love MARK[1]

To Marjorie Gertler

6 July 1932 *22 Kemplay Road, Hampstead*

Dearest Marjorie, I was saddened to hear that you are depressed as well as feeling rather feeble physically; all the same you *must not* talk of boring me—no such thing enters into it at all. I enjoyed both my week-ends with you *immensely*. Only the fact is I cannot get over the "tragedy" of leaving the studio. It came over me suddenly and I feel very, very wretched. It happens when I'm with you and when I'm not with you—so you must know that when I look bored I'm really struggling with an awful fit of depression and anxiety in connection with the studio business. It is a pity, because otherwise I should be fairly happy. Working in rooms—these rooms are not *really* as comfortable as working in a studio, though it may be more amusing—all sorts of difficulties crop up: one gets in one's own light, casts shadows on the model, or one has to pop one's head round the corner of one's canvas to see the model at all! It's quite surprising. Yesterday I tried a model in your bedroom, but it wasn't very successful. Probably the drawing-room will turn out to be the only possible work-room; but if I shall have to do my still-lifes there, it might be awkward. I may then have to make one of the other rooms into a reception room. After all this, you will feel inclined to suggest my keeping on the studio. But I simply cannot make up my mind to that either! No, the die is cast. I leave my studio and work here for the interval we're apart (not long I hope) anyhow. The fact is I'm not yet used to working in rooms and am probably a little hysterical as yet. The trouble is that for some time I shall get these fits of depression. But you must try not to mind them. I know that when I am on my holiday, it will come over me every now and then

[1] This was his last letter to Carrington, who took her own life very shortly after Lytton Strachey's death.

that for the first time in history almost I shall not have my studio—a real workshop to go back to. Yes, I shall have bad moments. But *you* must try and be happy. MARK GERTLER

To S. S. Koteliansky

[*2 August 1932*] *Hackness Hall, Scarborough*[1]

My dear Kot, I hope to finish the portrait tomorrow. I could leave on Saturday, but they seem to like having me so it would seem rather like running away.

I *hate* doing commissioned portraits. It never *works* exactly. It's always a sort of compromise and therefore dull—even degrading. Perhaps I shall never accept one again. This is indeed a lordly place; a beautiful eighteenth-century mansion and even the surrounding landscape looks as if it had been designed by God expressly for a lord; on the walls are efficient well-behaved old-masterish family portraits. The furniture is very special too, yet I should die of tedium if I had to live here six months.

Lord Derwent, Lady Derwent and her mother are all nice—especially Lord D., whom I like *very* much. He is genuine and a very decent young man, a great admirer of Lawrence. . . . MARK GERTLER

To Thomas Balston

[*21 September 1932*] *22 Kemplay Road, Hampstead*

My dear Tom, I have just come back from St Leonards, staying with Taylor. Last week-end I spent with the Mavros in Charmouth. I enjoyed that very much and felt well there for a wonder. Now I have just managed to get the illusion of having had a holiday sufficiently to desire to dig myself in for the winter and start work. But this is going to be far from easy because I now feel definitely I *can't* work here and so *must* get a studio or large room. I start hunting tomorrow.

Marjorie and Luke[2] are now thoroughly installed at Highgate and are doing well. Marjorie is coming to dinner here tonight! She is allowed out for two hours in the evenings.

Well, I start my "Saturdays" next Saturday in a feeble sort of a way. But do come in. MARK

[1] The home of the third Lord Derwent, whose portrait Gertler had been commissioned to paint.

[2] Gertler's son, born in 1932.

To Thomas Balston

7 October 1932 — *22 Kemplay Road, Hampstead*

My dear Tom, Just got back from my teaching[1] tired and nervous, but I feel I must immediately answer your very encouraging letter. Already I feel less nervous because of it.

As for your choice—both for Sadler and yourself—it shows good judgement as ever. You will be pleased to hear that I have a charming studio at last. I am absolutely thrilled. It *is* good to have a workshop again, a "sanctum"—to work and pray!—It's near Well Walk, practically on the Heath and only £8 a year more than my last studio! If only my show goes well, I shall be happy. MARK

To Marjorie Gertler

April 1933 — *Pavillon Bleu, Saint-Cloud*

Dearest Marjorie, All I'm looking forward to now is coming home! We had a good journey, and really this place is *most* beautiful. It would make an excellent painting holiday—for a few weeks. There is lots to paint and the proximity to Paris would be a very exciting addition. We must think of it. You would love this Hotel. It is rather like the "Cadran Bleu" of Fontainebleau. You would remember it, if you saw it. It stands just opposite the café we had tea at. We noticed it but thought it too expensive-looking for tea, and so it is! I really could have enjoyed it all much more if you were present, and even in Paris I keep thinking of all the things we did and saw together, and I long for your presence. We have seen a few good pictures; a dealer called Van Leer who looks like a white slave trafficker showed us one or two interesting ones. A show of *early* Utrillos was interesting too. But Paul Guillaume is away and the American also. Miss Krassin I somehow don't feel like seeing, so it has all rather gone flat. We had an excited card from the Moores[2] to say that they are coming over on Monday. Rather late in the day. However it will be nice to see them. It would have made all the difference if they had come with us. But Heavens! Why am I doomed to spend so many boring hours on holidays! How seldom they succeed with me. But I believe I know how to plan it in future. Anyhow it is always nice to get *back*. MARK

To Marjorie Gertler

[July 1933] — *53 Haverstock Hill, Hampstead*

Dearest Marjorie, . . . Tonight I sleep all alone in the house, for Luke

[1] At the Westminster School of Art.

[2] Henry Moore, the sculptor, and his wife.

has gone off to the Freres. He went this morning looking with terrific interest and absorption at the chauffeur. This morning I walked into his room, *just* as he was falling asleep. It was a fascinating sight. His eyes were already closed, but his little white arms were still waving about gently in the air, not yet having found, as it were, a place for themselves. At last they slowly descended to rest. He must have been awake only a moment before. He is looking wonderfully well; both his lower teeth are now out and the two upper starting. But he seems to get no more pain. Elsie is very good with him. Albert is good technically but Elsie is better humanely, because she talks to him, and that is what he loves and needs. I'm afraid I am not good at it myself....

Love M.

To Thomas Balston

24 August 1933 *Hackness Hall, Scarborough*

Dear Tom, I've just escaped from a very tedious lunch party. Some "relations" have arrived. People who talk about members of the Royal family as you or I might about Mavro and Christine, only I hope we are not so tedious.

The portrait ought to be finished tomorrow, and although I *could* leave on Satuday, I feel that it would look too much like running away, especially as I have a feeling that Lord Derwent rather likes having me here—so I'll return to London on Monday.

Lord Derwent is *really* nice—he is a genuine and simple person.

MARK GERTLER

To S. S. Koteliansky

29 August 1934 *Castelltersol, Spain*

My dear Kot, ... We are all quite happy here; only Tom, Wellington and myself have been poisoned by something we ate at the hotel and suffered much pain for several days ... but it is a good quiet simple life here and I am *really* reluctant to return to London with all its complexity and servant problems, telephone calls and above all my show, which I dread. Among other things it is so cheap to live here. The best drinks cost a few pence; we get lively for about 6*d*. each every night. I think if my show doesn't pay I shall come and live here. After all we've got the house for a year. Luke is very well, developing rapidly. He says a few words now and then and a good many we don't understand. But he is very noisy. In the village he is a great favourite. We took him to an open-air dancing (there has been a fiesta here); he caused a great sensation. He ran about laughing and excited during the intervals and the people threw confetti at him. As he ran the confetti showered from his head like golden rain....

MARK GERTLER

The Mandolinist

Oil painting (*30 × 22 in.*) *1934*

Reproduced by permission of Mr Thomas Balston

The Spanish Fan

Oil painting (42 × 48 in.) 1938

Reproduced by permission of Mrs Napier

To Marjorie Gertler

11 October 1934 — *53 Haverstock Hill, Hampstead*

Dearest Marjorie, It would be a great blessing if you *could* get back on the 26th for my sake as well as your own, as I badly need someone to have a word with. I am going through a very bad time. My show looks like a complete failure and the pictures generally very unpopular. There is not much chance of my receiving any more cheques from the Leicester Galleries—and this doesn't feel good—but I've got more work at teaching, and I have other plans[1] in my head for getting some money. I will tell you about them when you get back—if ever you do! With love MARK

To S. S. Koteliansky

30 October 1934 — *53 Haverstock Hill, Hampstead*

My dear Kot, . . . I have started the book[2] and am rather pleased and excited about it. But I saw at once that it can't be turned into a money matter right away—as I had hoped. It has to be done slowly and not to any time limit or primarily for money. So I must try and get money in other ways. . . .

To Thomas Balston

3 July 1935 — *Castelltersol, Spain*

My dear Tom, I had a pleasant enough journey. But I had to take a sleeper at Quai d'Orsay and got one all to myself—which was very comfortable indeed. Travelling is a matter of money. If you can afford to spend enough money on it, it becomes quite simple.

I don't know what to tell you about the house. It is much more primitive than the other, and to my mind not so comfortable. I don't know what you will think of it at all. Of course it is very beautiful, but *very* old—courtyards and stone stairs, etc.

The worst part is my own mood. I am going through an awful time, Tom. I am fundamentally upset and unhappy. I don't know how it will all end. I generally feel it worst at night—and last night was my worst. I have had this spell on me now for about seven weeks. Last night was so bad that I had to go and waken Marjorie twice during the night, as I felt I was going off my head. I am more composed today, but dread the night. I hope to have improved by the time you come. Anyway your company will be a great help, providing I don't depress you. I have practically decided on a bedroom for you, which I think will be best and most detached.

[1] Probably the writing of his memoirs.

[2] His autobiography, of which only a fragment was ever finished.

To Thomas Balston

3 September 1935 *53 Haverstock Hill, Hampstead*

My dear Tom, I am very glad to hear that your holiday is a success—you certainly deserve to have a good one, after the disasters of Castelltersol. I have had a good deal of trouble since my return. That girl who has that passion for me, turned up one afternoon when I was alone in the house and proved to be quite mad. She flung herself upon me, and wouldn't leave the house. I lost my nerve and began to beat and kick her out, but she kept returning through some window! just like a nightmare. At last I called the police. They got her home, but she returned at 1.30 in the morning! For a few days life was hell, but ultimately I interviewed her mother, and for many days there has been no sign—phew! Also I had no news from Marjorie for ten days after I left Spain, which made me imagine all sorts of horrible things, but it turned out that she was putting *35* instead of *53* on the envelopes!!!! I missed a splendid sailing expedition with the Herberts[1] on that account, because I was too anxious to leave London. This morning I had a wire from her asking me to telegraph £20 to Tossa and no proper address—and there is no bank in Tossa!—Alas poor me!

However, I am fairly calm now on the whole, just sitting tight and awaiting events, and I hope to start the old wheels going any moment in the studio.

I had a letter from Ivon Hitchens to say that he is more than engaged, that he is married, but a little apprehensive about the finances. It sounds as if she has no money, and he has and earns very little. Also a nice one from Moore. Ivon Hitchens speaks very highly of the picture of mine in your collection—says he envys you!

I have had many invitations to the country but I don't think I shall go anywhere. The best thing for me would be if I could start work. MARK

To Thomas Balston

23 June 1936 *53 Haverstock Hill, Hampstead*

My dear Tom, I am afraid an unfortunate thing has happened. Since I last saw you I felt very ill again and went to see Morland[2] and it seems that the condition of my chest is somewhat suspicious. He didn't find any actual activity in the lung, but the slight difference in the photographs from the last and above all the condition of my blood makes him feel that trouble *may* start any moment. He therefore strongly urges me to forgo the Spanish part of my holiday and go to the sanatorium for six weeks instead, and he thinks it ought to be all right about our South of France venture. If no activity starts, six weeks at the sanatorium ought to be sufficient. So that

[1] Mr and Mrs A. P. Herbert.

[2] Andrew Morland, Gertler's doctor at Mundesley.

is how the matter stands at present. It is very depressing but can't be helped. Life has been too much for me this last year and I felt that a crisis of some sort was inevitable—the strain was too great. MARK

To Thomas Balston

2 July 1936 *The Sanatorium, Mundesley, Norfolk*

My dear Tom, Your letter arrived this morning—my first morning here. I arrived last night. I have been feeling very ill and overstrained, in a way longing to get here—though dreading it too. I have been so unhappy at home that I longed for *any* change and, when I got here, I went through the usual fit of depression this place always gives me on arrival. But I soon got over it, and now feel thankful for the peace and rest, which I have not been able to enjoy for months and months.

I have a beautiful room (all modern), large open window looking on to a good landscape which I hope to paint as soon as I feel up to it. For the time being they are keeping me in bed for "observation". It is very tedious, but I'm not opposing it because I do really feel very weak still. I have been examined a good deal here already, but so far they are not able to discover any trace of real activity, and therefore our trip abroad is not threatened.
MARK

To Thomas Balston

10 July 1936 *Mundesley*

My dear Tom, I am afraid things have receded since I last wrote—I am having a hellish time. I'm running very high temperatures, 104! Horrible headaches and life isn't worth living. I don't know what will come of it all. I can't believe I shall be well enough to leave for France in August but I will let you know within the next week or ten days then you can make other plans if necessary. I am terribly sorry and it is abominable bad luck. But I have had so much bad luck this last year and there is no end to it. They don't quite know if it is the lung or what—whatever it is, it's horrible.

I won't write any more just now as I am tired but will let you know as soon as there is an improvement—so far I've got worse every day. MARK

To Marjorie Gertler

11 July 1936 *Mundesley*

Dear Marjorie, This must be a short note because since I last saw you I have become pretty ill—I am running temperatures of 104! which is like being on fire with terrible headaches. They don't quite know what it is yet, but it is horrible. But this must not interfere with your holiday. I really don't want anyone here. I lie all day with ice compresses on my head so it would be useless to have company.

Should it take a serious turn I will of course wire you and you can be here within two days. But I think it is just a matter of patience. Please explain to anyone in England when you write why I am not writing.

I'm afraid I cannot attend to the house. With love MARK

To Thomas Balston

27 July 1936 *Mundesley*

My dear Tom, I am not really fit enough to write letters. To begin with both my arms are injured—one I did myself,[1] the other due to a blood transfusion given with inadequate apparatus, which by the way was agonisingly painful. Only I want to say that it would be nice if you came on the 11th August. I have asked Marjorie to book you a room for a week. You can see how you feel about staying longer afterwards. If you bring your painting things you ought not be bored. Unfortunately it gets very full here, but Marjorie will try another hotel if hers is full. I am very ill still and it seems incredible that I shall ever be on my feet again. My temperatures are much lower but won't go down altogether. I hate being washed and helped on to the pot and until a few days ago I was fed! You must excuse me from going into my action more or describing my emotion. For one thing what I have to say would not make you very happy, neither would it help me to go over it all. But here I am still alive, with more problems than ever to face. But it will be nice to see you on the 11th and I do hope Marjorie will succeed in getting you a room—we will let you know in a day or two.

With love MARK

To S. S. Koteliansky

2 August 1936 *Mundesley*

My dear Kot, I am not really fit to write yet, but you have written so many nice and encouraging letters to Marjorie that I feel I must make the effort. I am getting better slowly but am still very ill. I have a long way to go before I shall be even as well as when you last saw me. I have lost a great deal of weight and that will take time to restore. Still, I am making progress. I can walk fifty yards. A week ago that would have seemed incredible, as up till then I was even being fed by nurses. Hateful not to be able to wash oneself or go to the lavatory. Up to about a week ago I was

[1] Gertler had tried to take his life by opening a vein in his arm.

watched day and night, in case I tried to do away with myself again. I had to do all the natural functions in front of a nurse. That's over now and soon I hope to be strong enough to go to the lavatory and bath. I *hate* being washed all over by a nurse. So much for the physical part. I have also to tackle the mental part. Can I take up life again as before? That is the question. For the moment it seems hateful. I have suffered so much this last year. Married life with Marjorie is so difficult and complicated; the accounts, and bills, etc. I feel I shall never have the strength to do it again, yet what else can I do? However, I am very ill now and all may seem different when I am stronger....

Mackie[1] suddenly appeared today. He tells me there is nothing wrong with you, so it must be nerves, a nervous breakdown—it is just a question of time. My trouble is mostly that too—too much unhappiness: we need a little joy in our lives....

With regard to money, it is awfully nice of Sidney Bernstein, but I shan't be able to earn any money for at least six months and so I am asking Philip Morrell to approach a few people—I will send him names.

I do hope, now that you *know* there's nothing organically wrong with you, that you will commence to improve. You *must* make an effort. Try and eat well. Food is good for the nerves. Guinness (beer) is also very good.

With love MARK GERTLER

To Marjorie Gertler

5 October 1936 *Mundesley*

Dearest Marjorie, I am so sorry you are feeling tired and depressed. I *thought* the house[2] would tire you out. I foresaw lots of difficulties and complications, but it sounds as if the result will make it worth while. I expect it is going to look very nice and, after all the work put into it, is of permanent value. I do wish you will see your way to coming here with Andrew.[3] If he leaves on Monday, 12th, he can take me back then. I am sure they won't mind my leaving two days earlier. It is difficult to know *how* well I am really. I *feel* all right, but then life is *so* slow and simple here. But whatever I feel like when I get away, I shall have to go slow at first, not to make the contrast too great right away, and shall have to try and keep on eating a lot, so that I don't lose my precious weight too quickly. But I feel calmer in my mind than I have felt for ages, and that is *very important*. I needed that more than anything. They have not yet taken another blood test. I expect they will before I leave. I'm not pressing it, because I *am so* tired of tests and temperatures and X-rays etc. I do so want to get away from it all. I have received £10 from Mavrogordato—says he cannot afford £25! So that's that. But I have boldly written to

[1] Stuart Mackie, famous Australian eye-surgeon.
[2] Grove Terrace, Highgate.
[3] Andrew Morland.

"Plucky little Gwen"—don't tell Kot—I somehow feel he won't like it. I am glad to hear of Kot's improvement. What a pity we hadn't thought of it, I mean to tell him he has a disease—almost anything would have done. He was obviously suffering from nothing more "grand" than fear of illness and death—not so much, after all, of that soul-suffering pity for the troubles of Mrs Farbman, etc. He wrote to me about this disease. And if he really has it, it can be serious. But I hope it isn't bad. Thanks for the cutting. I'm glad nice things are being said about Taylor—but they ought to say what a good artist he is himself.

Well, perhaps I shall see you next Saturday. Meanwhile all my love and let me tell you that I feel proud to be "linked" to a woman as beautiful, as exceptional and of such good taste as you. Why say all this? Well, because I just feel that way about you. MARK

To Thomas Balston

6 October 1936 *Mundesley*

My dear Tom, Your experience of being discouraged with your work[1] is everybody's experience. So take heart—one must get hardened. The great and important thing about being a painter is *to paint*—never mind the results. Also, next time you look at them they will probably look much better. MARK

To Thomas Balston

21 November 1937 *5 Grove Terrace, N.W.5*

My dear Tom, I have been working very hard—perhaps a bit too hard. I have still not got over the impetus received in Paris. But I think one can strain too much. Otherwise I am all right and tolerably contented. I have also had a bit of financial luck—I sold the sketch of the "Heather-Field" for £21, and the large flower piece I showed you. The latter sold at the London Group for £85 (minus 25 per cent of course)—both new buyers—so perhaps I am becoming fashionable after all!

I went and saw Macdonald of the Lefevre and fixed up a show for May 1939. I sometimes get panicky and feel it is too soon and that I shan't get enough work done in time. But I shall know within the next six months and can postpone it if necessary. MARK

To Thomas Balston

16 June 1938 *5 Grove Terrace, N.W.5*

My dear Tom, Marjorie and Luke are going off on Saturday morning. I

[1] Balston, under Gertler's tuition, had taken to painting.

have decided to stay here all the time until I join them myself. I am looking forward to being alone and working and thinking in that peaceful way one can only do when one is quite alone. So I shan't be coming down to Holt End[1] this side of August, but I daresay I shall get tired of it before the end, and then there will be time for me to stay with you a bit before school starts. I shall be leaving London about 10th July. I could go a week before, but I am particularly looking forward to three weeks of solitude. But if you happen to be up *do* let me know.

We stayed a week-end with the Sidney Bernsteins *with Luke.* It was awfully funny. Luke's place at meals was opposite Charles Laughton[2] and the latter found it extremely difficult to keep up the "great man" stunt with Luke's extraordinary questions being shot at him all the time!

To S. S. Koteliansky

20 July 1938 *Cassis*

My dear Kot, . . . So far I've suffered from continuous headaches which makes things difficult, but perhaps one will become acclimatised . . . only Luke seems perfectly well and happy. But how tiring and irritating a child can be. The fault is that there are no other children he can play with. He won't play with the native children because he cannot talk to them, and talking is his greatest pleasure. He *never* stops. But we have a girl who takes him out from 3 to 6 and that's a relief. We are neither of us, I'm afraid, good parents.

There is the Varda[3] contingent always at the cafés and restaurants. But they fill me with gloom and futility. And now Nelson has turned up too. How very futile the lives of Bohemian intellectuals and "artists" are!

I am very anxious to know about your foot. MARK GERTLER

To Thomas Balston

11 August 1938 *Cassis*

My dear Tom, . . . We are having a mixed time of it here. The place itself is charming and *could* make an excellent holiday resort, but it is *filled* with the "Bohemia" of London—absolutely packed—futile men and prostitute-like women. Mostly semi-acquaintances of a sort one tries to avoid like poison in London, and now Greville has turned up! Kate and her "boy" are coming[4]—Dick and his latest girl, etc. etc. Even a niece of mine suddenly appeared! So that the whole place seems like a lunatic asylum. The only *human* being is Braque, a tall handsome man, but he keeps well out of the

[1] Balston's house near Newbury, where Gertler often stayed.
[2] The actor.
[3] Janko Varda, the Greek painter, lived at Cassis.
[4] Greville and Kate Foster, sisters, and friends of Dick Carline.

way and one only gets a glimpse of him occasionally. I have found a lonely spot where I can bathe in the morning unobserved and from 2 to 6 I work. But I have had some bad fits of depression. Unfortunately Marjorie says she will go mad if I leave her here alone . . . and as she has to wait for her boat which doesn't sail before the 16th September, I shall have to hang on, though I hope to get away a few days before her—on the 12th September—as I long nowadays to be alone—*quite* alone. I do enjoy painting so much when I am living alone. I have never been more full of new ideas than now, and how I long for a year of bachelorhood, to work them out. But I'm afraid it is not possible as, ironically enough, Marjorie is again very much attached to me and dislikes being away from me—she gets quite miserable—whereas before she would not have minded so much. So for the time I must do the best under my circumstances. . . .

I forgot to say that Luke is the only one that is really flourishing here. He has never been better or happier. He knows everybody and unlike ourselves he just loves them and they him. He has a terrific social manner. He will be six on Tuesday!

With love

MARK

To Marjorie Gertler

10 September 1938 *5 Grove Terrace, N.W.5*

Dearest Marjorie, I had quite a comfortable journey and now here I am in my studio. My mood continued bad till I reached the studio, when it improved somewhat. I am so sorry, my dear, to have had so many bad moods in Cassis—I could have kicked myself, specially as you were more than ever lovable and desirable. But there it is. The last two or three years I have been going through a bad time and it is sometimes difficult to bear. For the most part I get irritable and depressed by things that disturb my life as a painter. Family life—you know, being a painter yourself—prevents me so often from getting just that detachment and isolation I need for my work and, by God, how I do enjoy it when for a little while I get it! What grieves one also is that these moods prevent me from expressing the fullness of my love for you. I don't believe you've ever realised how much I love you! I love your body so much for one thing! *So please remember this* in spite of my moods and go on tolerating them as you have done up to now. No, you need never fear my running off with another woman, unless it be the "Goddess of Painting"—the only true romance!

No, I shall adjust myself one of these days and then you'll see how happy we shall be—*the* most perfect couple! . . .

Love to you both

MARK

To Thomas Balston

27 September 1938 — *5 Grove Terrace, N.W.5*

My dear Tom, The "family" returned last Thursday, and I'm afraid I've been depressed ever since! This is distressing, but the desire to be undomesticated has by now become a sort of obsession—just to be left alone with my work—and so it is all very difficult. It is probably temporary, and adjustment to my circumstances would be best. However I've talked it all over with Marjorie and we agreed that, if my mood continues, some kind of more separate life might be preferable. We both know that the trouble is not fundamental, as we do really love one another. But there are two creatures in me—the painter and the man. It is the painter in me that causes difficulties. Unfortunately most ideas for living more detached cost more money. Anyway it would be a great upheaval so we are leaving things for the time being. Only one thing: I am going *out* for lunches, just as I do when I am alone here. That I know will greatly help as I shall be alone with my thoughts all day. MARK GERTLER

To Thomas Balston

10 October 1938 — *5 Grove Terrace, N.W.5*

My dear Tom, . . . When I last wrote to you, I had not yet read Hitler's speech and was not quite expecting that awful crisis we went through. That's why I aired my private "crisis" so much. That Wednesday I was trying to teach, and I don't think any of us at the school will forget the day as long as we live. What finished us off was that we were told that in the event of war the school would be closed instantly—and no salaries. From now till May my teaching money was to be my only maintenance. So you can imagine what I felt like.

To Edward Marsh

8 May 1939 — *5 Grove Terrace, N.W.5*

Dear Eddie, Thanks very much—it was nice to you to arrange it—though I think it deserves a better place. I do wish they would get a more recent and larger work for the Tate, but they just wait.

I'm afraid I am very depressed about my show.[1] I've sold only one so far! The large flower piece and tiny landscape were sold about a year ago. That show represents two years' hard work and there is all the expense, frames, etc., attached to it. It's very disheartening.

I was pleased to see you last Thursday and shall look forward to reading your book.

Ever yours — MARK

[1] At the Lefevre Galleries.

To Edward Marsh

[*11 May 1939*] *5 Grove Terrace, N.W.5*

My dear Eddie, Of course I am not angry with you for writing what you think—you are much too old a friend and have done so much for me in the past that you have a *right* to say what you think. Besides, what you say is, I suppose, true in a sense, as obviously a number of other people feel as you do about my recent works. The trouble is that I can never *set out* to paint to please. My greatest spiritual pleasure in life is to paint just as I feel *impelled* to do *at the time.*

Each time I get a change of conception I am thrilled, and it is such changes which makes painting worth while and prevents monotony. Of course I love it when people like my pictures. But to *set out* to please would ruin my process—and you know me well enough to realise that I am sincere, and to paint to the best of my capacity is, and has always been—my primary aim in life. I have sacrificed much by doing so. Also there *are* a number of people—whose taste I trust—who find some of the others as attractive as the "Flowers", even more so.

You must remember that many works by artists of the past were considered unattractive during their life time. My works may be more appreciated in the future....

In very friendly spirit, I am yours ever MARK

P.S. There is one other picture I think as attractive as the "Flowers", done in the same way, "The Garden" (No. 10), but it hasn't sold.

To Thomas Balston

13 May 1939 *5 Grove Terrace, N.W.5*

My dear Tom, Thank you so much for your letter. I am of course delighted that you liked the show, as you are one of the inner circle whose opinion I value. I must quote from a letter of Marjorie's: "I think the real mischief in England is that buyers never have any personal tastes. Tom is an exception. Even if people don't understand painting as well as Tom they can at least have the courage to buy independently and not what all their friends tell them. . . ."

That is true, and partly the reason, I suppose, why I am doing so badly. I am really very depressed and disheartened. I have only sold *one* picture, "Red Shawl", and that tiny dot (smallest nude, 12 guineas). The large "Flowers" was of course sold about two years ago at the London Group. And the sketch landscape "Heather" a year ago. So up to date, I've only realised about £50! which doesn't cover expenses of frames, etc. And, as you know, the first week—or even the first day—is the most important. It is extraordinary because there has been so much enthusiasm and I have a whole pile of letters of appreciation on my desk here. What is going to happen? I don't know. I have now arranged with Jamieson[1] to do the maximum amount of teaching—two days and three evenings—but even that is going to make it difficult for me to pay for materials, models and frames. However, I can just live on it. But my immediate worry is the summer. I only get one more payment until about the end of October! and unless I sell another two medium-sized pictures I shall be in a real hole.

Both Marjorie and Luke seem well. I've arranged to go to Paris over Whitsun to see Marjorie. But how I wish I hadn't, as I ought to save every penny for the summer. MARK

To Thomas Balston

[*26 May 1939*] *5 Grove Terrace, N.W.5*

My dear Tom, Thanks very much for your letter. I'm afraid I've not sold anything more to speak of. Just my self-portrait for £15. That's all 75 guineas—12 guineas and £15—is the lot and I get that minute 33⅓ per cent!

I felt so disgusted and disheartened that I really did not feel able to paint. So I searched out that piece[2] I showed you of "My Life" and showed it to Sylvia Lynd.[3] To my surprise, she was enthusiastic! and has been pressing me so much to go on with it that I *have* gone on a bit; and meanwhile she is going to get in touch with Gollancz, and hopes to get me an advance of £200! Though I shall be satisfied (as I told her) with £100. Just to carry me through the summer. She is also going to edit it, and correct the English a bit. Everybody seems excited at the idea, and everybody is most anxious for me to do it. But I can't *quite* get reconciled to the idea. On the other hand I *do* need the money for the summer, and it does keep me occupied, as for the moment I'm really off painting. I find it rather moving and over-emotional stuff to do, and feel almost feverish when I write, but perhaps that will pass with habit. However, if she does not succeed in getting me an advance of £100 at least, I shan't continue—so we shall see.

Well, I am off tomorrow, Saturday, to Paris. For the next week letters could get me at 7, Impasse du Rouet, Alesia, Paris 14.[e] MARK

[1] R. K. Jamieson, Principal of Westminster School of Art.
[2] See the fragment of autobiography, page 15.
[3] Wife of Robert Lynd, the essayist.

Mark Gertler by Sylvia Lynd

Mark Gertler took his own life on 22 June 1939. Sylvia Lynd wrote an obituary of him which was subsequently included in the catalogue of his Memorial Exhibition at the Leicester Galleries in 1941. It is here reprinted.

Mark Gertler is dead. Let me try to tell what he was like—to look at, as a companion, in character.

He was forty-six years old when he died, but he was one of those people of whose physical beauty youth seems to have been a part. It was impossible to regard him as a middle-aged man. Strangers took him for thirty-two. He was of medium height, lightly built, pale, with grey eyes and dark hair, which he wore cropped into a characteristic curly mound on the top of his head. His hands were of a feminine elegance, and his clothes had something of a feminine elegance, too, within their masculine convention. When I last saw him he was wearing a shirt of fawny-pink colour, a dark pink tie spotted with paler pink, a pale pink handkerchief, a fawn-coloured suit. Behind him, on my window-sill, there happened to be a bowl of pink peonies.

He was always decorative, but not with the decorativeness of his pictures which, apart from their deliberate skill, had, at their most characteristic, much in common with the folk-painting that can be seen on such things as merry-go-rounds and barrel organs and barges and cigar boxes. That sort of decoration he contrived in his surroundings; there were gilt-framed sofas and big embroidered pictures of tigers in his room, and the same sort of splendour often appeared either by chance or design in the clothes of the women friends whom one met at his house, so that one saw him within the frame, as it were, of one of his own pictures. This gipsy gaudiness and vehemence were part of his instinctive nature, not a deliberate taste. He consciously loved the unsensational English landscape. As a boy in Whitechapel he had been attracted by the superabundant vitality of the Jewish girls, he told me, the girls of his own nationality; but it was an encounter with an English girl who happened to quote a phrase of great literature to him which gave him, in a single moment, a passion both for her and for a wholly different kind of life. He never pretended to himself that his slum life had been enviable.

His manner in the presence of strangers was grave and inexpansive, and only the occasional flitting round his mouth and nostrils of his rather wry little smile indicated the intensity of his sense of humour. This humour was boundless and completely irreverent. It depended for its effects not on any verbal jest, but on accurate observation and aptness of mimicry. Mark describing an altercation in a restaurant, an incensed neighbour in a cinema, a Spaniard explaining to another Spaniard the difficulties that Mark was having with the water supply in his house, a friend missing train after train at a railway station because he had left his overcoat behind in the hotel, could not remember the French word *surtout*, and a friend uncertain what to pack for an elopement, a blind beggar, a man in uncomfortable boots walking along a road—with two words, two gestures, the person, the situation suddenly was there. His gentle low-pitched voice retained some of the Cockney vowels that were a legacy from Whitechapel, but it was a marvellous instrument for catching a tone or a phrase.

Not least often he made himself the butt of his own stories, and his account of his confusion in foreign cities, of his social solecisms in England of his adventures with over robust or excitable people were hilariously funny. I have never heard him repeat himself in the seventeen years of our acquaintance. Whatever befell him he turned into a fantasia of absurdity, and it is this running commentary of laughter that will be most missed by his friends.

His stories were not edifying, but they were the stories of a man of genius whose experience passed through the whole scale of living. It would be nonsense to call him a good man; his attitude to life was frankly sensual, and I doubt if his behaviour was ever consciously influenced by any moral consideration. But he was faithful to his friends, he had physical fastidiousness and a proud delicacy of feeling which gave him integrity and dignity. I have known him to avoid a chance meeting with people who had proposed to buy one of his pictures, lest his presence should be an embarrassing reminder to them of their obligation.

What impulse prompted him suddenly to end his life I do not know. Such impulses had come to him before, and he had always dreaded his bouts of depression, though these, like everything else, he turned into laughter. He had been through a cumulative year of worry, and some further touch of misfortune must have changed depression to despair. When I saw him, two days before his death, he was talking hopefully of the future. He had begun to write his autobiography and had brought me the first seven thousand words or so for my opinion. I thought them not only good, but supremely good. A publisher had been immediately found, and the project had upon it every sign of prosperity. He left me with the intention of taking the manuscript at once to a typist.

What changed his attitude to the future? I think the clue is to be found in the pages of that manuscript, in the two descriptions which he called his first and last "depressions"[1]—the first of a crowded room in Whitechapel where, on his second arrival in England, as a small boy, he woke in the night to see his mother and all his brothers sleeping on the floor; the last, of himself alone in an empty, echoing house—for so his life ended. He perceived the dramatic perfection of the contrast.

He is buried in rough grass among the unmarked graves of the unorthodox; but over him is one of London's tall grey-green poplars with leaves for ever in movement and one may imagine that he is not discontented to be at last wholly part of the England that he loved.

[1] See page 21.

APPENDIX

Mendel

Gilbert Cannan's novel *Mendel* was published towards the end of 1916. He was fairly well known as a writer at that time, having already written half a dozen novels, also speculative essays, poems and a study of Samuel Butler. He was perhaps even better known as having gone off with Sir James Barrie's wife, Mary, when he had been secretary to the dramatist. Gertler almost certainly met him through Eddie Marsh, as Gilbert Cannan had been involved in the launching of *Georgian Poetry*.

In May 1916 Gertler wrote to Lytton Strachey that Cannan had completed a novel which was based on his, Gertler's, life. Strachey answered that he would hardly welcome such an honour for himself. And in a letter of 29 August of the same year Gertler wrote that he had read to Cannan parts of his diary and the beginning of his "Currie" chapter. There is no evidence that I can discover in Gertler's own letters that he ever read the novel in manuscript. Equally there is nothing to show that at the time of its publication he repudiated it as a whole or in part. The fact that he lent a copy to D. H. Lawrence suggests otherwise. I have been told by a member of his family that they regarded it as "libellous", at least as regards the part that covered the early life. However, it would be impossible to discover how much was directly drawn from Gertler's own reminiscences and how much was Cannan's own embroidery. He was under no obligation to keep to the facts. Indeed as a novelist he could be expected to let the story "develop" on its own. There are plenty of departures from known fact. For instance in the novel Mendel goes with friends to Paris, whereas Gertler up to that time had never been further abroad than a week's trip to Ostend. Therefore the rather cruel caricature of his reception by the "Froitzheims" at a studio in Hampstead is very probably a travesty of Gertler's original story to Cannan, allowing for the fact that he was always touchy about dependence on rich patrons. Throughout the Slade period his letters to William Rothenstein certainly do not suggest ingratitude.

Amongst his own circle of friends the reception of *Mendel* was hardly favourable. Writing to Catherine Carswell (2 December 1916), D. H. Lawrence comments:

Zennor

. . . We had *Mendel*. Gertler lent us his copy. It is a bad book—statement without creation—really journalism. Gertler, Jew-like, has told every detail of his life to Gilbert—Gilbert has a lawyer's memory and has put it all down—and so ridiculously when it comes to the love affair. We never recognised ourselves—or Frieda—but now I remember she must be

Mrs Lipton—or whatever it was—wife of an artist. I only glanced through the book. . . .

Carrington (to whom the novel was dedicated) wrote to Gertler:

1 November 1916 *3 Gower Street, W.C.1*

. . . How angry I am over Gilbert's book! Everywhere this confounded gossip, and servant-like curiosity. It's ugly, and so damned vulgar. People cannot be vulgar over a work of art, so it *is* Gilbert's fault for writing as he did. . . .

and there is an undated letter from Gertler's friend and great admirer Montague Shearman:

Sunday night *26 Evelyn Gardens, S.W.*

Dear Mark, I have just finished Gilbert's book *Mendel* and am deeply moved by it. Not that I think it good. It fascinates and disgusts me. Fascinating it is because it is about yourself and, now that I am proud to call myself your friend, I feel in an intimate way a sense of delight in reading about you as the hero not only of some of my ideals but of a novel for the public. I am disgusted however at the vulgarity of revealing the hidden things and the sanctity of friendship and love to the world in this way. Perhaps some of it is not true. Some of it seems to me grotesquely absurd and impossible and unlike you. Some of it however is very like, as no doubt you will admit. I often wonder whether, if I did not know you and some of the others, I should regard some parts of the book as good as I do. I should very much like to discuss it with you and we will. But on the whole I am annoyed with the book. Except for the cutting picture of Conway which I thoroughly enjoyed. I think I recognised Geoff. Lawrence also. But is is all very baffling. . . . M.S.

Lastly we have at a later date two letters from William Rothenstein and Gertler's apologia.

30 June 1918 *Far Oakridge, Stroud, Gloucestershire*

Dear Gertler, I was staying with my brother and he showed me a book dealing with your life and adventures. In it I read an account you gave Cannan of your first meeting with me and of your impressions on that occasion. Why you should be at pains to show that you were repelled by the reception you had when you first came to see me, that my painting and myself were alike false and second-rate, is not easily understandable. I cannot see that, had you come with the simplicity of youth and believed that both I and my pictures were genuine, and that the interest we shared in your talent and welfare was equally real, there would be any need for shame. On the contrary, I think such an attitude would have been as honourable to your self as to me. You wrong both of us by giving so sordid and untruthful account of your own feelings and of mine, and the portrait of myself and of my motives in welcoming you as I did is as ungenerous as it is ignoble. I am deeply hurt that anyone could find it in his heart to turn the pleasure of helping a beginner into an ugly legend. It is true I hear and see nothing of you now but it never for a moment entered my head that you had such feelings regarding us. Let me tell you, young Gertler, that it is not a pose of mine to pretend to speak well of people belonging to a newer movement than yours. I have always been happy to admire the work of my own contemporaries, and of men older than myself. I have never been slow to express my admiration for any work which moved me by its power or its beauty. I am sorry you have not allowed me to believe that, however your own artistic development has changed your views, that the relations between an older and a younger man could be sweet and sound. Truly yours W. ROTHENSTEIN

3 July 1918 *Garsington Manor, Oxford*

Dear Rothenstein, Your letter was forwarded me here this morning. It was a shock to me and opened up an old wound. I have suffered a great deal from that wretched book and I feel that any person who can for a moment believe me responsible for such a piece of cheap trash cannot understand me. I was therefore hurt from that point of view alone—to get your letter. But first let me tell you its history as far as I know it.

Some years ago, I was feeling very wretched and Gilbert Cannan was suggested to me as a person to stay with in his country place. I went and was foolish enough to tell him a great deal about myself. Some years later, he asked me if I would mind him writing a novel *with a person something like myself in it.* Of course I consented and soon this awful and distorted affair came out. I have never, I assure you, ceased to blush over it. I could say much more, but it is not to the point, what I want to tell is this—

That I have never for a moment ceased to feel thankful to you for the way you received me at that time and for what you did. It was for me perhaps one of the most wonderful experiences in my life. Gilbert Cannan's version is, I assure you, *entirely false* and I am not responsible for it.

PLEASE UNDERSTAND THIS.

Nor could I ever be responsible for such an agglomeration of cheap trash as is contained in that awful novel.

Believe me, yours very sincerely MARK GERTLER

4 July 1918 *Far Oakridge, Stroud, Gloucestershire*

My dear Gertler, Your letter has just reached me; I accept it unreservedly. I have not read the book and knew nothing of the circumstances under which it was written. The part my brother showed me dealt with details so precise that I could not let it go unnoticed. If the whole book deals with incidents of a like kind it would naturally be difficult for you to explain to each person concerned that you were not responsible for the use of the facts you gave Cannan; otherwise, a line from you, in case the pages met my eye, would have been considerate. Let us both take warning and keep the more tender and beautiful things of life from ununderstanding eyes. If my letter shocked you it will help you to understand how shocked I was to find a charming happening turned into a mean and ugly thing. I could not but be shocked—I am glad to learn from you that you yourself consider it false and repugnant. Next time you want to unpack your heart, don't do it before a realistic writer. And remember too, that in those early days, your work was not very practical or inspiring; it was extraordinarily able but very dull, and by no means of a kind to make me afraid of a new comet, the tail of which was to destroy me. I knew when you got into touch with the people at the Slade that your talents would quickly flower and happily I was right. If, since then, you have found a vision of your own, different from that of my generation, this is as it should be. But this need not blind you to the artistic integrity of another's outlook, or spoil the relation, so charmingly begun, between an older and a younger man. Anything in the nature of gratitude is the last thing I want, but I do appreciate the sympathy and respect of men younger than myself, as I believe they care for these things themselves when they win them from older men. I see you are staying with the Morrells. Will you give them my kind remembrance and believe me always yours very sincerely,

WILLIAM ROTHENSTEIN

P.S. I hope your people are well—if they have not forgotten me will you give them my kind remembrances.

Select Bibliography

Mark Gertler. (British Artists of Today, No. 1.) Introduction by Hubert Wellington. The Fleuron, 1925.

Mark Gertler. Catalogue of Exhibition. Introduction by Aldous Huxley. Lefevre Gallery, 1937.

Collection of Montague Shearman. Foreword by St. John Hutchinson Redfern Gallery, 1940.

Mark Gertler. Retrospective Exhibition. Introduction by Sylvia Lynd. Leicester Galleries, 1941.

Mark Gertler. Memorial Exhibition. Introduction by Thomas Balston. Whitechapel Art Gallery, 1949.

Modern English Painters, Lewis to Moore. By Sir John Rothenstein. (Eyre and Spottiswoode, 1956.

Index of Correspondents

Index of Correspondents

Recipients of Letters from Mark Gertler

Letters from other Writers

Index

Index